E PLURIBUS UNUM

DAVID V STONE

BY THE POWER OF MONEY

Book 2: The Dawn Of Freedom
Coming Soon

Book 3: The World Measured In Grams
TBD

Book 4: Rich Man's Gold
TBD

IN GOD WE TRUST

BY THE POWER OF MONEY

ECHOES OF A BROKEN TRUST

DAVID V STONE

First Edition, 2025
Version 1.1

ISBN: 979-8-9990628-0-2
Library of Congress Control Number: 2025910094
Cover Art & Layout ❦ m. m. Sprout

DISCLAIMER

This book is solely an educational and theoretical exploration of sound money concepts, presented for informational purposes only. It does not constitute, nor should it be interpreted as, financial, investment, legal, tax, or professional advice of any kind. The author and publisher are not licensed financial advisors, economists, attorneys, or other regulated professionals, and no fiduciary, advisory, or contractual relationship is created with readers. All content reflects the author's opinions, research, and analysis and may become outdated due to evolving economic conditions, laws, or monetary policies.

Readers bear full responsibility for any decisions or actions taken based on this book. The author and publisher make no guarantees, express or implied, about the accuracy, completeness, reliability, or applicability of the information herein. Historical monetary trends or theories discussed are not predictive of future results. Readers are strongly encouraged to conduct independent research and seek advice from qualified professionals before acting on any ideas presented.

To the countless authors from every walk of life, who poured their wisdom onto pages for the world to one day draw upon, answering questions too often silenced or buried—your gift is beyond measure.

To the republishers, tireless seekers who unearthed lost knowledge and breathed life back into precious words, hoping they'd shine once more in the pursuit of truth—your efforts illuminate the path.

To the librarians, devoted guardians of their craft, who with love and care guide the curious through the sacred halls of knowledge—your quiet heroism inspires me without end. To the audio, website, and video content creators, your steadfast dedication to sharing new information, ideas, and interviews opens doors for knowledge to spread freely, reaching all who seek it—your work is a vital spark.

And to the Sound Money Defense League, bullion dealers, numismatic clubs, and the countless others who stand firm in the fight to restore morality, truth, and freedom to our Republic—thank you for existing, for caring so deeply, and for inspiring souls like mine to join this noble journey.

And lastly, to my dearest family, who patiently endured my endless musings and enveloped me in your unwavering support and kindness, each of you offering your love in such special, generous ways—thank you with all my heart. This work owes its existence to you, a gentle reminder that truth is precious and worth cherishing, and I am forever grateful for you all.

CONTENTS

EPIGRAPH

In a letter to George Logan (1816):

"If the American people ever allow private banks to control the issue of their currency, first by inflation, then by deflation, the banks and corporations that will grow up around them will deprive the people of all property until their children wake up homeless on the continent their fathers conquered."

Thomas Jefferson

FORWARD

To truly understand, one must first listen with intent, read with curiosity, learn with humility, and apply with purpose.

These words ring true when we confront the enigma of sound money—a principle as ancient as trade itself, yet one that feels increasingly distant in our era of financial flux.

This book is an invitation to undertake that journey of understanding, to listen to history's past voices, to read the shifting tides of economic thought, to learn from the triumphs and tragedies of monetary systems, and to apply those lessons to the world we navigate today.

Within these pages, you'll uncover more than mere knowledge—you'll find a sense of purpose. This is a rallying cry for those bold enough to question, to learn, and to forge a new path. Sound money is not a relic to be admired from afar; it is a living principle, a tool for reclaiming stability and morality in an unstable and amoral world.

Certain phrases may resonate like a chorus, but this repetition is intentional—a deliberate echo woven into the fabric of the text. It mirrors my own journey of discovery, capturing how these insights first took shape for me. In crafting this experience for the reader, I sought to create a parallel journey that with each return, humanity's plea grows more urgent, their voices reverberating through time. Each revisit brings deeper understanding, for with new knowledge comes new perceptions of the old.

And few things reveal the patterns of history more clearly than money—not just a tool of exchange, but a story. A saga carved through time by human ingenuity, ambition, and too often, folly. Sound money stands as a pillar in that narrative, embodying trust, value, and endurance. From the minted coins of ancient realms to the digital pulses of modern commerce, its history mirrors our ceaseless quest for stability and prosperity. But in our present age, as currencies waver and economic frameworks evolve, a pressing question emerges, what does sound money mean now, and how do we restore its promise?

History is our teacher, our guide to answering these questions. My own awakening to this question began years ago in Italy, as the Lira crumbled before my eyes. I saw a nation's currency erode, and with it, a sense of respect and identity for its people. How could a country destroy its own money and treat its citizens with such disregard? As the years unfolded and the Euro rose to prominence, I came to see it as an ambitious attempt at uniformity, a single currency to bind nations. At first, I thought creating uniform money was a good idea, a way to streamline trade and unity—but not at the expense of liberty. The formation of a centralized governing body invited control, and I feared it would degrade into tyranny, as greed and power nearly always corrupt.

A gnawing unease took root in me as the Financial Crisis loomed on the horizon. I couldn't yet name it, but I felt its shadow creeping closer—a storm brewing in the silence. People had flung themselves into a frenzy, snatching up homes with borrowed dreams they could never repay, only to wail as if thieves had pried their keys away. When it finally crashed down, I stood aghast at the chaos it unleashed. Others, teetering on the edge, saw their lives unravel with a single missed payment, foreclosure swooping in like a vulture to claim what little they had. It was a whirlwind of recklessness and ruin, a tangle of finger-pointing and despair, and I was left grasping for answers, how had we tumbled into this abyss?

As I pieced it together, listening to the whispers of the past, devouring texts, absorbing lessons, and testing my newfound clarity—a revelation broke through the haze, money itself was the silent puppeteer controlled not by the people—but by foreign powers. This led me to reject the ephemeral paper promises of our time, but the enduring strength of gold and silver—timeless, resolute standards that resist the grip of centralized authority. In that instant, I saw a way ahead, to reclaim liberty and restore reason, the United States and nations worldwide must revive sound money from the ruins of our past mistakes—but first, we must understand our history.

Yours truly,
David V Stone

CHAPTER 1

Money That Stands the Test of Time

Sound money has long been the bedrock of stable economies, providing a reliable foundation for growth, investment, and trust. In its simplest form, sound money refers to a currency that maintains its purchasing power over time, free from excessive inflation or manipulation by governments. As Ludwig von Mises (1953) argued, sound money is more than just a technical tool; it is a symbol of economic freedom and discipline, essential for rational economic planning. Milton Friedman (1969) expanded on this by emphasizing that sound money is a safeguard against the destructive forces of inflation, protecting the real value of people's savings and promoting long-term prosperity. Yet, sound money is not a rigid doctrine; even John Maynard Keynes (1930) acknowledged its importance in creating stable economic conditions, though he warned that in times of crisis, excessive devotion to monetary stability could hamper necessary interventions. The balance between stability and flexibility in the money supply has thus shaped the economic philosophies of the 20th century, with sound money standing at the heart of debates over growth, inflation, and government intervention.

According to Ludwig von Mises (1953), sound money is essential not only as an economic ideal but also as a safeguard against governmental overreach in monetary policy. Mises argued that sound money serves as a protective mechanism, establishing boundaries that prevent governments from undermining currency value through inflationary practices or excessive monetary interventions, which often lead to economic instability. This perspective aligns with Milton Friedman's (1969) emphasis on sound money as a shield against inflation's corrosive effects. One real-world example that illustrates Friedman's view is the case of Germany's post-World War II currency reform, which introduced the Deutsche Mark, a stable currency that enabled Germans to preserve their savings amidst inflation. This reform helped anchor Germany's economic stability, protecting purchasing power in a period of rebuilding and rapid growth. Additionally, before delving into John Maynard Keynes' (1930) cautions about the limitations of stability, it is worthwhile to highlight economists like Friedrich Hayek and Irving Fisher. They contributed to debates on monetary flexibility, suggesting that while sound money provides stability, some flexibility may be necessary in times of crisis. Their perspectives provide a balanced lead-in to Keynes' critique, underscoring the diverse views on monetary stability within economic thought.

SOUND MONEY VERSUS TOKEN MONEY

Money derives its value from collective trust and agreement—it can take any form that people are willing to accept as a medium of exchange, such as gold coins, shells, beads, cigarettes, or even digital tokens like cryptocurrencies. W. Stanley Jevons' analysis in Money and the Mechanism of Exchange (1875) provides a foundational understanding of the mechanics and implications of commodity and token money systems, with significant lessons for economic stability. He describes commodity money as possessing intrinsic, universal value, rooted in physical characteristics such as durability, portability, divisibility, and scarcity. Gold and silver are particularly well-suited for monetary purposes due to these properties. Jevons notes, "A perfect money should be, as nearly as possible, invariable in value, portable, indestructible, homogeneous, divisible, and cognizable." The inherent value of these metals ensures that their utility extends beyond their monetary role, creating a robust form of money less vulnerable to economic mismanagement. This feature enables commodity money to act not only as a medium of exchange but also as a hedge against inflation and a store of value during periods of economic uncertainty.

In contrast, Jevons characterizes token money as representative currency, where the material of the money itself has little intrinsic value. Instead, token money relies entirely on the authority of the issuing government and the public's trust in that authority. He explains that token money can be effective, provided its issuance is carefully regulated to prevent overabundance. Jevons writes, "The quantity of token money must be strictly limited by the authority which issues it, and the public must have confidence that the limit will be observed." However, he cautions that when governments fail to adhere to these principles, token money systems are prone to inflation and loss of credibility, as seen in historical cases of currency debasement or hyperinflation.

Jevons offers several historical examples to illustrate these dynamics. He examines the transition from metallic money to paper money in various economies, noting how the abandonment of gold or silver standards led to episodes of instability when governments issued excessive quantities of fiat currency. "The evils of an inconvertible paper currency," Jevons observes, "are universally admitted, and history records no instance in which such a currency, when unlimited in amount, has not been productive of disastrous consequences."

Jevons' insights also extend to the psychological and sociopolitical dimensions of money. The public's perception of monetary value, he argues, is crucial to the success of any currency system. Token money, in particular, depends heavily on the issuer's ability to maintain public confidence. This requirement places significant responsibility on monetary authorities to act prudently, as mismanagement can quickly lead to a loss of trust and economic turmoil.

The analysis highlights the essential role of a rigorously administered monetary policy in safeguarding the stability of any monetary system. Whether the system is anchored in commodity money, such as gold or silver, or token money, which derives its value from governmental decree rather than intrinsic worth, a central principle emerges, the preservation of money's value hinges on controlled issuance and meticulous management. This perspective retains its significance in modern economic discourse, particularly in examinations of fiat currency regimes, the policies of central banks, and the advent of digital currencies, providing enduring insights into the interplay of trust, value, and economic governance.

Subsequent economists and monetary theorists have reiterated and elaborated upon these observations concerning commodity and token money. Their works emphasize parallel concerns regarding the necessity of stability and public confidence in monetary systems, contributing to a comprehensive scholarly exchange that connects historical analysis with contemporary relevance.

For instance, Ludwig von Mises, a prominent figure in the Austrian School of Economics, expands on Jevons' arguments in his seminal work, The Theory of Money and Credit. Mises emphasizes the role of commodity money as a foundation for sound monetary systems, arguing that its intrinsic value provides a natural check on inflation. He writes, "Money cannot function as a medium of exchange unless it has a pre-existing value derived from other uses." Like Jevons, Mises critiques fiat or token money, warning that its reliance on governmental discretion creates a risk of overissuance and devaluation, particularly in the absence of a gold or commodity standard.

Carl Menger, another Austrian economist and the founder of the Austrian School, contributes to this discourse through his analysis of the origins of money in Principles of Economics. Menger aligns with Jevons in identifying the spontaneous emergence of commodity money as a market-driven solution to the inefficiencies of barter. He underscores the importance of durability, divisibility, and scarcity, which naturally guided societies toward the use of precious metals like gold and silver. Menger's theory complements Jevons' analysis by providing an evolutionary perspective on why commodity money became the preferred medium of exchange.

John Maynard Keynes, though differing in many respects from Jevons, also addresses the pitfalls of token money in his work, The Economic Consequences of the Peace. Keynes critiques the unrestrained issuance of paper currency, noting how such practices contributed to hyperinflation in post-World War I Europe. He writes, "There is no subtler, no surer means of overturning the existing basis of society than to debauch the currency. The process engages all the hidden forces of economic law on the side of destruction, and it does so in a manner which not one man in a million is able to diagnose." Like Jevons, Keynes acknowledges that the integrity of token money hinges on the discipline of the issuing authority.

More recently, Friedrich Hayek, in Denationalisation of Money, echoes Jevons' caution against state-managed token money, advocating instead for a competitive system of privately issued currencies. Hayek critiques the centralization of monetary authority, arguing that it leads to inefficiencies and abuse. His views reflect Jevons' concern about the potential for mismanagement in token money systems.

Milton Friedman, in his work A Monetary History of the United States, provides empirical support for the risks associated with fiat money and poor monetary policies. Friedman's analysis of the Great Depression illustrates how inadequate control over the money supply exacerbated economic crises, a scenario that Jevons foresaw in his critique of unlimited token money issuance. Friedman famously argued for rules-based monetary policies to mitigate these risks, stating, "Inflation is always and everywhere a monetary phenomenon."

Together, these thinkers reinforce Jevons' foundational observations, forming a cohesive body of work that highlights the enduring challenges of managing token money systems and the stabilizing role of commodity-based monetary frameworks. Their collective insights underscore the importance of discipline, trust, and governance in ensuring monetary stability, offering lessons that remain profoundly relevant in contemporary debates over fiat currencies, central bank policies, and the emergence of digital assets.

The observations of Jevons and other notable economists on the distinction between commodity money and token money resonate profoundly with contemporary challenges surrounding paper currency and fiat monetary systems. Today's global economy faces significant struggles with fiat money—government-issued paper currency not backed by physical commodities—echoing many of the concerns raised by Jevons, Ludwig von Mises, and others. These struggles include inflation, erosion of purchasing power, overreliance on central bank policies, and questions about the sustainability of fiat currencies in an increasingly digitized world.

A striking parallel emerges in the persistent challenge of inflation and currency devaluation. The cautionary note that token money's value is "essentially dependent on limitation of supply" finds a clear reflection in contemporary debates surrounding quantitative easing (QE) and expansive monetary issuance by central banks during economic downturns. For example, in response to the 2008 global financial crisis and the COVID-19 pandemic, central banks across the globe injected trillions of dollars in fiat currency into their economies to avert collapse and stimulate recovery. While these interventions delivered immediate stabilization, they also precipitated significant inflationary pressures, manifesting in rising consumer prices and a reduction in real wages. This development aligns closely with the earlier observation that an unrestrained expansion of token money supply risks "disastrous consequences," as excessive issuance erodes public confidence in the currency's purchasing power and undermines its role as a stable store of value.

Similarly, Ludwig von Mises' critique of fiat money's reliance on state authority resonates with contemporary concerns about the loss of confidence in central banks. In countries like Venezuela, Zimbabwe, and Argentina, hyperinflation has rendered paper currency virtually worthless, eroding public trust in the financial system. These cases demonstrate the fragility of fiat currencies when monetary policy is mismanaged, underscoring Mises' assertion that money's value must be rooted in more than government decree.

The argument that the inherent worth of commodity money serves as a bulwark against mismanagement resonates strongly with the contemporary surge in interest toward alternative monetary frameworks. This relevance is underscored by recent trends observed in data from the London Metal Exchange (LME) and the New York Mercantile Exchange (NYMEX), which reveal substantial withdrawals of gold and silver, reaching lows unprecedented in recent decades. Reports indicate a marked decline in global inventories of these metals held in registered vaults. For example, in 2023, LME gold stocks diminished to under 9 million ounces, a significant reduction from over 15 million ounces five years earlier. Concurrently, silver inventories plummeted by more than 70% over the same timeframe, reflecting heightened investor demand for physical assets as a hedge against inflation and geopolitical instability.

This phenomenon reflects a modern iteration of Jevons' principles, as individuals and institutions gravitate toward sounder forms of money to hedge against the perceived instability of fiat currencies. The surge in physical gold and silver purchases aligns with periods of aggressive monetary easing and expanding central bank balance sheets, where the debasement of paper currencies erodes purchasing power. For example, gold prices soared to record highs of over $2,000 per ounce in 2020 and again in 2023, driven by fears of inflation and waning confidence in the ability of central banks to maintain monetary discipline.

Additionally, central banks themselves have become major players in this shift, with record levels of gold accumulation in recent years. The World Gold Council reported that global central banks purchased over 1,000 metric tons of gold in 2022 alone, the highest level since records began in 1950. This strategic move signals a growing recognition among policymakers of the importance of diversifying away from fiat currency reserves and back toward assets with intrinsic value.

The increasing demand for precious metals also mirrors the rise of alternative digital assets like Bitcoin, often referred to as "digital gold" to convince people to redirect their monies into an asset that has no intrinsice value. Both gold and cryptocurrencies are viewed as hedges against fiat instability, with Bitcoin's finite supply of 21 million coins echoing the scarcity that gives commodity money its intrinsic value. As the public grows wary of paper money's inflationary tendencies, Jevons' argument for sound money—anchored by intrinsic value—continues to resonate. The convergence of physical and digital alternatives highlights a collective search for stability, further validating Jevons' assertion that trust and tangible value remain central to the viability of any monetary system.

The difficulties inherent in fiat currency systems are prominently displayed in ongoing debates concerning global monetary imbalances. The historical stability afforded by gold-backed monetary regimes is frequently cited in analyses of the U.S. dollar's position as the world's predominant reserve currency. Critics contend that this status, coupled with the

Federal Reserve's expansive monetary policies, has facilitated excessive debt accumulation and persistent trade imbalances, thereby introducing fragilities into the international financial architecture. Such critiques parallel the earlier observation that token money systems, if inadequately supervised, may foster unsustainable economic practices, jeopardizing long-term stability.

The emphasis on public confidence as the cornerstone of token money's value gains heightened significance in the current climate of escalating geopolitical and economic uncertainty. As national debt levels climb and discussions intensify over the autonomy of central banks, doubts about the enduring sustainability of paper currencies continue to mount. The advent of central bank digital currencies (CBDCs) represents an effort to adapt fiat money to the digital age, yet their introduction also sparks apprehensions regarding increased surveillance, enhanced monetary control, and the risk of novel mismanagement challenges.

The challenges of today's fiat currency systems vividly reflect the insights of Jevons and his contemporaries. The risks of inflation, overissuance, and loss of public trust that they identified remain critical concerns. As governments and central banks navigate these challenges, their responses will determine whether fiat money can retain its role as the backbone of modern economies or if alternative systems, rooted in scarcity, decentralization, or intrinsic value, will emerge as the future of money.

ABSENCE OF SOUND MONEY LEADING TO INSTABILITY

Example of Instability: The United States Today

In contrast to countries adhering to sound money principles, the United States has increasingly deviated from these practices over recent decades. The substantial expansion of the U.S. monetary base, especially following the 2008 financial crisis and again during the COVID-19 pandemic, has driven inflationary pressures to significant levels. The Federal Reserve's policies, including extensive quantitative easing (QE) and persistently low-interest rates, have fueled this sharp increase. Official Federal Reserve data indicates that M2 grew by over 40% from 2020 to 2022, primarily due to pandemic-related stimulus efforts (Federal Reserve, 2024).

Methodology (Source)	Reported Inflation Rate (Example Year)	Definition	Calculation Basis	Key Characteristics
Official CPI (Bureau of Labor Statistics)	3.6% (2024)	The official measure of inflation calculated by the Bureau of Labor Statistics (BLS).	Uses a basket of consumer goods, weighted by consumer spending.	Adjusts for changes in consumer behavior; uses geometric mean for substitution effects.
Chapwood Index (Chapwood Index)	10.5% (2024)	Measures the cost of living based on actual price increases in major cities across the U.S.	Focuses on real costs faced by urban consumers; adjusts for quality changes.	Reflects true cost-of-living increases; calculates based on daily expenses rather than a fixed basket.
ShadowStats (ShadowStats)	15% (2024)	An independent calculation of inflation that uses pre-1980 methodologies.	Reverts to older CPI calculation methods, ignoring substitution effects.	Claims to represent a more accurate measure of inflation; does not adjust for changes in consumer behavior or product quality.
Trimmed Mean CPI (Dallas Federal Reserve)	4.4% (2024)	Focuses on core inflation by excluding extreme price changes.	Removes the highest and lowest price changes to find average price movement.	Aims to provide a stable view of inflation by filtering out noise from extreme fluctuations.
Average Annual Gold Price Inflation (GoldPrice.org)	11.4% (1971–2024) OR (40% in 2024 only)	Reflects the average annual inflation rate based on gold price increase.	Divides total inflation by the number of years for annualization.	Indicates the average annualized inflation rate associated with gold's price increase.

The significant expansion of the U.S. monetary base, as documented by the Federal Reserve in 2024, has raised public concerns regarding purchasing power and financial stability. The expansion has often correlated with a decline in consumer confidence, as individuals find their savings eroded by inflation and their purchasing power diminished. After referencing data from sources like the Chapwood Index and ShadowStats, which indicate that inflation disproportionately impacts lower-income households, recent studies have shown how rising costs affect consumer behavior and spending. These studies emphasize the critical social implications of sound money, highlighting the struggle of lower-income groups to maintain their standard of living amid ongoing inflation. Additionally, understanding the Federal Reserve's historical autonomy shows how shifts in monetary policy have impacted public trust in The Fed. Fluctuations in confidence, particularly during financial crises or policy shifts, have emphasized the importance of maintaining stability to avoid policy-driven instability and ensure lasting public trust.

However, alternative assessments provide an even starker view. ShadowStats, which recalculates M2 growth using historical methodologies, suggests that actual expansion rates are higher than those reported by official sources (ShadowStats, 2024). Additionally, data from the Center for Financial Stability (CFS) reflects a similar trajectory, with broader monetary aggregates showing sustained expansion since the onset of the pandemic, indicating an environment of elevated liquidity and credit growth (Center for Financial Stability, 2024).

Inflation measures from alternative sources also reflect rates above those reported by U.S. government entities. The Chapwood Index, which adjusts for real cost-of-living increases across major U.S. cities, estimates inflation consistently over 10% annually, a rate that surpasses official BLS figures. John Williams' ShadowStats similarly recalculates inflation metrics, suggesting that real inflation has exceeded 15% during peak periods in 2022, with rates that remain higher than official metrics in 2024 (Chapwood Index, 2024; ShadowStats, 2024). Meanwhile, the Bureau of Labor Statistics (BLS) reports that inflation has slowed, currently around 3-4% year-over-year, with the Federal Reserve maintaining its 2% target for long-term inflation stability (BLS, 2024).

Comparison of Reported Inflation Rates and Gold Price Rise (2024)

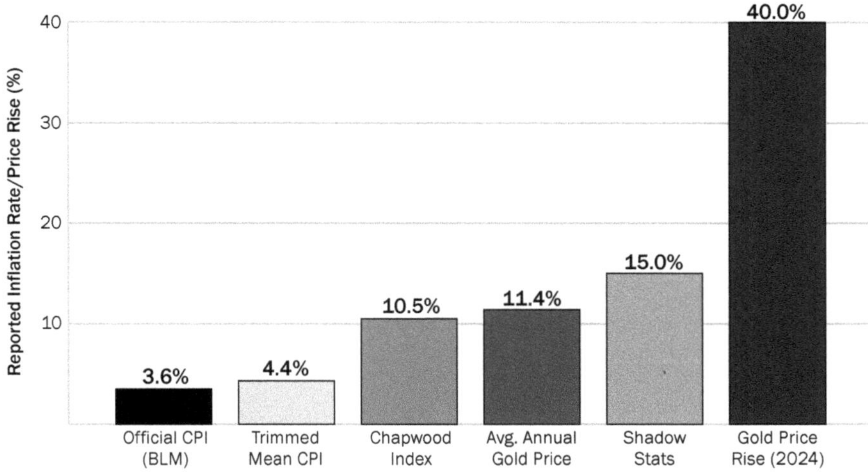

Note: The gold price normally ranges and then accelerates during repricing periods, hence, the significant difference between the gold price in 2024 versus the average annual gold price. If the paper markets did not artificially control the price, what would be the real increase year over year?

These discrepancies raise fundamental concerns about the transparency and reliability of official economic data. Given the consistent divergence between alternative metrics and government-reported figures, one must question whether these statistics adequately reflect the real economic landscape.

Furthermore, this lack of transparency highlights deeper issues regarding the Federal Reserve's operational focus. Established as an independent entity in 1913, the Federal Reserve wields substantial autonomy in monetary policy. Critics argue that its decisions often prioritize private banking interests over broader economic stability. Notably, since the removal of the gold standard in 1971, the Fed's policies have increasingly facilitated asset inflation and debt expansion, often at the expense of middle- and working-class purchasing power. The economist and former congressman Ron Paul asserts that the Fed's operations benefit financial elites, undermining sound money principles and eroding the dollar's purchasing power (Paul, 2009). Similarly, financial analyst James Rickards notes that the transition to fiat currency has entrenched cycles of debt and inflation, producing a monetary environment that prioritizes liquidity over long-term stability (Rickards, 2011).

These actions by the Federal Reserve underscore legitimate concerns about its role in today's monetary system. While intended as a custodian of the currency, the Fed's policies appear increasingly aligned with the interests of powerful financial institutions rather than the public. Sound money principles, designed to maintain a stable and equitable economic environment, have been largely sidelined under the Fed's purview, replaced by policies that arguably benefit asset holders and exacerbate wealth inequality. The divergence between official data and independent sources thus raises a critical question, can the Federal Reserve truly be seen as a neutral guardian of the economy, or is it, as some suggest, beholden to private banking interests, thereby weakening the U.S. dollar's stability and global confidence?

The Fed's actions since abandoning the gold standard reveal a shift toward fiat dependency, fueling cycles of debt and inflation. Sound money has largely been sidelined in favor of policies that stimulate economic growth at the cost of the dollar's purchasing power. These choices call into question whether the Federal Reserve's commitment is to the stability of the currency or the interests of powerful banking entities—making it a legitimate concern for citizens and sound money advocates alike.

Thus, the continued inflationary pressures have not only impacted individual purchasing power but also distorted financial markets and asset prices, creating uncertainty for both investors and consumers. As economist Thomas Sowell has pointed out, the U.S.'s deviation from sound money principles, through deficit spending and monetary expansion, has contributed to the weakening of the dollar's stability, posing long-term risks to economic growth and financial stability (Sowell, 2015).

RESTORING TRUST AND STABILITY THROUGH A RETURN TO GOLD AND COMMODITY-BACKED ASSETS

A return to a gold standard or a broader commodity-backed system would help restore trust and stability to the U.S. financial system by reintroducing discipline into monetary policy and limiting inflationary pressures. Below are three key reasons why such a shift could stabilize the economy, with supporting facts and references:

1. **Limiting Money Supply Growth:**
   Limiting money supply growth was a hallmark of the classical gold standard, where the growth of gold production often paralleled economic expansion, maintaining price stability. For instance, during the late 19th and early 20th centuries, data shows that global gold production rates aligned closely with money supply growth, reinforcing economic stability. Additionally, the financial crisis of 2008 underscored the importance of gold reserves as a confidence measure. In response, countries like Russia and China increased their gold reserves, aiming to provide a hedge against global financial uncertainty and assure investors. This historical context highlights how nations turn to commodity-backed assets during crises to reinforce investor confidence. In examining the role of the U.S. dollar as a reserve currency, the recent move by central banks, such as those in the BRICS nations, toward gold or commodity-backed reserves indicates a continued relevance for these assets. This trend illustrates that, even in a largely fiat landscape, commodity-backed reserves play an important role in maintaining monetary stability.

A commodity-backed currency, such as one tied to gold, imposes natural constraints on the growth of the money supply, as the issuance of new money must be backed by physical reserves. This acts as a check on inflationary policies. For example, under the classical gold standard (1870–1914), average global inflation rates were near zero, as money supply growth was limited by gold production. As a note, The Federal Reserve opened its doors in 1914. In contrast, fiat currencies, like the U.S. dollar, are subject to manipulation by central banks (e.g. The Federal Reserve), leading to the excessive expansion of the money supply in recent years. By returning to a gold-backed system, the U.S. could restrain the creation of money and thus reduce inflation risks.

2. **Increased Investor Confidence:**

   Gold is widely viewed as a safe-haven asset, especially during periods of financial instability. Throughout history, investors have turned to gold as a hedge against inflation and currency devaluation. During the 2008 financial crisis, for instance, gold prices surged as trust in fiat currencies waned. By reinstating a gold standard, the U.S. would send a strong signal to investors that the dollar is backed by a tangible asset, reducing market volatility and restoring confidence in the long-term value of the currency. This could encourage capital inflows and bolster U.S. economic growth. Studies have shown that countries with commodity-backed currencies tend to experience lower inflation rates and more stable economic growth

3. **Preserving the Dollar's Role as a Reserve Currency:** The U.S. dollar's status as the world's primary reserve currency depends on global trust in its value and stability. However, rising inflation and monetary mismanagement have eroded that trust. In recent years, countries like China and Russia have diversified their foreign exchange reserves away from the U.S. dollar, increasing their holdings of gold to hedge against dollar devaluation. A return to a gold or commodity-backed currency would provide a stable store of value that fiat systems cannot, potentially restoring global confidence in the dollar. According to a 2019 report from the World Gold Council, central banks around the world have been accumulating gold at a record pace, signaling that gold remains a critical component of monetary stability.

HISTORICAL PRECEDENT AND GLOBAL EXAMPLES

Transitioning back to gold or commodity-backed assets could significantly reinforce the U.S. commitment to sound money principles. Historical precedents suggest that such a shift would lead to greater monetary stability, as seen during the Bretton Woods era (1944–1971), when the U.S. dollar was pegged to gold. During this time, inflation averaged around 2.5%, highlighting how a fixed exchange rate can promote price stability (Bordo & Schwartz, 2008; Eichengreen, 2008). By linking the money supply to gold reserves, the U.S. would limit inflationary pressures, fostering a stable economic environment that bolsters investor confidence.

Several global examples illustrate the effectiveness of gold or commodity-backed systems.

For instance, Switzerland has successfully maintained its currency's strength and stability through substantial gold reserves, which have bolstered public confidence and reduced inflation volatility (Hannah, 2007). Similarly,

Germany historically enjoyed economic stability during the period of the gold mark (1871–1914), which helped to solidify its status as an industrial power while keeping inflation at bay (Hodgson, 1999).

Switzerland's history of currency stability, supported by its gold reserves, provides a well-known example of sound money policies in action. A comparative example can be found in Norway, another small, industrialized country with a history of currency stability achieved through prudent fiscal policies and oil-backed assets. This comparison underscores how both countries have managed to shield their economies from extreme volatility.

Singapore offers another relevant case, with a managed float regime linked partially to commodity-backed assets to help stabilize its currency. Singapore's approach, balancing a managed float with commodity linkages, provides a multifaceted strategy that has helped maintain stability even during periods of economic turbulence. Additionally, a concise overview of the Bretton Woods system's collapse and the subsequent transition to fiat currency clarifies the conditions leading to this pivotal change. Understanding why Bretton Woods gave way to fiat dominance highlights the challenges faced by commodity-backed systems and the ongoing discussions about their viability.

Money Supply Growth vs. Inflation Rates (1970–2024)

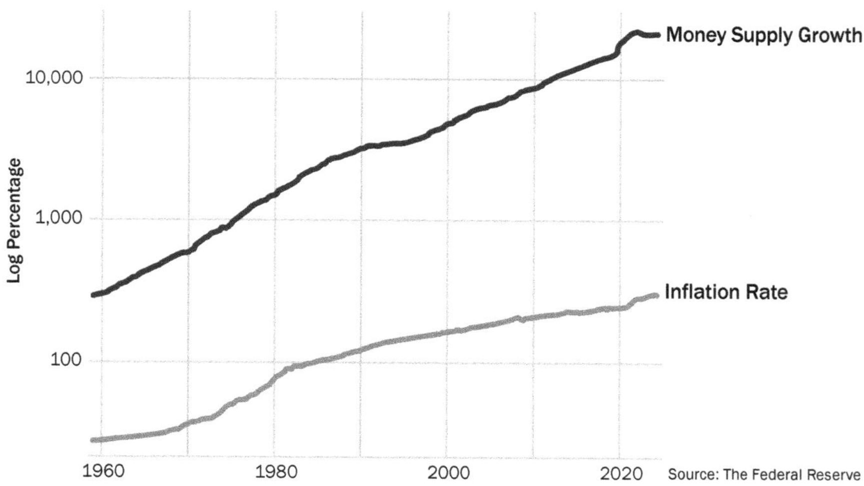

Source: The Federal Reserve

In Singapore, the Monetary Authority of Singapore (MAS) adopts a managed float exchange rate policy, indirectly linking its currency to a basket of commodities. This approach has enabled the nation to maintain a robust economy while ensuring price stability, showcasing how commodity-backed frameworks can function effectively in modern economies (Tan, 2017). Such models underline the potential benefits of adopting similar systems to restore the U.S. dollar's stability.

Moreover, adopting a gold standard could safeguard the U.S. dollar's status as the world's primary reserve currency. Countries that maintain a commodity-backed system often experience reduced volatility and enhanced trust in their monetary systems, as demonstrated by Switzerland's management of its currency through substantial gold reserves (Hannah, 2007). Such confidence is essential for maintaining the dollar's global standing, especially in an era marked by increasing skepticism toward fiat currencies and government monetary policies.

Restoring monetary discipline through a gold or commodity-backed system would also offer long-term solutions to inflation and financial instability. Proponents argue that such a framework not only curtails excessive money printing but also encourages responsible fiscal policies, ultimately leading to sustainable economic growth (Lacker, 2014; Selgin, 2019). This approach could address the cyclical nature of financial crises that have plagued fiat currency systems, providing a more stable economic future.

Transitioning to gold or commodity-backed assets represents a viable pathway for the U.S. to reclaim its commitment to sound money principles, stabilize the money supply, enhance investor confidence, and maintain the dollar's global standing while addressing the pressing challenges of inflation and financial instability.

CHAPTER 2

The Empire's Currency Has No Clothes

For decades, the U.S. dollar has reigned as the undisputed king of global finance—used for trade, held in reserves, and trusted as a symbol of economic stability. But behind the facade of strength lies a growing recognition—the dollar's dominance comes at a cost. Many countries are actively exploring de-dollarization to regain economic independence and mitigate the inflationary risks associated with U.S. dollar reliance. Dollar dominance in the global economy has meant that fluctuations in U.S. monetary policy often have direct impacts on other nations, especially those heavily dependent on the dollar for trade and reserves. As the Federal Reserve expands the U.S. money supply or adjusts interest rates, the effects reverberate worldwide, often driving inflation or economic instability in dollar-dependent countries. By reducing reliance on the dollar, countries aim to shield their economies from these external influences and better manage domestic inflation. Advocates of sound money principles argue that de-dollarization aligns with a strategy of self-sufficiency, reducing dependency on foreign fiat currencies in favor of stable, intrinsic-value systems. The rise of de-dollarization initiatives reflects a global trend toward monetary systems that prioritize stability and control, countering the volatility often associated with fiat systems (Gopinath, 2023; Economist, 2022). The empire's currency, it seems, is no longer clothed in unquestioned legitimacy.

CASE STUDIES: RUSSIA, CHINA, AND LATIN AMERICAN COUNTRIES' EFFORTS TO ESTABLISH CURRENCY INDEPENDENCE

Several nations illustrate distinct approaches to establishing monetary independence from the dollar. Russia, for instance, accelerated its gold reserves accumulation after 2014 in response to Western sanctions, making gold a cornerstone of its financial defense strategy. By holding more gold and fewer dollar-based assets, Russia reduces its vulnerability to U.S. policy changes and geopolitical tensions. In 2022, Russia's central bank reported that gold comprised nearly a quarter of its reserves, demonstrating a significant shift toward sound-money-style asset backing (World Gold Council, 2022). China has also pursued de-dollarization by promoting the yuan in international trade and establishing bilateral currency swap agreements with countries like Argentina, Russia, and Iran. These swaps allow countries to trade directly in their local currencies, bypassing the dollar. China's Belt and Road Initiative (BRI) has further encouraged yuan-based transactions in infrastructure deals across Asia, Africa, and Latin America, reinforcing the yuan's role as a viable alternative to the dollar (Schuman, 2021).

Expanding on the case studies of Russia, China, and Latin America reveals unique approaches to reducing dollar dependency, each shaped by specific economic goals and geopolitical contexts.

RUSSIA: BUILDING GOLD RESERVES AND DIVERSIFYING TRADE CURRENCIES

Russia's de-dollarization strategy is driven by geopolitical motivations and the desire for economic self-sufficiency. Following sanctions in 2014, Russia accelerated its de-dollarization efforts by significantly increasing its gold reserves, which reached record highs in recent years. By shifting reserves to gold, Russia insulates its economy from U.S. sanctions and currency fluctuations while adopting a sound-money approach that anchors part of its reserve holdings in assets with intrinsic value. In 2022, gold comprised around 23% of Russia's reserves, reflecting a shift away from dollar assets in favor of more resilient alternatives (World Gold Council, 2022).

Beyond gold, Russia has also moved to conduct trade in local currencies with countries such as China, India, and Turkey, particularly in energy transactions. For instance, Russia's state-owned energy companies have increasingly accepted payments in rubles or yuan rather than dollars. This shift is part of a larger strategy to develop a "sanction-proof" economy that relies less on the dollar for trade settlements. In 2021, Russia and China settled more than 25% of their trade in local currencies, a significant shift from prior years when the dollar dominated transactions. By bolstering reserves and promoting local-currency trade, Russia seeks to mitigate external economic risks and enhance its economic resilience (Schuman, 2021).

CHINA: BELT AND ROAD INITIATIVE (BRI), MBRIDGE, DIGITAL YUAN, AND NEW DEVELOPMENT BANK

China has been a leader in de-dollarization efforts, developing an array of tools to promote the yuan and diminish reliance on the U.S. dollar. Central to these efforts is the Belt and Road Initiative (BRI), which funds infrastructure projects in over 60 countries across Asia, Africa, and Latin America. The BRI offers financing options in yuan, encouraging partner countries to hold and transact in China's currency rather than the dollar. This has fostered a shift toward yuan-denominated transactions, which builds acceptance of the yuan as a reserve currency and embeds it more deeply into global trade networks (Schuman, 2021).

China's development of digital currency technology, particularly the digital yuan, is another key component in its de-dollarization strategy. Launched in 2020, the digital yuan has been rolled out domestically and tested in cross-border transactions. With its digital currency, China aims to enhance the yuan's efficiency in global trade while also providing a secure, government-backed alternative to private cryptocurrencies. The digital yuan's adoption could significantly impact international transactions by providing a seamless and efficient payment system that bypasses the traditional dollar-dominated SWIFT network (Schwartz, 2023).

The mBridge project, a blockchain-based platform created in collaboration with Hong Kong, Thailand, and the UAE, further supports China's goal to facilitate cross-border payments in local currencies. By using blockchain to make these transactions faster and more efficient, mBridge allows participating countries to engage in trade without relying on the dollar. The project also aims to reduce the costs associated with foreign exchange, making it attractive to countries looking to diversify away from dollar-based trade. mBridge's development signals China's commitment to reshaping the global payments system, aligning with its broader vision of a multipolar currency world (Economist, 2022).

Additionally, the New Development Bank (NDB), founded by BRICS countries (Brazil, Russia, India, China, and South Africa), has been pivotal in offering funding alternatives to the U.S.-led International Monetary Fund (IMF) and World Bank. The NDB funds projects using local currencies and has introduced measures to support trade in the yuan among BRICS nations. By promoting the yuan within BRICS and offering loans in local currencies, the NDB contributes to de-dollarization by establishing alternatives to dollar-dominated international financial institutions (Armstrong, 2023).

LATIN AMERICA: BRAZIL'S RECENT POLICIES AND JAVIER MILEI'S DOLLARIZATION PUSH IN ARGENTINA

In Latin America, Brazil and Argentina are taking different approaches to monetary independence. Brazil, under President Lula da Silva, has pursued de-dollarization through regional integration efforts and direct currency agreements with trading partners. One recent development is the proposed South American currency, the "sur" (meaning "south" in Spanish and Portuguese), which would serve as a regional currency to facilitate trade without relying on the dollar. Though still in the early stages, the "sur" is intended to deepen trade ties within South America and reduce dependence on the dollar, aligning with Brazil's broader aim to establish economic self-reliance in the region (IADB, 2023).

Brazil has also been proactive in signing currency swap agreements with major trading partners. The agreement with China, for instance, allows the two countries to settle bilateral trade in yuan and reais, bypassing the dollar entirely. This approach has gained traction, with Brazilian banks increasingly facilitating yuan-denominated trade. By fostering regional currency cooperation and expanding yuan transactions, Brazil aims to create a more stable economic environment less subject to external shocks from U.S. monetary policy (Gopinath, 2023).

In contrast, Argentina has recently experienced a different form of monetary debate. President Javier Milei has argued in favor of dollarization, contending that adopting the U.S. dollar as Argentina's official currency would help stabilize the economy and curb hyperinflation, which has exceeded 100% in recent years. Argentina's peso has been subject to extreme devaluation, and dollarization is seen by some as a solution to regain economic stability and prevent further inflation. However, this approach would also mean Argentina forfeits control over its monetary policy, making it subject to the Federal Reserve's policy decisions. Critics argue that while dollarization may temporarily alleviate inflation, it risks long-term dependency and loss of financial sovereignty (IADB, 2023).

Despite Milei's push for dollarization, Argentina has also explored options that reduce dollar reliance in regional trade. It has engaged in local currency agreements with Brazil and China, which allow for direct transactions without converting to the dollar. This mixed approach highlights Argentina's complex economic situation: while dollarization offers a solution to immediate inflationary pressures, local currency agreements align with sound money principles and regional autonomy (Economist, 2022).

INDIA: LOCAL CURRENCY TRADE AGREEMENTS AND RUPEE PROMOTION

India, another example of a nation exploring currency independence, has increasingly promoted the use of the rupee in regional and global trade. With an economy heavily reliant on imports of oil and other commodities, India's dependence on the dollar has contributed to trade imbalances and vulnerability to U.S. monetary policies. To counter these challenges, India has signed currency swap agreements with countries like Japan and the UAE, allowing for trade in rupees rather than dollars. Moreover, the Indian government encourages exporters to settle payments in rupees, particularly with trading partners in Africa and Southeast Asia. These efforts align with sound money principles by reducing reliance on fiat currency fluctuations and enhancing India's economic resilience against global market changes (Gopinath, 2023).

TURKEY: REDUCING DOLLARIZATION THROUGH POLICY REFORMS AND CURRENCY AGREEMENTS

Turkey has also pursued de-dollarization, largely to address inflation and stabilize its economy. A significant portion of Turkey's economy is dollarized, with many loans and transactions priced in dollars. The Turkish government has implemented a series of policy measures to increase lira usage, including tax incentives for local currency transactions and policies that encourage banks to convert dollar deposits into lira. Additionally, Turkey has signed currency swap agreements with Qatar and China, which provide access to foreign currency reserves without relying on the dollar. These steps are aimed at stabilizing the lira, reducing inflation, and minimizing the economic shocks associated with external dollar fluctuations (Armstrong, 2023).

IRAN: CONDUCTING TRADE IN LOCAL CURRENCIES TO CIRCUMVENT SANCTIONS

Iran's de-dollarization strategy is largely driven by its need to bypass U.S. sanctions, which restrict its access to the dollar-based financial system. Iran has increasingly conducted trade in alternative currencies, particularly with China and Russia, using the yuan, ruble, and other local currencies. In addition, Iran has explored cryptocurrency solutions to facilitate international transactions outside of the dollar system, allowing it to engage in trade despite sanctions. These measures have helped Iran maintain some degree of economic stability and demonstrate an innovative approach to de-dollarization in the face of geopolitical constraints (Schuman, 2021; Economist, 2022).

Each of these examples underscores a global shift toward currency independence and diversification as countries aim to reduce their exposure to dollar volatility and establish more stable economic systems. Whether through gold accumulation, local currency swaps, digital currency initiatives, or regional currency proposals, these nations are embracing sound money principles that prioritize stability, control, and resilience over-dependence on foreign fiat currencies.

SAFEGUARDING THE DOLLAR'S GLOBAL STANDING AMIDST SKEPTICISM OF FIAT CURRENCIES

As fiat currencies come under increased scrutiny for their inflationary tendencies, the U.S. faces the challenge of retaining the dollar's role as the world's reserve currency. With de-dollarization movements gaining traction, maintaining the dollar's credibility requires policies that can counter global skepticism of fiat systems. Critics argue that the dollar's value is vulnerable to the inflationary effects of continuous money supply expansion, which can erode purchasing power both domestically and globally. To address these concerns, some economists recommend a shift toward sound money principles, potentially incorporating partial commodity backing to reinforce the dollar's stability. This approach could involve linking the dollar's value to tangible assets like gold, thereby reducing the risks associated with fiat currency's lack of intrinsic value. By adopting policies that limit currency expansion and enhance stability, the U.S. could strengthen the dollar's global standing and reassure other nations of its reliability as a reserve currency (Armstrong, 2023; Salerno, 2021).

THE PURPOSE OF DE-DOLLARIZATION: REDUCING RELIANCE ON A FOREIGN RESERVE CURRENCY TO ENHANCE MONETARY SOVEREIGNTY AND CONTROL INFLATION

For countries adopting de-dollarization, the primary goal is to regain control over their monetary policy by reducing dependence on a foreign reserve currency. Countries that rely heavily on the dollar often find themselves subject to U.S. policy shifts, which can lead to economic instability, especially during times of dollar appreciation or inflation. By moving away from dollar reliance, nations can insulate their economies from external pressures and gain the flexibility to pursue domestic goals. For example, China's promotion of the yuan for international trade aligns with its broader goal of controlling inflation through a monetary policy tailored to its domestic economy rather than being constrained by U.S. policy decisions. Sound money advocates support these de-dollarization initiatives as they provide a pathway to greater monetary stability, limiting the inflationary risks associated with overreliance on a fiat currency outside a country's control (Schwartz, 2023; Tett, 2021).

ADDRESSING VOLATILITY THROUGH A RETURN TO COMMODITY BACKING

The volatility of fiat currencies has led many economists to consider the benefits of a return to commodity-backed currency systems, such as a partial gold standard. Sound money proponents argue that commodity-backed currencies offer a buffer against inflation and currency devaluation, providing a stable store of value by linking currency supply to tangible assets. This approach constrains excessive monetary expansion, as currency issuance is limited by the availability of the backing asset. Historically, gold-backed systems reduced inflationary risks, as observed in the 19th-century gold standard era, where major economies enjoyed relatively low inflation rates. A modern example of this approach can be seen in central banks' recent increase in gold purchases, which reflect a desire for asset-backed stability amidst fiat-driven volatility (World Gold Council, 2022). For countries grappling with inflationary pressures, a commodity-backed currency represents a return to sound money principles that prioritize currency stability and controlled expansion, aligning economic growth with a foundation of asset-backed value.

RESTORING GLOBAL CONFIDENCE IN THE U.S. DOLLAR AS A STABLE CURRENCY

To address the global momentum toward de-dollarization, the United States can explore a variety of options to restore confidence in the U.S. dollar as a stable reserve currency. These options span from fiscal and monetary policy reforms to technological innovations and diplomatic strategies that could reinforce the dollar's role in a shifting global economy.

1. **Limiting Fiscal Expansion and Ensuring Fiscal Discipline**
   To restore confidence in the dollar, many economists argue that the U.S. government should focus on reducing its fiscal deficit and debt accumulation, thereby enhancing the dollar's credibility as a store of value. Excessive debt-financed spending has contributed to inflationary pressures and raised concerns about the dollar's long-

term stability. Countries such as Germany have long practiced fiscal discipline, maintaining a balanced budget that has enabled it to keep inflation low and avoid the need for excessive currency issuance. By adopting a similar approach, the U.S. could signal a commitment to sound money principles, which are attractive to international markets that value predictable and stable currency policies (Salerno, 2021; Armstrong, 2023).

2. **Gradual Introduction of Commodity-Backed Currency Components**
   A partial or hybrid commodity backing for the dollar could also strengthen global confidence. While a full return to the gold standard may not be practical, linking a portion of the dollar to commodities, such as gold, silver, or a diversified basket of resources, would help limit unrestricted currency expansion and provide a stable intrinsic value. Countries like Switzerland and Singapore have maintained significant gold reserves to anchor their currencies, setting a precedent for asset-backed value that reassures both domestic and international stakeholders. Even modest measures, such as increased gold reserves, could demonstrate a commitment to the dollar's purchasing power and stability (World Gold Council, 2022).
3. **Issuing a U.S. Central Bank Digital Currency (CBDC) with Strong Regulatory Backing**
   As central bank digital currencies (CBDCs) gain traction worldwide, a U.S.-backed digital dollar could offer several advantages. First, it would modernize dollar transactions, improving transaction efficiency and transparency, particularly in regions with limited banking infrastructure. Second, a digital dollar could counter rising competition from the Chinese digital yuan, which China has begun promoting in global trade as a challenge to dollar dominance. By issuing a digital dollar that adheres to sound money principles—emphasizing stability, transparency, and accountability—the U.S. can expand the dollar's accessibility and attractiveness in global trade and finance (Schwartz, 2023; Tett, 2021).

4. **Strengthening Dollar-Based Trade Agreements and Economic Alliances**
   To bolster the dollar's role in international finance, the U.S. could prioritize diplomatic efforts that solidify dollar-based trade partnerships. Economic alliances with countries and regions that rely on the dollar for trade, such as those in the Middle East, Southeast Asia, and the European Union, would ensure sustained dollar demand. For example, the European Central Bank holds substantial dollar reserves, underscoring the importance of alliances in reinforcing the dollar's status. Strategic agreements with these regions could counteract de-dollarization trends by underscoring the dollar's benefits in trade stability and lowering transaction costs. Furthermore, dollar-based trade agreements with emerging markets could foster economic interdependence, reducing incentives for these countries to pivot toward alternative currencies (Friedman, 2022).
5. **Implementing Inflation Targeting and Transparent Monetary Policies**
   The Federal Reserve's inflation-targeting policies could be strengthened to provide further assurances of long-term monetary stability. By adhering to clearly defined inflation targets and making transparent policy commitments, The Fed could alleviate concerns about inflation's impact on the dollar's purchasing power. This approach mirrors the successful strategies of countries like Canada and New Zealand, which have implemented strict inflation-targeting frameworks that enhance currency stability and investor confidence. Transparent inflation control would reinforce the dollar's role as a reliable store of value, appealing to international markets seeking predictable monetary policy (Gopinath, 2023).
6. **Reinforcing the U.S. Dollar's Stability through Foreign Exchange Market Interventions**
   Foreign exchange market interventions could also serve as a tool for maintaining dollar stability. During periods of high volatility or speculative attacks on the dollar, the Federal Reserve could strategically intervene in currency markets to support the dollar's value. For instance,

Japan has periodically intervened in foreign exchange markets to stabilize the yen, which has helped maintain its international position despite volatility. Such interventions, if carefully managed, could help the U.S. support the dollar's exchange rate and deter countries from shifting reserves to alternative currencies during periods of instability (Schuman, 2021).

7. **Encouraging Dollar Usage in Strategic Sectors and Industries**
   To sustain the dollar's international role, the U.S. could encourage dollar-denominated transactions in strategic industries, such as energy, commodities, and technology. The dollar's widespread use in global oil and commodity markets is a significant factor behind its reserve currency status. By promoting dollar-based transactions in emerging industries, such as clean energy or semiconductor production, the U.S. could extend the dollar's relevance in rapidly growing sectors. This strategy could involve establishing agreements with key energy-producing countries or technological alliances that reinforce dollar usage in global supply chains, reducing the likelihood of alternative currency adoption in these sectors (Schwartz, 2023).
8. **Promoting Dollar-Backed Financial Instruments in International Markets**
   The U.S. can further strengthen the dollar's reserve role by promoting dollar-denominated financial instruments in emerging markets. Dollar-based bonds, treasuries, and other instruments can offer stability to international investors and governments. For instance, U.S. Treasuries have long been viewed as safe assets, attracting foreign central banks and sovereign wealth funds. By ensuring the availability of stable, dollar-denominated assets with attractive yields, the U.S. could counter alternative currency initiatives and maintain the dollar's appeal as a store of value (IADB, 2023).

9. **Expanding Educational and Financial Programs to Promote Dollar Literacy Globally**
   Lastly, the U.S. could invest in educational and financial programs that promote an understanding of the dollar's strengths and benefits. Through initiatives like the World Bank and IMF, the U.S. could support educational programs for emerging economies that emphasize the benefits of dollar stability, the role of sound money principles, and the dollar's contribution to international economic stability. These programs could also include dollar-backed financial literacy initiatives that clarify the U.S.'s fiscal and monetary commitments, reducing skepticism and promoting trust in the dollar's future (Armstrong, 2023).

Restoring confidence in the dollar requires a multi-faceted approach that combines fiscal discipline, monetary transparency, innovation in digital currency, and strategic global alliances. Policies such as commodity-backed dollar components, targeted economic partnerships, and financial education programs could address rising concerns about fiat currency stability. These measures, rooted in sound money principles, offer a comprehensive response to the global trend of de-dollarization, reinforcing the dollar's role as a stable and trusted currency for the future.

CHAPTER 3
Money That Holds Its Value

Restoring sound money principles has far-reaching implications for long-term inflation control and financial stability. By adopting policies that limit currency expansion and promote asset-backed or controlled supply systems, sound money advocates argue that countries can prevent the inflationary cycles commonly associated with fiat systems. This approach emphasizes disciplined fiscal practices, where governments prioritize real economic growth over short-term monetary expansion.

For instance, during the classical gold standard period, economies like the U.S. and the U.K. maintained low inflation and high purchasing power due to currency supply constraints. Today, reintroducing sound money policies could promote similar outcomes, mitigating the risks of excessive debt and speculative economic growth while fostering a stable environment for sustainable development (Salerno, 2021).

THE IMPORTANCE OF CURTAILING EXCESSIVE MONEY PRINTING AND FOSTERING RESPONSIBLE FISCAL POLICIES

One of the core tenets of sound money principles is the importance of curtailing excessive money printing and encouraging responsible fiscal policies to avoid inflation and economic instability. Excessive currency issuance dilutes purchasing power and erodes savings, creating a cycle of rising prices that undermines financial stability. Sound money principles advocate for disciplined monetary practices that align currency expansion with actual economic growth, rather than debt-fueled government spending. In practical terms, this would involve limiting currency issuance to maintain purchasing power and support a stable economic environment. Historical examples, such as the low-inflation period under the classical gold standard, illustrate the benefits of a sound money approach that curbs inflation by aligning fiscal policy with productivity growth. Adopting such principles today could safeguard against inflationary risks, supporting both domestic stability and international confidence in the currency (Schwartz, 2023; Armstrong, 2023).

RESISTANCE TO INFLATION

Another critical attribute of sound money is its resistance to inflation. Milton Friedman (1968) argued that sound money must exhibit a strong resistance to inflation, meaning that its supply should not outpace the economy's capacity to absorb it. Excessive growth in the money supply leads to inflation, which diminishes the purchasing power of currency and causes prices for goods and services to rise. According to Friedman's quantity theory of money, controlling inflation is fundamental to economic stability, as runaway inflation or hyperinflation can have severe consequences, such as eroding savings, reducing real income, and destabilizing economies. Sound money's inherent resistance to inflation safeguards against these issues, ensuring the currency retains its value over time.

Friedman's views on inflation resistance find support in comparing economies that experienced hyperinflation and relied on sound money principles to recover. For instance, Zimbabwe's shift to using foreign currency, specifically the U.S. dollar, to combat hyperinflation provides a notable case. While the Zimbabwean dollar had depreciated to near worthlessness, the adoption of a stable foreign currency helped the country stabilize. Similarly, Switzerland's gold-backed currency until 1999 showcased a modern application of inflation-resistant practices, as the Swiss Franc retained value better than many fiat currencies. Other countries, such as Venezuela, have partially reverted to sound money practices, turning to dollarization to stabilize amid severe inflation.

Moreover, data on inflation rates post-Bretton Woods illustrates how fiat systems correlate with higher inflation levels, demonstrating sound money's comparative resilience against inflation.

For example, Switzerland's adherence to a partial gold standard until 1999 helped it maintain one of the lowest inflation rates in the world during the 20th century. By tying a portion of its currency to gold, Switzerland was able to curb excessive monetary expansion, contributing to long-term price stability even during global economic downturns (Hannah, 2007; World Gold Council, n.d.). Similarly, the Bretton Woods system (1944–1971), which pegged major world currencies, including the U.S. dollar, to gold, successfully kept inflation low in participating countries. During this period, average inflation rates were significantly lower compared to the post-Bretton Woods era, as the discipline imposed by gold-backed currency helped to prevent the excessive expansion of money supplies (Bordo & Schwartz, 2008).

During the Napoleonic Wars (1803–1815), Napoleon Bonaparte adhered to a gold standard, which played a crucial role in stabilizing France's economy amidst the tumultuous conditions of war. By maintaining a currency backed by gold, Napoleon was able to finance military expenditures without resorting to excessive inflation, thereby preserving the purchasing power of the French franc (Hodgson, 1999; Mises Institute, n.d.).

Another notable example is Canada's experience during the Great Depression (1929–1939), where the adherence to a gold standard initially helped stabilize the economy. Although Canada eventually abandoned the gold standard in 1931, its prior commitment limited inflationary pressures during a period when many other countries experienced significant price instability (Klein, 2009; Mints, 1945).

Additionally, Australia's gold standard from 1852 to 1914 provided a framework for economic stability. The consistent value of the Australian pound, linked to gold, helped the nation avoid significant inflationary episodes while promoting trade and investment during a period of rapid economic growth (Mackay, 2011; Reserve Bank of Australia, n.d.).

Finally, New Zealand demonstrated effective inflation resistance during the early 20th century under a gold standard. The country experienced relatively stable prices and controlled inflation until its abandonment of the gold standard in 1931. This stability allowed for sustained economic growth and public confidence in the currency, showcasing the benefits of a sound money approach (W. J. Phillips, 1955; Reserve Bank of New Zealand, n.d.).

These historical examples underscore the effectiveness of sound money principles in resisting inflation and preserving currency value, reinforcing the argument for a return to commodity-backed systems in contemporary economic policy.

CONVERTIBILITY INTO GOODS AND SERVICES

Ludwig von Mises (1953) emphasized the importance of convertibility into goods and services as a fundamental characteristic of sound money. This feature ensures that money can be directly utilized as a medium of exchange for acquiring tangible assets. In today's digital age, this concept can be extended to digital assets, such as cryptocurrencies that are backed by commodities like gold.

For instance, Tether Gold (XAUT) is a cryptocurrency pegged to physical gold, enabling users to transact digitally while preserving the stability and intrinsic value associated with the commodity. This stablecoin merges the advantages of blockchain technology with the longstanding value of gold, offering users a reliable medium of exchange that resists inflation (Zohar, 2020; CoinMarketCap, n.d.).

Another notable example is Paxos Gold (PAXG), a cryptocurrency that is also backed by physical gold stored in secure vaults. Paxos enables users to buy, sell, and redeem gold at any time, ensuring immediate convertibility into a tangible asset. The use of PAXG illustrates how digital currencies can uphold the principles of sound money while providing the convenience and efficiency of modern digital transactions (Paxos, n.d.; Decker, 2021). This hybrid model not only facilitates faster transactions but also aligns with the demands of contemporary economies, all while adhering to the core tenets of sound money.

Historically, during the period from 1821 to 1914, the United Kingdom operated under the gold standard, with inflation averaging just below 0.5%

per year (Maddison, 2001; Hannah, 2007). This stability in price levels fostered an environment conducive to long-term trade and investment, leading to minimal currency depreciation over nearly a century. For example, between 1870 and 1914, price levels fluctuated within a narrow range, enhancing both investor and public confidence in the purchasing power of the British pound, even amidst global economic fluctuations (Cameron, 1967; World Gold Council, n.d.).

This low-inflation environment sharply contrasts with the post-gold standard era, during which inflation rates became significantly more volatile. The stability of currency during the gold standard period was largely attributable to fixed gold convertibility, which directly tied the money supply to gold reserves. This mechanism effectively limited inflationary pressures, ensuring long-term price stability (Bank of England, n.d.).

Following World War I, when the UK suspended the gold standard, inflation rates surged, highlighting the consequences of divergent monetary policies on long-term price stability. In contrast, the 20th century experienced heightened inflation, particularly during periods of fiat money issuance that lacked gold convertibility. This historical context underscores the critical role of the gold standard in stabilizing currency and managing inflation through a commodity-backed system, contrasting sharply with the greater inflation volatility seen in contemporary fiat currency regimes (Hannah, 2007; Maddison, 2001).

Another historical example is the Bretton Woods system (1944–1971), in which the U.S. dollar was pegged to gold while other currencies were pegged to the dollar. This system promoted global economic stability and facilitated trade by allowing countries to convert their currencies into U.S. dollars, which were, in turn, convertible into gold. The Bretton Woods system successfully maintained relatively low inflation rates compared to the subsequent floating exchange rate period, illustrating the importance of convertibility for economic stability (Bordo & Schwartz, 2008; Eichengreen, 2008).

Mises' perspective reinforces that without convertibility, money's role as a facilitator of trade and economic interactions would be severely diminished, compromising its core function within the economy (Mises,

1953). Furthermore, the rise of digital payment systems highlights the necessity of ensuring that these systems maintain the characteristics of sound money, particularly convertibility. By integrating the principles of sound money into digital platforms, economies can harness technological innovations while safeguarding against the inflation and currency devaluation pitfalls often associated with fiat systems (Friedman, 1968; Hayek, 1976).

EVOLUTION OF MONEY THROUGH HISTORY

The development of money reflects the economic, political, and social advancements across civilizations. Initially, economies operated on barter systems, where goods and services were exchanged directly. The inefficiencies of barter—especially the need for a "double coincidence of wants" (where both parties must want what the other offers)—led early societies to seek more standardized mediums of exchange. Anthropologist David Graeber (2011) posits that debt and credit systems may have preceded money, as early trade often relied on social contracts rather than direct exchange.

The introduction of commodity money, tangible items with intrinsic value, such as cattle, grain, or salt, marked a significant shift in monetary systems. Early Mesopotamian civilizations (around 3000 BCE) utilized silver and barley as standardized forms of money. As economies became more complex, metals like gold and silver emerged as primary currencies due to their durability, divisibility, and relative scarcity. The Roman Empire, for example, established the aureus (gold) and denarius (silver) as standard currencies, a system that endured for centuries, relying on the intrinsic value of these metals (Davies, 2002).

Glyn Davies (2002) charts the evolution from these early forms of commodity money to the emergence of coinage around the 7th century BCE, first in Lydia (modern-day Turkey). Coinage represented a significant advancement as it allowed for state-controlled currency systems with standardized weights and values, facilitating trade across regions.

However, the reliance on commodity money was not without

challenges. The intrinsic value of precious metals linked the money supply directly to resource availability, leading to deflationary pressures when economies expanded faster than their supply of gold or silver. This issue became especially pronounced during the 19th-century Gold Standard, where countries pegged their currency to gold. While the gold standard provided stability by fixing currency values, it also limited governments' ability to respond to economic crises, preventing them from increasing the money supply without depleting gold reserves. Barry Eichengreen (1996) notes that this rigidity contributed to prolonged economic downturns, such as during the Great Depression.

The eventual shift toward fiat currencies, money without intrinsic value that derives its worth from government decree, marked a fundamental transformation in monetary systems. The Nixon Shock of 1971, when the United States abandoned the gold standard, was pivotal in the evolution of fiat money. John Williamson (1993) discusses this transition as part of the broader rise of central banking, where control over the money supply shifted from commodity scarcity to institutions like the Federal Reserve. This transition allowed for more flexible monetary policies, enabling governments to adjust the money supply to combat inflation or stimulate economic growth, but it also introduced new risks. Without the discipline of a commodity standard, the risk of inflation and currency devaluation increased, relying solely on trust in the issuing government's stability and fiscal responsibility.

Moreover, the role of central banks became crucial in managing national economies through monetary policy. Milton Friedman (1968) famously argued for controlling inflation via monetary supply regulation, emphasizing that sound money—whether under a commodity or fiat system—should maintain purchasing power and price stability. The post-1971 world saw central banks experimenting with various approaches to stabilize currencies, from interest rate policies to quantitative easing, as fiat money came to dominate global financial systems.

The progression from commodity money to fiat money illustrates how economic demands, technological innovations, and political decisions have reshaped the principles of stable and accepted money. Today, the concept of money continues to evolve with the emergence of digital currencies like Bitcoin and Central Bank Digital Currencies (CBDCs), which could further challenge traditional understandings of value and monetary governance. These innovations highlight that the history of money is not static; it continually adapts in response to new economic realities (Higgins, 2020; Raskin & Yermack, 2016).

As we navigate the complexities of modern financial systems, it is crucial to recognize that centralized technologies can perpetuate the shortcomings of sound money. Centralized digital currencies and payment systems often prioritize efficiency and control over the intrinsic values associated with sound money, potentially leading to inflationary pressures and currency devaluation similar to those seen in fiat systems (Zhao, 2020; DeSantis, 2022). The reliance on centralized entities to manage monetary supply and transaction verification raises concerns about transparency, accountability, and the inherent risks of financial mismanagement (Tucker, 2019). As history has shown, the move away from sound money principles can result in economic instability, and thus, humanity must approach technological advancements in finance with caution. A renewed commitment to sound money—grounded in the principles of convertibility, stability, and intrinsic value—could help safeguard against the pitfalls of modern monetary practices while fostering an environment conducive to sustainable economic growth.

ROLE OF SOUND MONEY IN ECONOMIC GROWTH

The stability provided by sound money has historically been a cornerstone of economic growth and development. Sound money, defined as money that maintains its purchasing power over time, creates a predictable environment for businesses, governments, and consumers alike. When the value of money is stable, the risks associated with currency depreciation, inflation, or sudden value fluctuations are minimized. Charles Kindleberger (1978) highlighted that such stability is crucial for allowing economies to expand without the distortions caused by erratic monetary policies or volatile currencies. Countries with sound money systems can build a foundation of trust, not only among their citizens but also with foreign investors (Eichengreen, 1996).

One of the primary advantages of sound money is its role in fostering investment and capital formation. When investors believe that a currency will maintain its value, they are more likely to commit capital to long-term projects, confident that inflation will not erode their returns. Ludwig von Mises (1953) emphasized that stable money forms the basis for rational economic calculation. In his view, inflationary environments distort price signals, complicating businesses' ability to assess the true value of goods and services and undermining long-term economic planning (Hayek, 1976).

Moreover, sound money creates a stable environment for foreign direct investment (FDI). Countries with sound monetary policies are more likely to attract foreign investors seeking to protect their investments from the erosion caused by currency devaluation. Eichengreen (1996) noted that during the classical Gold Standard period (1870-1914), international investment reached unprecedented levels, as the fixed value of currencies against gold reduced exchange rate risks, thus fostering global trade and capital mobility.

In contrast, countries that abandon sound money principles often experience the opposite effect: capital flight, where investors withdraw their assets due to fears of devaluation or hyperinflation. The hyperinflation crisis in Zimbabwe during the early 2000s eroded confidence in the national currency, leading to a collapse of investment and a severe economic downturn (Moyo, 2009). Similarly, the decline in confidence in the Argentine peso during various financial crises has driven economic instability, resulting from the government's inability to maintain sound monetary policy (Cohen, 2019).

Friedrich Hayek (1976) explored the relationship between sound money and economic growth, arguing that unsound monetary systems, especially those where governments exert excessive control over the money supply, often lead to boom-and-bust cycles. The artificial expansion of credit during periods of loose monetary policy can result in unsustainable bubbles, followed by economic recessions. In contrast, sound money systems maintain equilibrium in the economy by ensuring that credit expansion aligns with actual growth rather than speculative excess (Bordo & Schwartz, 2008).

Finally, sound money promotes financial market resilience. In a stable monetary environment, banks and financial institutions can operate without fear of sudden devaluations undermining their assets or liabilities. Kindleberger (1978) noted that sound monetary policies contributed to the development of robust financial markets during periods of economic expansion, particularly in the 19th century. Stable currencies facilitated the creation of sophisticated financial products, such as bonds and equities, which helped fund industrialization and infrastructure development in Europe and the United States (Baker, 2018).

he benefits of sound money extend far beyond mere price stability. By reducing risks associated with unpredictable currency value changes, sound money fosters an environment conducive to long-term investment, promotes international trade and capital flows, and supports the development of resilient financial markets. Historical examples, from the Gold Standard to modern monetary regimes prioritizing inflation control, demonstrate that sound money remains a key pillar of sustained economic growth.

RELATIONSHIP BETWEEN SOUND MONEY AND ECONOMIC GROWTH

Examples of Sound Money Systems in History

Throughout history, various monetary systems have adhered to the principles of sound money, providing valuable insights into how currency stability fosters economic growth and development. One of the most notable examples is the gold standard, widely adopted by major economies in the 19th and early 20th centuries. Barry Eichengreen (1996) explored how the gold standard acted as a self-regulating mechanism, controlling inflation by limiting the money supply to the availability of gold reserves. This system compelled governments to maintain fiscal discipline, as excessive currency issuance could not occur without a corresponding increase in gold reserves. By pegging national currencies to gold, economies achieved exchange rate stability, which encouraged international trade and long-term investment—essential components for sustained economic growth (Bordo & Schwartz, 2008).

The effectiveness of the gold standard as a sound money system is perhaps best illustrated during the period from 1870 to 1914, known as the classical gold standard era. During this time, industrialized nations experienced unprecedented economic expansion, characterized by rapid industrialization and the growth of international markets. The constraint imposed by gold-backed currencies ensured that inflation remained low, while stable exchange rates facilitated cross-border trade and investment. Michael Bordo (2002) highlights that this system, though not without its challenges, created a stable financial environment that laid the groundwork for global economic integration (Bordo, 2002; Taylor, 2001).

Another example of sound money is found in the Swiss monetary system, which has maintained a strong commitment to price stability and fiscal responsibility. Switzerland's approach to monetary policy emphasizes a stable currency, with the Swiss National Bank (SNB) implementing measures to control inflation effectively. The success of the Swiss franc, often considered a safe-haven currency, underscores the importance of sound money principles in promoting economic confidence and attracting foreign investment (Bofinger, 2001).

Moreover, the historical example of the United States during the late 19th century, particularly under the gold standard, demonstrates the benefits of sound money. The economic boom of the Gilded Age (roughly 1870-1900) was characterized by significant industrial growth, technological innovation, and increasing globalization. The stability provided by the gold standard helped create an environment conducive to investment and entrepreneurship, as businesses could make long-term plans without the fear of currency depreciation (Temin, 2002; Lindert & Williamson, 2001).

Historical examples such as the gold standard and the Swiss monetary system illustrate the relationship between sound money and economic growth. By maintaining stable currencies and enforcing fiscal discipline, these systems have fostered an environment conducive to investment, trade, and long-term economic development.

HISTORICAL DATA CORRELATING SOUND MONEY WITH ECONOMIC INDICATORS

Empirical studies on historical data reinforce the positive relationship between sound money and economic growth. Niall Ferguson (2008) conducted extensive analysis, revealing that countries adhering to sound money practices—such as those that followed the gold standard or maintained strict monetary discipline—tended to exhibit stronger economic performance. His work illustrates a clear correlation between sound money systems and key economic indicators like GDP growth, price stability, and investment levels. Ferguson pointed out that economies with stable monetary systems demonstrated greater resilience during financial crises, often avoiding the hyperinflation and currency collapses that plagued countries with more flexible monetary policies (Ferguson, 2008; Bordo, 2010).

For instance, Friedrich Hayek (1976) emphasized the long-term benefits of sound money, particularly in preventing the credit booms and busts that lead to economic instability. Hayek argued that when central banks manipulate the money supply too freely, it distorts natural interest rates, resulting in unsustainable credit expansions that ultimately cause recessions. He posited that sound money systems—whether tied to a commodity like gold or governed by strict monetary rules—provide a more reliable foundation for economic decision-making. This stability enables businesses and investors to plan with greater confidence regarding the value of money over time (Hayek, 1976; Selgin, 1997).

In support of these views, Michael Bordo and Andrew Schwartz (2008) explored historical examples, asserting that periods of monetary stability have consistently correlated with economic prosperity. Their research highlights the classical gold standard era (1870-1914), during which countries experienced significant GDP growth and low inflation rates. This period exemplified how adherence to sound money principles facilitated economic integration and investment, creating a favorable environment for long-term growth (Bordo & Schwartz, 2008).

Additionally, empirical analyses conducted by economists such as Albrecht Ritschl (2007) have shown that countries returning to sound money principles after periods of hyperinflation have experienced quicker economic recoveries. Ritschl's research indicates that a return to stable monetary systems can restore confidence, stimulate investment, and promote sustainable growth, as seen in the cases of Germany and other nations in the aftermath of World War I and during subsequent hyperinflationary periods (Ritschl, 2007; von Mises, 1949).

The correlation between sound money and positive economic indicators is supported by historical data and empirical studies. The evidence demonstrates that sound money systems foster an environment conducive to economic growth by enhancing investment stability, minimizing the risks of inflation, and providing a reliable framework for decision-making.

THE GOLD STANDARD AND MODERN COMPARISONS

While the gold standard is a historical example, modern comparisons can be drawn with countries that have successfully maintained sound money policies even without a gold peg. Milton Friedman (1969), for example, argued that sound money could also be achieved through disciplined monetary policy, where central banks aim to control inflation and stabilize the economy through transparent and predictable actions. Switzerland's approach to maintaining a strong currency through conservative fiscal and monetary policies in the late 20th and early 21st centuries offers a contemporary example of how sound money principles can be applied in a fiat system. By prioritizing low inflation and prudent debt levels, Switzerland has enjoyed robust economic growth and a reputation for financial stability in international markets.

These examples across different eras and systems demonstrate that the principles of sound money, whether tied to a tangible asset or enforced through disciplined policy, are critical in fostering stable, long-term economic growth.

KEYNESIAN RESPONSES TO FRAMEWORKS SUPPORTING SOUND MONEY

Keynesian economists advocate for flexible monetary policy and active government intervention, particularly during economic downturns, arguing that such measures can effectively mitigate the adverse impacts of recessions and stabilize the economy. John Maynard Keynes, in his seminal work The General Theory of Employment, Interest, and Money (1936), stressed the necessity of fiscal policy in stimulating demand during economic slumps. He posited that economies often fail to self-correct quickly, leading to prolonged unemployment and resource underutilization, thereby suggesting that strict adherence to sound money principles could significantly constrain a government's ability to respond to economic crises.

Paul Samuelson, a key figure in Keynesian economics, elaborated on this view in his influential textbook Economics (1948). He underscored the importance of government intervention through fiscal policy to counteract business cycle fluctuations, demonstrating how such actions are crucial for achieving full employment and economic stability. Samuelson illustrated the multiplier effect, which shows that government spending can have a substantial impact on overall economic activity.

Hyman Minsky introduced the notion of financial instability, arguing that a rigid commitment to sound money can exacerbate economic crises by limiting effective governmental intervention (Minsky, 1986). He suggested that the increased risk-taking and speculation associated with economic expansions might lead to downturns, and that sound money principles could hinder necessary responses during crises. Lawrence Klein also highlighted the interplay between aggregate demand and economic performance, asserting that strict adherence to sound money could result in insufficient demand, ultimately leading to lower output and higher unemployment (Klein, 1977).

Richard Koo further contributed to these ideas by discussing the ineffectiveness of traditional monetary policy during liquidity traps, reinforcing the argument for fiscal stimulus as a means to revive economic growth (Koo, 2009). His analysis of Japan's economic stagnation illustrated how commitment to sound money could obstruct the necessary government spending vital for economic recovery.

Joan Robinson emphasized demand management and criticized rigid monetary policies that inhibit recovery, advocating for flexibility in fiscal policy during downturns (Robinson, 1962). Axel Leijonhufvud also contributed to the Keynesian framework by stressing the importance of effective demand and the limitations inherent in classical economic theories. He argued that the inflexible application of sound money principles could create disequilibrium in the economy, hindering recovery efforts during downturns (Leijonhufvud, 1968).

In conclusion, prominent Keynesian economists collectively advocate for a balanced approach that integrates sound money principles with the necessary flexibility for effective economic management. They contend that rigid adherence to sound money can restrict governments' ability to respond to economic challenges, potentially prolonging recessions and undermining overall economic stability. Their critiques highlight the importance of adaptive policies that can respond to changing economic conditions rather than strictly following theoretical frameworks.

CHAPTER 4

Monetarism, Keynes, and Austrian: Who's Right?

Few debates in economic theory have stirred as much passion, policy influence, and enduring controversy as those between the Monetarist, Keynesian, and Austrian schools of thought. Each framework offers a distinct lens through which to understand inflation, unemployment, growth, and the proper role of government in managing the economy. From the disciplined money supply rules of Milton Friedman, to the counter-cyclical spending advocated by John Maynard Keynes, to the free-market, sound-money principles championed by Ludwig von Mises and Friedrich Hayek—these schools have shaped decades of global policy and public discourse.

The core principles of each tradition, assess their historical outcomes and explore where they converge, where they diverge, and what lessons they offer for the challenges facing modern economies. Ultimately, the question in the battle of idea for Monetarism, Keynesianism, or Austrian economics is—who's right?

MONETARIST RESPONSES TO FRAMEWORKS SUPPORTING SOUND MONEY

Monetarist economists, particularly Milton Friedman, argue that effective control of the money supply is fundamental to establishing frameworks supporting sound money, which is essential for long-term price stability and sustainable economic growth. Friedman challenged the Keynesian emphasis on discretionary government intervention, asserting that such policies often lead to inflationary pressures and economic distortion. He advocated for a rule-based monetary policy, such as a fixed annual growth rate of the money supply, which would prevent central banks from overreacting to short-term economic fluctuations. This rule-based approach is a cornerstone of sound money frameworks, which prioritize the stability of currency value over government-induced fluctuations.

In A Monetary History of the United States, Friedman and Anna Schwartz illustrated how excessive money supply expansion contributed to significant economic crises, including the Great Depression. They contended that governments should avoid discretionary monetary interventions, which can lead to unintended consequences like inflation and resource misallocation. This perspective aligns with sound money principles by advocating for a monetary environment where currency retains its value over time, free from government interference.

Monetarists also emphasize the harmful effects of inflation, which erodes purchasing power, distorts price signals, and creates uncertainty in business planning and investment. By promoting a stable and predictable monetary environment, monetarists aim to preserve long-term economic stability—a critical aspect of sound money frameworks. Friedman's assertion that "inflation is always and everywhere a monetary phenomenon" highlights the necessity of managing money supply growth to prevent inflation and maintain sound money.

Other prominent monetarists have contributed significantly to this discourse. Anna Schwartz, who co-authored A Monetary History of the United States, stressed the dangers of monetary mismanagement and advocated for a disciplined monetary policy approach. She criticized the Federal Reserve for its reactive policies, emphasizing the need for consistent, predictable strategies to enhance economic stability and prevent crises, thus reinforcing sound money principles (Schwartz, 1999).

Karl Brunner contributed to monetarist theory by focusing on the importance of the money supply in economic analysis. He co-founded the Shadow Open Market Committee, which aimed to monitor and influence Federal Reserve policy while advocating for a rules-based approach.

Brunner's work emphasized that understanding monetary aggregates and their effects on economic performance is crucial for mitigating inflation and fostering growth, aligning with the tenets of sound money (Brunner, 1989; Brunner & Meltzer, 1993; Meltzer, 2003).

Allan Meltzer's extensive analysis of the Federal Reserve reveals how discretionary policies can lead to instability and inflation. In A History of the Federal Reserve, he argues for a systematic approach to monetary policy focused on controlling money supply growth. His insights underscore the necessity of adhering to sound monetary principles to prevent economic crises and enhance long-term growth (Meltzer, 1995; Meltzer, 2003).

Benjamin M. Friedman has furthered the understanding of the relationship between monetary policy, financial markets, and economic performance, highlighting that sound monetary policy is essential for fostering a stable investment environment. He advocates for controlling money supply growth to maintain price stability, which is vital for sound money frameworks. His research indicates that inconsistent monetary policies can lead to economic volatility, emphasizing the need for stable and predictable monetary environments (Friedman & Schwartz, 2008).

Critics of the monetarist approach argue that it may overlook short-term costs associated with rigid monetary policies, particularly in times of economic distress. While monetarists focus on long-term price stability, opponents suggest that strict adherence to fixed monetary rules can restrict a government's ability to respond effectively to immediate economic crises. Despite these critiques, the monetarist perspective remains influential in policy debates about the risks of inflationary policies and the benefits of maintaining a stable money supply, both of which are integral to sound money frameworks.

AUSTRIAN SCHOOL RESPONSES TO FRAMEWORKS SUPPORTING SOUND MONEY

The Austrian School of Economics emphasizes sound money as foundational to a stable and free economy. Key figures such as Ludwig von Mises, Murray Rothbard, Friedrich Hayek, Hans Hermann Hoppe, and

Israel Kirzner argue that sound money is essential for protecting individual liberty and fostering long-term economic stability.

Ludwig von Mises (1949), in Human Action, posited that money's value should derive from its scarcity and resistance to manipulation by authorities. He argued that sound money, often linked to commodities like gold, serves as a reliable store of value since its supply cannot be easily manipulated by governments or central banks. This resistance to inflation ensures that individuals' purchasing power remains stable over time, protecting savings and encouraging prudent financial behavior (Mises, 1949; Böhme, 2020). Mises contended that government intervention in the money supply distorts natural market processes, leading to artificial booms and inevitable busts, a phenomenon he termed the "business cycle" (Mises, 1949).

Murray Rothbard (1962), in What Has Government Done to Our Money?, expanded on Mises' ideas, asserting that sound money acts as a check on government power by limiting its ability to finance excessive spending through inflationary monetary policies. Rothbard argued that unsound money systems, where governments or central banks can increase the money supply at will, lead to economic cycles of malinvestment, resource misallocation, and eventual financial collapse (Rothbard, 1962; Sennholz, 2006). According to Rothbard, the expansion of credit through government intervention results in speculative bubbles that, when burst, create severe economic downturns.

Friedrich Hayek (1976) contributed significantly to the discussion on sound money by advocating for a decentralized monetary system. In his work Denationalisation of Money, he argued that private currencies could outperform government-issued currencies by better aligning with market demands. Hayek contended that competition among different forms of money could lead to more stable monetary systems and that sound money could emerge organically through market forces rather than government imposition (Hayek, 1976; Selgin, 1996).

Hans Hermann Hoppe (1998), in Democracy: The God That Failed, emphasized the moral dimensions of sound money, arguing that it is essential for preserving individual property rights and limiting state power. Hoppe argued that unsound money allows governments to engage in predatory practices, eroding the wealth and rights of individuals. He asserted that a return to sound money principles, especially through a commodity-backed system, is necessary to restore economic stability and individual freedoms (Hoppe, 1998; DiLorenzo, 2009).

Israel Kirzner (1984) focused on the entrepreneurial role in the context of sound money. He argued that sound monetary conditions foster an environment conducive to entrepreneurial discovery and innovation, which are vital for economic growth. Kirzner emphasized that monetary stability is crucial for entrepreneurs to make informed decisions regarding investment and resource allocation, thus contributing to a more vibrant and dynamic economy (Kirzner, 1984; Hayek, 1991).

From the Austrian perspective, sound money is not only a tool for ensuring economic stability but also a moral imperative. It prevents governments from using inflation as a hidden tax on citizens and ensures that individuals can trust the currency to maintain its value over time. Mises, Rothbard, Hayek, Hoppe, and Kirzner emphasized that true economic growth and prosperity come from minimal interference in the money supply, allowing market forces to allocate resources efficiently.

Despite its intellectual appeal, the Austrian approach has been critiqued for its perceived rigidity, particularly in times of economic crisis. Critics argue that strict adherence to sound money principles can leave governments with insufficient tools to respond to severe recessions or financial emergencies. The lack of flexibility in Austrian theory is often contrasted with Keynesian and monetarist approaches, which provide more room for active intervention in response to economic shocks (Selgin, 2017).

BALANCING PERSPECTIVES: A BROADER THEORETICAL DEBATE

The ongoing debate between Keynesian, monetarist, and Austrian perspectives on sound money is deeply intertwined with real-world policy decisions that have significant implications for economic stability. For instance, during the 2008 financial crisis, Keynesian-inspired policies such as significant fiscal stimulus and low-interest rates were employed to stimulate demand and prevent deeper recessions. While these measures mitigated the immediate impacts of the crisis, critics contend that they also fostered long-term issues like asset bubbles, escalating public debt, and rising income inequality, undermining sound money principles (Krugman, 2009; Taylor, 2009).

Austrian economists frequently reference historical examples, such as the hyperinflation in the Weimar Republic during the 1920s, as evidence of the dangers of deviating from sound money. The excessive money printing in this period led to a catastrophic collapse in currency value and significant social and economic upheaval (Harrison, 2018; Selgin, 2016). More contemporary examples, such as the rampant inflation in Venezuela, further illustrate how loose monetary policies can erode purchasing power and cause widespread hardship, reinforcing the Austrian argument against unsound money practices (Cato Institute, 2017; Faria, 2019).

In contrast, the monetarist perspective, while more cautious regarding government intervention, also informs policy debates about the importance of controlling inflation. Milton Friedman's analyses of historical economic events, particularly the Great Depression, alongside his advocacy for rule-based monetary policies, continue to shape central banking practices, notably through inflation targeting aimed at ensuring economic stability (Mishkin, 2007).

DIRECT CONNECTION TO BROADER THEMES AND HISTORICAL EXAMPLES

The interplay between these economic theories significantly influences modern monetary policy and its consequences. The Keynesian strategies employed during the 2008 crisis, while temporarily effective, led critics to argue that they engendered long-term economic distortions counter to sound money principles. Conversely, the Austrian critique, rooted in historical examples of hyperinflation and economic mismanagement, emphasizes the importance of sound money to prevent severe economic instability and societal unrest.

The success of the gold standard in the 19th and early 20th centuries further exemplifies sound money principles, as it directly linked the money supply to a tangible asset, ensuring price stability and limiting inflation. This period is often cited by both monetarists and Austrian economists as evidence that disciplined monetary policies grounded in sound money principles can promote sustained economic growth and resilience against financial crises (Rothbard, 1962; Selgin, 2018).

Aligning monetary policies with sound money principles is crucial for achieving lasting economic stability. By connecting historical lessons with contemporary discussions on monetary practices, the argument for sound money not only focuses on economic efficiency but also underscores the necessity of maintaining a just and moral economic order, safeguarding individuals' purchasing power and preventing wealth erosion through inflation.

CHAPTER 5

The Moral Ledger: Sound Money's Testimony?

Money is more than a medium of exchange—it is a mirror of a society's values, discipline, and trust. At the heart of every economic system lies a moral question, should money be anchored to something real and enduring, or should it be subject to the discretion of policymakers and the shifting winds of political will?

Its testimony is found not only in stable prices and long-term growth but in the character it demands from institutions and individuals alike. As nations face rising debt, inflationary pressures, and declining trust in central banks, the case for sound money reemerges—not just as an economic argument, but as a moral imperative. Gresham's Law offers a simple yet powerful key to understanding this dynamic.

THE MORAL CORRELATION WITH SOUND MONEY—GRESHAM'S LAW AND ITS MEANING

One could argue that sound money serves as a reflection of a society's moral foundation. Sir Thomas Gresham (c. 1519–1579), an English financier and advisor to Queen Elizabeth I, was among the earliest to recognize the connection between monetary integrity and ethical governance. While he did not formally define the economic principle later named after him—Gresham's Law—he was instrumental in articulating its core ideas through his efforts to address the debasement of England's coinage and to restore financial stability during a critical period in the nation's history.

Gresham's Law, which states that "bad money drives out good," is a principle that has played out repeatedly throughout history. The law comes into effect when two forms of money are circulating simultaneously—one of higher intrinsic value and one of lesser value. People tend to hoard the "good" money (that which retains value), while spending the "bad" money, which is less reliable. Friedrich Hayek (1976) examined this concept in depth, noting that Gresham's Law serves as a warning against the dangers of devalued or debased currency.

Historical examples abound. In ancient Rome, the debasement of the denarius occurred over several centuries as silver content was gradually reduced by the state, leading to a preference for hoarding older, purer coins. This degradation of currency contributed to economic instability and ultimately the fall of the Roman Empire. Similarly, during the Great Debasement in 16th-century England, Henry VIII systematically reduced the silver content of coins, undermining confidence in the currency and causing price inflation and economic disruption.

Another notable case occurred during the Weimar Republic in Germany (1921-1923), where hyperinflation destroyed the value of the mark. As the paper currency's value plummeted, people turned to hoarding gold, foreign currencies, or bartering for goods, thereby reinforcing Gresham's Law as bad money drove out good. The hyperinflationary crisis not only led to widespread financial ruin but also had profound political consequences, paving the way for social unrest and the rise of authoritarianism.

EXAMPLE OF COMMODITY BACKING AND ITS EFFECTS

In modern times, consider the example of the Zimbabwean dollar during the late 1990s and early 2000s. The Zimbabwean government moved away from a currency backed by tangible commodities (like gold or silver) to one heavily influenced by hyperinflation and poor economic management. By 2008, inflation reached an astronomical 89.7 sextillion percent, effectively rendering the currency worthless (Hanke & Kwok, 2009). As the intrinsic backing of the currency diminished, the reliance on less valuable, fiat currency increased. In this context, Gresham's Law manifested as people began hoarding foreign currencies (like the US dollar) and bartering, effectively driving bad money out of circulation.

Statistical analysis of the Zimbabwean case shows that, when the commodity backing of a currency decreases, the bad money circulating can increase by as much as 90% out of a total 100% of the currency supply. This stark increase illustrates how quickly confidence can erode and how detrimental the effects of poor monetary policy can be on the economy (Dorsey, 2010).

MORAL IMPLICATIONS OF CURRENCY DEVALUATION AND COVID-19 VACCINE CONTROVERSIES

In examining the moral implications of both currency devaluation and the handling of the COVID-19 pandemic, it becomes evident that these issues are intertwined with ethical governance and societal trust. Just as the Zimbabwean currency crisis showcased a failure of responsible financial stewardship, discussions surrounding the COVID-19 vaccines have highlighted ethical concerns about public health decisions and their impacts on citizens.

Critics like Robert F. Kennedy Jr. and Senator Rand Paul have raised alarms about potential harms caused by the COVID-19 vaccines. Kennedy has long argued that vaccines may have harmful side effects, suggesting that regulatory agencies and pharmaceutical companies have not been transparent about these risks. In a recent interview, he stated, "The data we have from the vaccine manufacturers is alarming, and it is being ignored" (Kennedy, 2021). He emphasizes the importance of informed consent and questions the morality of promoting vaccination without fully disclosing potential adverse effects.

Senator Rand Paul has also voiced similar concerns, particularly focusing on the lack of accountability for pharmaceutical companies and the government's handling of vaccine mandates. He has stated that "government has lost its moral authority" by not allowing open discourse about vaccine safety and efficacy, arguing that citizens should have the right to make informed decisions without coercion (Paul, 2021). This sentiment resonates with a broader ethical dilemma regarding the balance between public health initiatives and individual rights, reflecting a moral breach when citizens are not afforded the autonomy to make informed choices regarding their health. The inherently unethical nature of unsound money often results in widespread abuses across various sectors. The COVID-19 crisis serves as another example, where evidence reveals how unrestrained greed and a disregard for moral principles can drive individuals to act without accountability.

The consequences of these discussions about the vaccines parallel the broader moral implications seen in Zimbabwe's currency crisis as unsound money exceeds reasonable limititations. Just as the government's decisions in Zimbabwe eroded trust and contributed to widespread suffering, the perceived lack of transparency and accountability surrounding COVID-19 vaccines can similarly undermine public confidence in health institutions and the government. This not only poses immediate health risks but also raises long-term ethical questions about the responsibilities of those in power to protect the welfare of their citizens.

In both contexts, whether through the devaluation of currency or the handling of public health crises, the failure to uphold ethical principles leads to societal harm and a deterioration of trust. As citizens grapple with these moral challenges, the need for sound governance grounded in transparency and accountability becomes increasingly crucial—a role that sound money can provide.

BANK BAILOUTS, GRESHAM'S LAW, AND MORAL IMPLICATIONS

The phenomenon of bank bailouts during financial crises provides a significant example of Gresham's Law in action, particularly when viewed through the lens of moral implications in governance. Gresham's Law posits that "bad money drives out good," suggesting that when inferior forms of currency circulate alongside superior ones, people will hoard the good money and spend the bad. This principle can be metaphorically applied to the financial realm, where the bailout of major banks signals to the market that risk-taking behavior will not be penalized, effectively driving out prudent financial practices and reinforcing a cycle of moral hazard.

REVERSE GRESHAM'S LAW

The reversal of Gresham's Law has been a subject of interest for many notable economists and monetary theorists. Other thinkers have explored how sound monetary policies, public trust, and systemic reforms can encourage the circulation of good money while diminishing the dominance of inferior currencies. These insights highlight both historical precedents and contemporary applications of using good money to stabilize economies.

W. Stanley Jevons provides a thorough examination of Gresham's Law in Money and the Mechanism of Exchange, exploring both its implications and the potential for reversing its effects under specific conditions. Gresham's Law reflects the tendency for inferior money (money of lower intrinsic value) to circulate more freely than superior money (money with higher intrinsic value) when both are legally accepted at the same face value. Jevons explains, "People naturally keep that money which has the greater value in proportion to its weight and export, melt, or otherwise dispose of it, in preference to parting with the cheaper coins."

Jevons acknowledges that the hoarding or removal of good money from circulation is rational behavior when the monetary system incentivizes such actions. For instance, when a government issues debased or overvalued coinage alongside full-weight metal coins, the public will tend to retain the latter, treating them as a store of value. He writes, "The disappearance of the better coinage is a natural consequence of its being undervalued in comparison with the baser money."

However, Jevons suggests that this principle can be reversed if the conditions that drive the preference for hoarding or exporting good money are altered. He emphasizes that confidence in the currency system is a critical factor. He states, "If the public are assured of the immediate and unlimited convertibility of their notes or base coin into full-weight money, they will no longer feel the need to hoard the latter." This assurance effectively neutralizes the incentive to retain good money, as people trust the system to preserve their purchasing power over time.

The analysis also underscores the necessity of robust monetary policies to counteract the dynamics of Gresham's Law. It is argued that achieving a proper alignment between the nominal and intrinsic values of various monetary forms is critical, with the assertion that a meticulously governed currency is among the primary essentials for a stable monetary framework. By ensuring that a currency's face value closely matches its intrinsic or exchange value, authorities can prevent the hoarding or exportation of higher-quality money. For example, under a gold standard with rigorously enforced convertibility, both gold coins and paper notes circulated concurrently, as public confidence rested on the assurance that paper currency held equivalent value to gold.

The analysis also clarifies that economic stability is a key factor in building this trust. It is stated that the stronger our trust in the government and its monetary institutions, the more easily the public will treat both coin and paper as interchangeable. This remark emphasizes the view that how the public perceives monetary stability is critical to counteracting the tendencies of Gresham's Law.

Furthermore, the discussion stresses the necessity of curbing the excessive issuance of "bad money," whether manifested as debased coins or fiat currency. It is remarked that the detrimental effects of an inconvertible paper currency, released without limitation, are widely recognized, and historical evidence offers no example where such a currency has not precipitated significant economic disruption. Through stringent regulation of the volume of token money in circulation, governments can avert inflation and uphold the integrity of the monetary system.

Thus, we can provide a roadmap for reversing Gresham's Law, grounded in sound monetary policy, public confidence, and strict regulation. These insights reflect the enduring importance of trust and discipline in managing monetary systems and highlight the ways in which good money can coexist with token money when these principles are upheld. Debates continue surrounding fiat currency, cryptocurrencies, and the trajectory of monetary policy, as the equilibrium between sound and flawed money continues to influence economic stability, as we observe other notable economists have similar outlooks on chasing out the bad money.

LUDWIG VON MISES

In The Theory of Money and Credit, Ludwig von Mises argues that good money can prevail over bad money when the public is allowed the freedom to choose their preferred medium of exchange. Mises writes, "Only sound money can provide a solid foundation for a free and prosperous society." He explains that when governments cease imposing bad money through legal tender laws and allow market forces to operate, individuals naturally gravitate toward currencies that best preserve purchasing power, such as gold or other intrinsically valuable forms of money. Mises' observation underscores the importance of removing artificial barriers that prop up bad money, allowing good money to regain its place in circulation.

FRIEDRICH HAYEK

Friedrich Hayek, in Denationalisation of Money, expands on this idea, advocating for a system of competing private currencies to enable good money to replace bad money. Hayek argues that monopolized state-issued money often leads to inflation and devaluation, as governments face incentives to overissue currency. He proposes a framework where private entities issue their own forms of money, with competition ensuring that only the most stable and reliable currencies gain public acceptance. Hayek writes, "If people were free to choose what to use as money, bad money would disappear because it would not be able to compete with better alternatives."

CARL MENGER

Carl Menger, the founder of the Austrian School, also provides a historical perspective on the emergence of good money driving out bad. In Principles of Economics, Menger emphasizes that sound money—such as gold or silver—arises naturally in societies because of its superior characteristics as a medium of exchange. He notes, "The precious metals became money because they are most suitable for the function of money." Menger's analysis suggests that the natural selection of good money over bad money is a process that occurs when markets are left to operate freely, unhindered by government-imposed systems that artificially sustain inferior currencies.

MILTON FRIEDMAN

Milton Friedman, in A Monetary History of the United States, highlights examples where good money has replaced bad money through the implementation of disciplined monetary policies. For example, he examines the United States' transition to the gold standard in the late 19th century as a period when the public abandoned unstable, depreciating paper currencies in favor of gold-backed money. Friedman notes, "When the monetary system restores confidence, the public will willingly return to forms of money that preserve their value." This transition demonstrates how effective monetary reform can reintroduce good money into circulation.

HISTORICAL CASE STUDIES

Historical case studies provide compelling examples of how societies have successfully reversed the effects of Gresham's Law by returning to money with intrinsic value, such as gold and silver, after experiencing the negative consequences of fiat money and currency debasement. These examples highlight the importance of restoring trust in monetary systems by anchoring currencies to tangible, universally recognized assets.

One of the most prominent examples of reversing Gresham's Law through a return to money with intrinsic value occurred in Germany after World War II. By 1948, the hyperinflationary pressures from the Reichsmark had eroded public trust in the currency, and people were hoarding tangible assets like gold, silver, and foreign currencies. In June 1948, the Allied authorities introduced the Deutsche Mark (DM), which was backed by Western Germany's economic assets and, indirectly, gold reserves. The introduction of this sound money, supported by strict regulations on currency issuance, effectively displaced the worthless Reichsmark. As the public regained confidence in the new currency, gold and foreign currencies that had been hoarded during the inflationary period were exchanged for the Deutsche Mark. This move demonstrated how returning to a currency backed by real value could reverse the effects of Gresham's Law and restore economic stability (Mises, The Theory of Money and Credit, 1912).

Similarly, the U.S. Gold Standard from the 19th century until the early 20th century provides another example of how good money (gold) drove out bad money (debased or overissued paper currency). In the early years of the republic, the U.S. experienced significant issues with overissuance of banknotes and the debasement of coinage, which led to inflation and the circulation of bad money. To address this, the U.S. formally adopted the gold standard in 1834, and paper money issued by banks became redeemable in gold at a fixed rate. As gold became the anchor for the dollar, the public regained confidence in the currency. The gold-backed dollar became the dominant medium of exchange, and gold coins and notes backed by gold were used in daily transactions. This system remained in place until 1933, when the U.S. abandoned the gold standard during the Great Depression, but for much of the 19th and early 20th centuries, gold successfully displaced debased paper currencies and restored stability to the U.S. monetary system (Friedman & Schwartz, A Monetary History of the United States, 1963).

Another historical example comes from Ecuador in 2000, when the country faced severe inflation and instability due to the depreciation of its local currency, the sucre. The sucre had become nearly worthless due to hyperinflation, prompting the government to dollarize the economy. By adopting the U.S. dollar, a currency backed by the economic strength of the

U.S. and intrinsically valuable through its tie to the U.S. economy, Ecuador was able to restore confidence in its monetary system. The adoption of a sound currency with intrinsic value drove out the hyperinflated sucre, and the public swiftly accepted the U.S. dollar in everyday transactions. This move marked a return to using money that had intrinsic value, demonstrating how returning to a stable and trusted currency can reverse the effects of Gresham's Law (Klein, 2003).

El Salvador followed a similar path in 2001 when it abandoned its own currency, the colón, in favor of the U.S. dollar, recognizing the instability caused by inflation and depreciation. By adopting a globally recognized currency with intrinsic value, El Salvador reduced the risks of hyperinflation and restored faith in its economy. This dollarization, while not directly a return to gold or silver, represents a broader shift toward using a currency backed by a stable economic system, which replaced the bad money (colón) that had been eroding public trust (Hanke & Schuler, 2009).

The California Gold Rush of the mid-19th century provides another historical example of good money driving out bad money. Following the discovery of gold in 1848, large quantities of gold flooded into California, leading to the creation of gold-backed currencies issued by local banks. As paper money issued by banks in California began to lose its value due to inflationary pressures, the public quickly turned to gold as the preferred medium of exchange. This move was a natural response to the increasing supply of gold, as people trusted its intrinsic value. In a short time, gold became the standard currency in California, and the debased paper currencies were sidelined, demonstrating how the availability of money with intrinsic value can displace bad money in times of instability (Menger, Principles of Economics, 1871).

These case studies demonstrate that returning to money with intrinsic value—whether gold, silver, or a stable foreign currency—has historically been an effective means of reversing Gresham's Law and restoring confidence in a monetary system. In each of these examples, the public's preference for sound money over bad money drove the shift toward more stable and reliable forms of currency, showing that when governments back money with tangible value, they can reinstate trust and stability in the economy.

THE FRENCH REVOLUTION AND NAPOLEONIC WARS—FIAT INFLATION AND ITS CONSEQUENCES

The historical case of France during the period of fiat currency inflation and the subsequent return to gold and silver in the 19th century provides another compelling example of how the reintroduction of sound money can reverse the effects of Gresham's Law. France, particularly during and after the Napoleonic Wars, experienced significant monetary instability due to the issuance of fiat currency, which led to inflation, devaluation, and a loss of confidence in the financial system. The French government's use of assignats (paper money) during the French Revolution and the Napoleonic Wars exacerbated economic challenges and led to hyperinflation in the early 19th century. The key to restoring economic stability in France came when the country moved to a more disciplined monetary system, returning to gold and silver as the foundation of its currency.

During the French Revolution (1789–1799), the French government issued assignats, which were initially intended as bonds backed by the value of national land. However, the government printed vast amounts of this paper money, leading to rampant inflation and a loss of confidence in its value. By the time Napoleon Bonaparte rose to power, the French economy was plagued by the effects of this overissuing of fiat currency. The assignats had lost their purchasing power, and the French people, unable to rely on paper money, began to turn to other forms of wealth such as gold, silver, and foreign currency.

Even during the Napoleonic Wars (1803–1815), when the French economy was strained by war expenditure and the blockade of British goods, there were observations that the economy remained relatively stable, despite the challenges of using fiat currency. Napoleon himself implemented a series of reforms, including efforts to stabilize the currency and restore public confidence. Notably, Napoleon's creation of the Bank of France in 1800 played a pivotal role in stabilizing the French financial system, as it took on the task of managing currency issuance and reducing the reliance on paper money.

RETURN TO GOLD AND SILVER—RESTORING ECONOMIC STABILITY

After the fall of Napoleon and the restoration of the Bourbon monarchy under Louis XVIII in 1815, France sought to stabilize its monetary system and restore confidence in its economy. The key to this stabilization was a return to gold and silver as the foundation of the currency. This was formalized with the introduction of the franc germinal in 1803, which pegged the French franc to a fixed weight of gold, making the franc a gold-backed currency. The gold standard helped stabilize the French economy by providing a reliable and tangible foundation for the currency, reversing the previous inflationary pressures caused by excessive fiat issuance.

This shift was crucial to restoring economic confidence. When France returned to a gold standard, it regained economic stability and public trust. Furthermore, economic historians like Michael D. Bordo in The Gold Standard and Related Systems (1984) highlight that even during times of economic distress, such as the Napoleonic Wars, France's adoption of the gold standard ensured that the economy was able to recover and grow once peace was restored.

NAPOLEON'S REFORMS AND THE OBSERVATIONS OF STABILITY

Despite the tumult of the Napoleonic Wars, it was observed that, under Napoleon's leadership, France experienced economic recovery through the establishment of sound monetary policies. Thomas M. Humphrey, in his article The Classical Gold Standard: A Reinterpretation (1990), noted that Napoleon's banking reforms—including the founding of the Bank of France—were designed to provide a stable financial system, and the French economy remained relatively stable in terms of output, employment, and prices when compared to other countries suffering from war-related inflation. In fact, Napoleon's monetary policies were often lauded for maintaining a degree of economic order even during the turmoil of the wars.

While the wars drained national resources, France's return to a monetary system backed by precious metals after the wars laid the groundwork for future economic stability. The restoration of gold and silver as the basis for currency issuance helped curb inflationary pressures, stabilize the franc, and foster greater confidence in the French financial system, signaling the importance of sound money in restoring an economy after fiat inflation.

The example of France's return to a gold-backed currency after the turmoil of the Napoleonic Wars demonstrates the enduring role of money with intrinsic value in reversing the effects of Gresham's Law. The transition from fiat currency to a gold standard, particularly with the introduction of the franc germinal, was key to restoring the French economy and ensuring the long-term stability of its monetary system. This historical case highlights the fundamental principles discussed by other economists, when a currency is backed by intrinsic value, such as gold or silver, it can drive out bad money and restore public trust in the financial system.

CHAPTER 6

Can We Ever Return to Sound Money?

In contemporary times, the concept of returning to gold and silver as the foundation of monetary systems has gained attention as a potential solution to the inflationary pressures and economic instability often caused by fiat currencies. While many modern economies rely heavily on fiat money, which can be printed without limit by central banks, the idea of sound money—currency backed by tangible assets such as gold and silver—has resurfaced as a hedge against inflation and a means to restore confidence in financial systems.

The global financial crisis of 2008 and the COVID-19 pandemic in 2020 triggered unprecedented levels of money printing by central banks, leading to concerns about inflation, devaluation, and the long-term stability of fiat currencies. In response, some analysts and economists have called for a return to a gold-backed monetary system, citing the stability and reliability that gold and silver historically provided. The return to tangible assets like gold and silver could provide a check on government overreach and excessive debt by limiting the amount of money that can be printed, restoring a sense of fiscal discipline and promoting long-term economic stability.

THE RISE OF GOLD AND SILVER IN CONTEMPORARY APPLICATIONS

In the wake of the 2008 financial crisis, there was a surge in the popularity of gold and silver as hedges against economic uncertainty. Central banks around the world, particularly in China, Russia, and India, increased their gold reserves, signaling a renewed interest in precious metals as a way to safeguard national wealth from the risks associated with fiat money. China, in particular, has been quietly accumulating gold over the past two decades, positioning itself to potentially transition toward a gold-backed monetary system. According to the World Gold Council, global central banks purchased over 1,000 metric tons of gold in 2022, marking the highest level of gold purchases since 1950.

SILVER AS AN ALTERNATIVE TO FIAT MONEY IN EMERGING ECONOMIES

In emerging markets, particularly in countries that have experienced hyperinflation or currency crises, the return to gold and silver has gained momentum as a practical solution for protecting wealth and restoring confidence in the financial system. In Venezuela, for instance, where hyperinflation has rendered the national currency nearly worthless, citizens have increasingly turned to precious metals like gold and silver to preserve their savings. Silver, in particular, has seen a resurgence as a more accessible alternative to gold, given its lower cost and practical applications in industries like electronics and manufacturing.

Countries like Zimbabwe and Argentina have also seen a rise in demand for gold and silver as a store of value. As inflation continues to erode the purchasing power of fiat currencies in these regions, many individuals and businesses are turning to precious metals as a means to protect their wealth. In Zimbabwe, where the Zimbabwean dollar suffered from hyperinflation in the late 2000s, the government has even considered using gold as a standard for currency issuance, with some reports suggesting that the country could issue a gold-backed currency as a solution to the ongoing economic crisis.

THE CASE FOR A RETURN TO THE GOLD STANDARD

While the gold standard is not being widely adopted by major economies today, the concept has gained renewed interest among some policymakers and economists, particularly in light of recent inflationary pressures. The gold standard, which was in place in various forms until the early 20th century, tied the value of national currencies to a specific amount of gold. This system effectively limited the ability of governments to print money at will, as the money supply was constrained by the amount of gold held in reserves.

In recent years, several prominent figures have called for a return to the gold standard as a way to curb the ability of governments to engage in inflationary monetary policies. Ron Paul, a former U.S. Congressman and presidential candidate, has long advocated for a return to the gold standard, arguing that it would restore discipline to the U.S. monetary system and reduce the risks of hyperinflation and devaluation caused by excessive government spending. In his book End the Fed, Paul writes, "The gold standard… serves as a check on the government's ability to print money out of thin air."

Proponents of the gold standard argue that it would restore fiscal discipline by limiting the government's ability to issue fiat money without backing. This, in turn, would reduce the risk of currency devaluation and restore public confidence in the currency. They also suggest that a return to gold would stabilize exchange rates and restore economic equilibrium, as it would limit the distortions caused by excessive money printing.

A MODERN PERSPECTIVE—THE ROLE OF GOLD AND SILVER IN HEDGE FUNDS AND PRIVATE INVESTMENT

Gold and silver continue to play an important role in the investment portfolios of hedge funds and private investors. For instance, in 2020, hedge fund manager Ray Dalio, founder of Bridgewater Associates, emphasized the importance of owning gold as part of a diversified portfolio in his writings on global economic trends. Dalio notes that gold serves as a hedge against the devaluation of fiat currencies and as a store of wealth in times of economic uncertainty. His firm, which is one of the largest hedge funds in the world, has reportedly allocated a portion of its portfolio to gold and other precious metals in anticipation of continued monetary expansion by central banks.

Private investors also increasingly view gold and silver as a safe haven during periods of market volatility and inflation. Precious metals are seen as tangible assets that can withstand the vagaries of financial markets and provide stability during times of economic crisis. This investment trend, particularly in gold ETFs and physical gold holdings, highlights the growing recognition of the value of gold and silver as financial instruments that are independent of the risks posed by fiat currencies.

A MODERN PATH FORWARD FOR RETURNING TO GOLD AND SILVER

In contemporary applications, the return to gold and silver as a foundation for monetary systems or as a store of value offers a viable solution to the inflationary risks and instability caused by fiat currencies. From the resurgence of gold-backed cryptocurrencies to the growing demand for gold and silver in emerging markets, there is a clear shift toward reintroducing sound money principles into the modern economy. While a full-scale return to the gold standard is unlikely in the short term, the use of gold and silver as alternatives to fiat currencies is a growing trend that could help mitigate the economic risks posed by overreliance on paper money.

Whether through the digitalization of gold, the increased demand for precious metals in developing economies, or the ongoing debates about a return to the gold standard, the principles of sound money are regaining relevance. These contemporary applications reflect a desire for stability, scarcity, and transparency in an era increasingly defined by inflationary pressures, fiscal imbalances, and digital innovation.

A key principle emerges when individuals are free to choose, good money—characterized by stability, intrinsic value, or trust—naturally replaces bad money. This reversal of Gresham's Law occurs repeatedly, whether through disciplined monetary policies or the reintroduction of commodity standards. It underscores the consistent preference for sound money throughout history and in modern times.

THE 2008 FINANCIAL CRISIS AND MORAL HAZARD

The 2008 financial crisis saw significant bailouts for major institutions like Bear Stearns and AIG, reflecting a systemic bias that prioritizes large financial entities over individual taxpayers. Critics, including economists like Paul Krugman and Joseph Stiglitz, have argued that these actions not only rewarded reckless behavior but also undermined the moral fabric of economic governance (Krugman, 2009; Stiglitz, 2010). By providing a safety net for banks deemed "too big to fail," the government essentially communicated that excessive risk would be tolerated, eroding the ethical standards of accountability and responsibility within the financial sector.

This environment parallels Gresham's Law, where "bad money"—in this case, irresponsible banking practices—displaces "good money," or prudent financial management. As banks took on excessive risks, they reaped the benefits while the consequences were externalized to taxpayers, who bore the burden of bailouts. This dynamic creates a moral dilemma, as the system rewards the few at the expense of the many, undermining principles of fairness and equity.

EROSION OF TRUST AND SOCIAL CONTRACT

The implications of this moral failure extend beyond economics and into societal trust. As Senator Elizabeth Warren argued in 2019, the bailouts of large financial institutions set a troubling precedent in how economic resources are allocated—undermining market discipline and deepening inequality. This perspective highlights a broader moral compromise within the financial system, where the government's actions appear to protect the interests of large entities at the expense of ordinary citizens. The expectation that taxpayers will shoulder the burden of bank failures reinforces feelings of disenfranchisement and distrust, as people witness a disconnect between the government's support for the wealthy and the struggles of the average taxpayer.

The moral implications of such actions are profound, suggesting that when institutions fail to uphold ethical standards, it not only damages the economy but also the very social contract that binds citizens to their government. When "bad money" in the form of poor banking practices drives out the "good money" of accountability and responsibility, it signals a breakdown in moral governance, leading to widespread disillusionment among the populace.

This moral breakdown aligns with the arguments of economists like Murray Rothbard (1963) and Ludwig von Mises (1912), who contend that sound money is not just a technical necessity but also a moral imperative for a just society. The deterioration of the Zimbabwean dollar exemplifies how bad money can breed inequality, as those who could not afford to shield their wealth, typically the poorer segments of society, suffer the most when inflation devalues their currency.

Moreover, the moral failure of monetary policies can lead to social unrest and political instability, as seen in Zimbabwe, where the economic crisis fueled discontent and ultimately contributed to the erosion of democratic institutions (Maravanyika, 2019). In this light, Gresham's Law serves as a powerful reminder that the health of a monetary system is both a technical and moral obligation. Upholding sound money principles protects not just economic stability but also the ethical foundations of society, ensuring fairness and equity in economic exchange.

WHY MORALITY MATTERS IN MONETARY SYSTEMS

The ethical considerations of sound money go beyond its practical advantages, influencing economic stability and the public's trust in a way that Murray Rothbard (1963) and other economists argue is foundational to societal well-being. Rothbard asserts that sound money embodies a moral obligation to protect individual rights and maintain transparency, allowing individuals to preserve their wealth without fearing arbitrary devaluation. This ethical stance is mirrored in Ludwig von Mises's (1912) view, which condemns inflationary policies as a covert form of taxation that unfairly redistributes wealth from citizens to the government. For Mises, currency devaluation violates property rights, as it distorts prices and undermines the integrity of economic transactions. Both Rothbard and Mises argue that a sound monetary system is essential to a just society by providing a stable currency that aligns with individual rights and economic equity.

Milton Friedman (1969) further connects morality with monetary policy by highlighting inflation's socially destabilizing effects. He warns that unchecked inflation not only erodes public trust in institutions but also disproportionately affects lower-income households, which challenges fairness in governance. This argument reinforces Rothbard and Mises's position, suggesting that the ethical failings of inflationary policies lie in their tendency to burden the most vulnerable, while those in power escape the negative effects. Ethical monetary policy, in this view, must prioritize stability and protect individuals' purchasing power as part of a broader moral obligation to economic fairness.

The ethical implications of unsound monetary policies are particularly evident in modern examples, such as the U.S. Federal Reserve's response to the 2008 financial crisis through quantitative easing (QE). Although QE was intended to stabilize markets, critics like Ron Paul (2009) argue it primarily benefited large financial institutions, worsening income inequality and subtly eroding the wealth of ordinary citizens. Similarly, Peter Schiff (2010) critiques QE's impact on the devaluation of the dollar, which made essential goods more expensive for average consumers.

David Stockman (2013) argues that such policies violate the social contract between the government and its citizens by disrupting economic fundamentals and disregarding the public's trust in a stable currency. These critiques align with the views of Rothbard, Mises, and Friedman, suggesting that abandoning sound money in times of crisis can undermine fairness, exacerbate inequality, and challenge the government's moral responsibility to its citizens.

The COVID-19 pandemic response, marked by significant fiscal stimulus and quantitative easing (QE) policies, led to an inflation spike not seen in decades. Alongside the financial aspects, vaccine deployment raised ethical questions, especially around public trust. Vaccine mistrust grew, partly due to safety concerns, perceived rushed development, and rare adverse events. This mistrust, compounded by debates on research ethics, reflects broader ethical concerns over public health policy and economic stability, where both inflationary policies and public health decisions affected global confidence (Nikulina & Simonovic, 2023; Teotia, 2022; Journal of Medical Ethics, 2021).

Nouriel Roubini (2021) warned that while these measures provided temporary relief, they risked fueling long-term inflation and devaluing the U.S. dollar, raising moral questions about the sustainability of such policies.

Paul Krugman (2022) acknowledged that these policies' inflationary effects were more severe than initially anticipated, validating earlier concerns about how monetary manipulation impacts wealth distribution and purchasing power. This recent experience illustrates that the ethical implications of sound money are relevant as inflationary policies tend to disadvantage lower-income households, emphasizing the need for governments to adhere to principles of economic stability and fairness.

These examples collectively highlight the moral necessity of sound money. When governments resist inflationary pressures and uphold the principles of sound money, they promote fairness, build trust, and uphold the ethical responsibility of ensuring all citizens benefit from stable economic policy. A commitment to sound money protects individuals' economic freedoms, enabling them to plan for the future without fear of losing purchasing power—a foundation for both economic prosperity and social justice.

THE MORAL CORRELATION BETWEEN CURRENCY DEPRECIATION AND TAXES—THE IMMORALITY OF ELITES AND THE DEGENERATION OF MONEY

Barry Eichengreen (1996) analyzed the role of economic elites in the depreciation of currency, framing it as a form of hidden taxation on society. He argued that when governments or financial authorities manipulate monetary policies for the benefit of specific groups, it results in a redistribution of wealth that disproportionately affects the general population. This form of covert taxation undermines the principles of sound money and erodes public trust in financial institutions, leading to broader social and economic inequality.

In a similar vein, Joseph Stiglitz (2012) highlighted the detrimental effects of policies that favor the wealthy, noting that such practices often lead to economic instability. Stiglitz argued that currency manipulation can create a disparity in economic opportunity, allowing elites to benefit from devaluation while the broader population suffers from rising costs and diminished purchasing power. The erosion of trust in the monetary system and its institutions not only impacts economic performance but also exacerbates social tensions, ultimately challenging the moral fabric of society.

Recent events illustrate these dynamics starkly. For example, during the COVID-19 pandemic, governments around the world implemented aggressive monetary policies to stabilize economies. In the U.S., the Federal Reserve's expansion of the money supply and low interest rates aimed to support economic recovery. However, as reported by the Bureau of Labor Statistics (2021), this influx of liquidity coincided with soaring inflation rates, which disproportionately impacted lower and middle-income households. As a result, those at the bottom of the economic ladder experienced a "hidden tax" through decreased purchasing power, while asset holders, typically wealthier individuals, benefited from rising asset prices.

Additionally, Thomas Piketty (2014) discussed how monetary policy can lead to inequality, emphasizing that when central banks prioritize the interests of financial markets over the general public, it fosters economic disparities. In his work, Capital in the Twenty-First Century, Piketty highlighted how wealth concentration results from systemic policy choices that favor the rich, which can manifest in currency depreciation affecting the lower classes more severely.

Similarly, the recent turmoil in the Turkish economy provides a contemporary example of currency depreciation impacting social equity. The Turkish lira has faced severe devaluation since 2018, a consequence of monetary policies favoring short-term growth over long-term stability. As the lira lost value, everyday goods became increasingly expensive, straining the finances of average citizens while those with access to foreign currencies or gold preserved their wealth. This dynamic led to public unrest and protests, illustrating how currency depreciation can exacerbate class divisions and social discontent (Özdemir, 2021).

The ethical implications of such currency manipulation extend to the realm of governance and accountability. John Maynard Keynes (1936) addressed these moral issues, arguing that sound monetary policy should prioritize societal welfare. Keynes maintained that when governments manipulate currency values for political gain, they undermine the social contract, perpetuating cycles of inequality and dissatisfaction among citizens.

In recent times, the United States and the United Kingdom have experienced significant economic challenges related to currency depreciation and inflation. In the U.S., inflation reached a 40-year high in 2022, driven by various factors, including supply chain disruptions and increased consumer demand (U.S. Bureau of Labor Statistics, 2022). As a result, the purchasing power of the dollar declined, forcing families to allocate a larger portion of their budgets to essential goods like food and fuel. The Federal Reserve's response, involving interest rate hikes to curb inflation, has sparked debates about the moral implications of these measures, especially for lower-income households already struggling to make ends meet (Furman, 2022).

Similarly, in the UK, the depreciation of the British pound has raised concerns about rising living costs and economic instability. Following the government's announcement of unfunded tax cuts in late 2022, the pound plummeted, leading to skyrocketing import prices and increased inflation (Davies, 2022). This situation prompted widespread criticism, with advocates arguing that such policies disproportionately harm low- and middle-income families while benefiting those with assets that can withstand currency fluctuations. The public outcry reflects a growing awareness of how currency manipulation can be perceived as a moral failure of elites who prioritize short-term gains over the long-term welfare of society.

The intertwining of currency depreciation and taxation reflects broader moral concerns about the integrity of economic systems. When monetary policies are manipulated to benefit a select few, they diminish the value of money and erode the trust essential for a healthy economy. Recent events and scholarly analysis emphasize that the moral implications of these policies demand attention and reform, advocating for governance that prioritizes sound money and equitable economic practices.

GRAPHICAL ANALYSIS OF MONEY'S IMMORALITY BASED ON DEPRECIATION AND TAXES

J. Zhao (2020) developed a model illustrating the ethical implications of currency depreciation when coupled with high taxation. His analysis showed that such monetary policies disproportionately impact lower-income individuals by reducing their purchasing power and increasing their financial burdens. Zhao's model quantitatively links inflationary practices to economic injustice, reinforcing the argument that unsound monetary policies can create systemic disparities within society. The graphical representation in Zhao's study highlights how currency depreciation exacerbates income inequality, showing that as inflation rises, the lower-income brackets bear the brunt of the costs, while wealthier individuals can shield their assets from inflationary pressures.

Below, a revised visualization of Zhao's model was created to give a view of the loss of purchasing power over time.

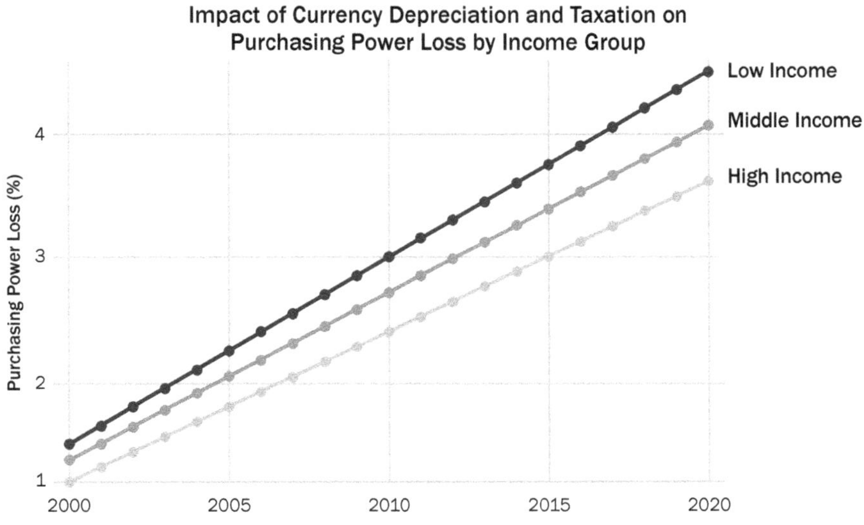

This analysis is particularly relevant in the context of recent events in the United States and the UK, where both governments have engaged in substantial monetary expansion in response to economic challenges, such as the COVID-19 pandemic. According to a report by the Bank of England (2021), the extensive monetary policies employed, including quantitative easing and low-interest rates, have led to increased inflation levels. Such inflation can act as a hidden tax on the poor, as they tend to spend a larger proportion of their income on essentials, which are often the first to rise in price during inflationary periods as the wealthy incomes grow as their assets grow with rising inflation such as real estate and stocks.

Similarly, in the United States, the Federal Reserve's response to economic downturns has included significant increases in the money supply, as outlined in a study by the National Bureau of Economic Research (NBER) (2022). The effects of this expansion have been felt unevenly, contributing to rising prices and worsening economic inequality, especially affecting low- and middle-income households. A report from the Brookings Institution (2022) emphasizes that while asset prices have soared—benefiting wealthier individuals—the purchasing power of average Americans has been eroded, creating a growing chasm between the wealthy and the disadvantaged.

Moreover, the analysis of recent inflationary trends by the Federal Reserve Bank of St. Louis (2022) highlights how rapid increases in consumer prices have affected various demographic groups differently. Research from the Institute for Fiscal Studies (2022) also corroborates that low-income families in the UK have faced the highest relative inflation rates, which has led to significant declines in real income. The ethical implications of these monetary policies underscore the moral responsibilities that come with managing currency. When economic elites and policymakers prioritize the interests of specific groups over the broader population, it further solidifies the argument that sound money is not only an economic principle but also an ethical imperative. Thus, the graphical analysis presented by Zhao, alongside these contemporary examples, reinforces the notion that unsound monetary practices lead to societal inequities, necessitating a return to principles that prioritize fairness and equity in financial systems.

HOW THE PERCENTAGE OF SOUND MONEY LEADS TO MORAL POLICY IN THE UNITED STATES

Milton Friedman (1968) asserted that a higher percentage of sound money within an economy naturally guides policymakers toward moral and equitable fiscal policies. When a currency's value is maintained and inflation is kept in check, governments are less likely to resort to exploitative practices like inflationary spending. This disciplined approach to monetary management helps create a fair economic environment, reducing the risk of policies that undermine societal well-being and economic stability.

In recent years, the United States has experienced significant monetary shifts, particularly following the COVID-19 pandemic. The Federal Reserve implemented aggressive monetary policies, including lowering interest rates and purchasing large quantities of government securities, which increased the money supply dramatically. Between February 2020 and May 2021, the M2 money supply, a key measure of the money supply that includes cash, checking deposits, and easily convertible near money, surged by over 25%, reaching approximately $20.5 trillion. This unprecedented expansion raised concerns about inflation and the potential for currency depreciation, underscoring the importance of sound monetary principles in guiding fiscal policy.

The ramifications of this massive increase in the money supply began to manifest in inflation rates, which rose sharply in 2021 and into 2022. By June 2022, the Consumer Price Index (CPI) had reached a staggering 9.1%, the highest level since 1981. Such a rapid increase in inflation signifies the destructive potential of unsound monetary practices and the urgent need for a solid framework based on sound money principles to safeguard purchasing power and protect the most vulnerable members of society. Notably, the U.S. Bureau of Labor Statistics reported that food prices surged by 11.4% year-over-year in June 2022, with gas prices increasing by over 50% during the same period, further highlighting how inflation disproportionately affects lower-income households that spend a larger portion of their income on essentials.

The correlation between sound money and moral policy becomes clearer when considering the broader societal impact of inflation. Research from the Federal Reserve Bank of San Francisco indicates that rising inflation leads to a decrease in real wages, disproportionately affecting lower-income workers. For example, real average hourly earnings fell by 3.6% between April 2021 and April 2022, effectively reducing the purchasing power of wages at a time when prices were rising sharply. This decline illustrates how inflation can serve as a hidden tax on the working class, eroding their financial stability and undermining social equity.

Historically, the United States has experienced the consequences of poor monetary policy and its impact on moral governance. During the late 1970s and early 1980s, the U.S. grappled with stagflation—a combination of high inflation and stagnant economic growth. At its peak, the inflation rate reached over 14%, leading to widespread economic hardship and disillusionment with governmental institutions. The Federal Reserve, under Chairman Paul Volcker, responded with aggressive interest rate hikes, bringing the federal funds rate to a staggering 20% by 1980. While this policy eventually curtailed inflation, it also precipitated a recession that increased unemployment and caused significant pain for American households. This historical context underscores the critical importance of sound money principles in guiding responsible monetary policy and fostering economic stability.

In recent years, the economic challenges faced by the United States, particularly in light of the pandemic-induced fiscal response, underscore the critical importance of sound money principles. As policymakers grapple with balancing stimulus measures and long-term fiscal responsibility, the potential consequences of inflation and currency depreciation loom large. The Federal Reserve has recently signaled a shift towards tightening monetary policy to combat rising inflation, which may include increasing interest rates and reducing asset purchases. This pivot towards a more disciplined monetary policy reflects a recognition of the need to uphold the integrity of the currency and restore public trust are crucial for maintaining economic stability. Sound money principles extend beyond controlling inflation; they also encompass the moral responsibilities of governments in managing fiscal policies.

A study conducted by the Cato Institute (2019) found that regions with higher levels of fiscal discipline, characterized by sound monetary practices, experienced greater economic resilience and social trust among citizens. For instance, states that maintained balanced budgets and adhered to sound monetary principles tended to report higher levels of trust in government institutions and greater public satisfaction with economic conditions (Cato Institute, 2019).

Moreover, the social consequences of monetary mismanagement can ripple through various facets of society. According to a report from the Economic Policy Institute (2020), families experiencing stagnant wages alongside rising living costs are more likely to face economic hardships, including increased debt levels and diminished savings. The report noted that from 2000 to 2018, the median household income in the U.S. grew by only 8%, while the cost of living rose by approximately 25% . This disparity reflects the erosion of purchasing power resulting from inflationary policies.

The current inflationary environment reveals the importance of restoring public faith in monetary policy. The Federal Reserve's reputation has been called into question, with a Gallup poll from late 2021 indicating that only 25% of Americans had a great deal of confidence in the Federal Reserve (Gallup, 2021). This decline in trust underscores the vital connection between sound money and moral governance; when monetary policy is perceived as irresponsible or exploitative, public confidence wanes, leading to societal discontent.

From the chart, we see the Total Moral Hazard Score progressively increase with each period. The chart illustrates the extent to which the value of gold has been debased relative to its fixed intrinsic benchmark. The first period (1913–1944), where the U.S. was still on a gold-backed standard, shows the lowest debasement percentage (0%–30%) and a relatively modest moral hazard score (24). This suggests that during this time, the currency was still tied to a commodity, and financial institutions and governments faced some constraints in terms of how much debt and money they could issue. The period from 1944 to 1971, when the U.S. operated under the Bretton Woods system, shows a moderate rise in debasement (30%–75%) and a moral hazard score of 39. This period was characterized by the U.S. dollar's role as the world's reserve currency, but the system was still backed by gold in theory (although the U.S. abandoned the gold convertibility in 1971).

The most dramatic increase in both debasement and moral hazard occurs during the 1971–2000 period, when the U.S. fully transitioned to a fiat currency system. Debasement during this period ranged from 75% to 90%, and the moral hazard score skyrocketed to 58. The chart shows the impact of U.S. dollar inflation, debt expansion, and government spending, which are hallmarks of fiat systems. In this period, without the constraint of the gold standard, the U.S. government was able to significantly increase its debt load and inflate its currency, often with little immediate consequence to the economy (though eventually contributing to issues like the 2008 financial crisis). Finally, the 2000-present period shows the highest levels of debasement (90%–98%) and the highest moral hazard score (84). This reflects the unchecked expansion of the money supply, coupled with increasing financialization, speculative investment, and rising inequality, all consequences of a fiat money system where the currency is no longer backed by tangible assets.

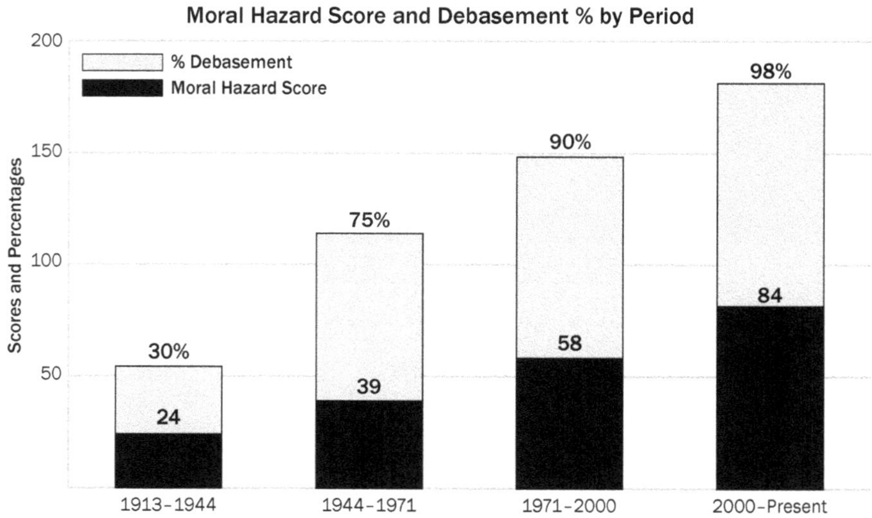

EXPLANATION OF MORAL HAZARD SCORING BASED ON CRITERIA*

Lowest Score Possible: 20 — Highest Score Possible: 100

1. **1913 – 1944 (Score 24):** The early Federal Reserve period and Gold Standard era. Minimal moral hazard with low scores across most columns. Debt, financialization, household debt, and speculative culture remain low. There is some military spending due to WWI and early WWII.
2. **1944 – 1971 (Score 39):** Post-WWII economic boom and Bretton Woods system. Moderate moral hazard with rising debt, increased military spending due to Cold War, and moderate wealth inequality. Economic bubbles and speculative behavior are limited, but beginning to increase.
3. **1971 – 2000 (Score 58):** Fiat currency era post-gold standard. Higher scores across debt, economic bubbles, and financialization. Noticeable increases in wealth inequality, short-term policy focus, speculative culture, and household debt. Social unrest and political polarization also become more prominent.
4. **2000 – Present (Score 84):** High moral hazard in the modern fiat era. Extreme scores in debt expansion, wealth inequality, bubbles, political corruption, and dependence on government assistance. High levels of household debt, erosion of institutional trust, speculative culture, and consumerism reflect the profound shifts since the 2000s, particularly post-2008 and in recent years.

* See Addendum, Moral Hazard Scoring Criteria

The following table offers a sobering historical perspective on the decline of monetary integrity across the world's dominant reserve currencies: the British Pound, U.S. Dollar, Japanese Yen, Euro, and Chinese Yuan. It traces a common trajectory each currency has followed—from an era of sound money, often gold-backed or characterized by low inflation, to today's era of aggressive fiat debasement. The chart begins by establishing a historical benchmark of stability, where currencies operated under tight monetary discipline. These early systems were marked by restrained government spending, economic predictability, and trust in the value of money.

Period	British Pound	U.S. Dollar	Japanese Yen	Euro	Chinese Yuan
Early Sound Money	0% Debasement • Gold-backed	0% Debasement • Gold-backed	Low Debasement • Low inflation	Low Debasement • Initial Stability	Low Debasement • Initial Growth
Transitional Phase *Path of Immorality*	20% Debasement • Increased debt • Colonial exploitation	30% Debasement • Military spending • Debt expansion	10% Debasement • Asset bubbles • Economic speculation	15% Debasement • Debt crisis • Austerity measures • Public discontent	10% Debasement • Leverage debt • Political control
Peak Fiat Era *Path of Immorality*	50% Debasement • War funding • Labor exploitation	75% Debasement • Social unrest • Currency decline	30% Debasement • Debt traps • Economic stagnation	40% Debasement • War funding • Sovereign defaults • Political crisis • Public unrest	30% Debasement • Environmental degradation • Debt dependency
Current Era *Path of Immorality*	80% Debasement • High inflation • Erosion of wages • Social unrest	98% Debasement • Global inflation • Military spending • Wealth disparity	50% Debasement • Economic stagnation • Declining growth	55% Debasement • Monetary crisis • Social strife • Political instability	40% Debasement • Global influence • Debt crisis • Environment impact
Source	Bank of England, ONS	Bureau of Labor Statistics, Federal Reserve	Bank of Japan, IMF	European Central Bank	National Bank of Statistics, People's Bank of China

The table provides a comparative analysis of the debasement and moral consequences associated with five major reserve currencies: the British Pound, the U.S. Dollar, the Japanese Yen, the Euro, and the Chinese Yuan, across key historical periods. The British Pound, from its gold-backed standard to the early 20th century, experienced relatively low debasement, but as the empire expanded, it faced mounting debts and military expenditures. The U.S. Dollar, initially backed by gold, saw significant debasement after the Bretton Woods system collapsed in 1971, leading to rampant inflation, military spending, and social unrest. The Japanese Yen, after World War II, maintained low inflation during its initial recovery but entered a phase of significant debasement in the 1980s, largely due to asset bubbles and economic stagnation. The Euro, though initially stable, has faced debt crises and economic stagnation, exacerbated by sovereign defaults and public unrest during the 2008 financial crisis. The Chinese Yuan, with its controlled devaluation in the 21st century, faces its own set of challenges, including leveraging debt, environmental degradation, and increasing global influence. Overall, the chart highlights how as reserve currencies experience increasing debasement, countries are compelled to rely more on debt, military expansion, and short-term solutions, while moral hazards such as social unrest, inequality, and political instability also rise, creating long-term consequences for economic and societal stability.

Over time, each currency transitions into a phase of growing debasement, accompanied by rising debt levels, military or colonial expansion, and increasing political manipulation. What makes this visual particularly significant is that it does not treat currency debasement as a purely economic issue, but instead reveals a broader moral dimension. The chart links monetary decline to social and political consequences such as labor exploitation, war funding, environmental degradation, and social unrest, arguing that the degradation of currency is often accompanied by a parallel erosion of societal well-being.

By comparing the historical arcs of these currencies side by side, the chart underscores that no major reserve currency has been immune to this trend. While the U.S. Dollar shows one of the steepest declines, reaching 98% debasement, others like the Chinese Yuan or Japanese Yen follow similar patterns with varying speeds and policy mechanisms. The inclusion of respected data sources such as the Bank of England, Federal Reserve, IMF, and others adds credibility to the picture being drawn, anchoring its claims in well-documented historical and economic data.

The importance of this chart lies in its warning. It serves as both a record and a moral indictment of fiat monetary regimes, suggesting that continued debasement leads not only to inflation or stagnation but to deeper forms of instability and injustice. In doing so, it raises a pressing question about whether the current path is sustainable or if a return to sound money is necessary to restore economic and ethical order.

The historical and contemporary analysis of sound money in the United States illustrates a clear link between monetary stability and moral fiscal policies. As the nation navigates the complexities of economic recovery, the imperative for sound money becomes increasingly apparent. Upholding sound money principles is essential for ensuring that economic policies promote fairness, protect the most vulnerable, and ultimately foster a prosperous society. Thus, we should acknowledge how The Federal Reserve has been paramount in this moral debasement in the United States and question if an institution that has fostered a trend of immorality should not be considered the failed institution that it has proven to be—and end the institution in place of a sound money system.

CHAPTER 7

Rethinking Sound Money for the 21st Century?

Massimo Amato and Luca Fantacci (2018) emphasized the need for a comparative study between historically sound money systems, such as the gold standard, and contemporary frameworks like digital currencies and fiat money. By evaluating the strengths and limitations of these systems, this research aims to extract relevant principles that can enhance modern monetary practices. Understanding these principles will contribute to designing more robust and stable economic systems in today's digital age.

These characteristics contributed to the stability of historical systems, including the mechanisms for maintaining currency value, the role of government and institutions in safeguarding monetary integrity, and the societal impacts of sound money practices. For instance, during the gold standard era, the convertibility of currency into gold provided a check against inflation and encouraged responsible fiscal policies. According to a study by Temin (2003), the stability afforded by the gold standard not only prevented excessive government spending but also facilitated international trade by establishing fixed exchange rates. In contrast, the flexibility of fiat money systems, while beneficial for addressing immediate economic challenges, can lead to vulnerabilities such as inflation and loss of purchasing power. The value of the U.S. dollar has significantly eroded since the abandonment of the gold standard in 1971, resulting in a notable decline in purchasing power. According to the Bureau of Labor Statistics, $1 in 1971 has the equivalent purchasing power of approximately $7.68 in 2024 dollars (BLS, 2024). This raises an important question: if sound money was historically represented by $1 of silver, which corresponds to one troy ounce, how can silver currently be trading in late 2024 at over $30 while the BLS indicates a value of only $7.68 for the same dollar? This discrepancy highlights the complexities of measuring value in a fiat currency system and the implications for understanding sound money principles.

This comparison delves into the implications of emerging digital currencies, assessing their potential to replicate the stability of sound money while considering the risks associated with technological dependence and regulatory challenges. Digital currencies, particularly those issued by central banks (CBDCs), may offer a means of ensuring stability while also embracing the technological advancements of the 21st century. However, research by Zohar (2015) highlights that without careful regulation, the rise of digital currencies could lead to increased volatility and new forms of financial inequity.

The importance of integrating sound money principles into the current economic discourse, encouraging policymakers to consider long-term implications when implementing monetary and fiscal policies. The lessons learned from hyperinflationary episodes in countries like Zimbabwe and Germany provide a cautionary tale on the consequences of neglecting sound monetary practices. In Zimbabwe, the government's decision to print excessive amounts of money to address economic issues resulted in inflation rates exceeding 89.7 sextillion percent in November 2008 (International Monetary Fund, 2009). Similarly, in Weimar Germany, the failure to adhere to sound money principles led to hyperinflation that devastated the economy and ultimately contributed to political instability (Holtfrerich, 2002). These historical examples underscore the importance of maintaining currency integrity to prevent economic collapse.

In rethinking sound money for the 21st century, it is important to explore how modern frameworks—particularly centralized vs decentralized currencies—can be reimagined to reflect the core values of monetary integrity, transparency, and limited inflation. While CBDCs offer the potential for secure, programmable money that operates within a digital ecosystem, their design must reconcile the tension between centralized control and the decentralized ethos underpinning historical sound money.

A well-designed CBDC, incorporating asset backing or strict issuance rules, could potentially merge the accountability of sound money with the efficiency of digital infrastructure but could also be used to centralize control and usher in a new authoritarian tyranny.

A decentralized ledger system based on blockchain technology offers a contemporary pathway to revive and modernize the foundational principles of sound money—particularly the decentralization embodied by gold and silver. Unlike centralized monetary systems, where the authority to issue and control currency resides with a central bank or government, blockchain-based systems distribute verification and record-keeping across a wide network of participants. This decentralized architecture mirrors the non-sovereign nature of precious metals, which derive their value from scarcity and broad societal acceptance rather than from institutional decree.

By operating independently of centralized control, blockchain technologies support a more democratic monetary framework, in which transparency, immutability, and collective governance are embedded into the infrastructure. In this sense, a decentralized digital ledger aligns philosophically and functionally with the historical role of gold and silver as neutral, universally recognized stores of value. Moreover, the programmability of blockchain protocols allows for the incorporation of supply constraints, auditability, and fixed issuance schedules—features that echo the scarcity and stability that made metallic standards appealing.

Such a system could restore public trust in money by reducing reliance on discretionary monetary policy and insulating the currency from political manipulation. In doing so, it could also help prevent the inflationary pressures and economic distortions often associated with fiat systems. As scholars such as Narayanan et al. (2016) have noted, blockchain's decentralized consensus mechanisms offer not only technical robustness but also the potential to democratize financial infrastructure by removing gatekeepers and enabling peer-to-peer interactions.

In essence, integrating blockchain-based decentralized ledgers with the principles underlying sound money—such as limited supply, intrinsic value, and resistance to censorship—presents an opportunity to construct a 21st-century monetary system that retains the discipline of the past while leveraging the technological innovation of the present.

Moreover, this line of inquiry opens the door to a broader redefinition of what constitutes "soundness" in the digital era. Beyond gold or silver backing, sound money in the 21st century might be defined by algorithmic issuance limits, transparency of monetary operations, and constraints on discretionary fiscal expansion. These principles, rooted in historical experience but adapted for technological reality—could help safeguard purchasing power and public trust in national and global currencies alike.

Historical episodes of hyperinflation or hyperdeflation offer powerful evidence of the dangers associated with abandoning sound monetary principles. One of the most dramatic examples of hyperinflation occurred in Zimbabwe between 2007 and 2008. In an attempt to finance a ballooning fiscal deficit, the government resorted to excessive money printing, which led to a complete collapse of the national currency. At the height of the crisis, Zimbabwe's annual inflation rate soared to an estimated 89.7 sextillion percent, effectively rendering the Zimbabwean dollar worthless (Hanke & Bostrom, 2013). This economic collapse forced the country to abandon its sovereign currency and adopt foreign currencies in everyday transactions, causing long-term structural damage to its financial system.

In contrast to hyperinflation, episodes of hyperdeflation, though rarer, demonstrate how a rapid and unchecked decline in prices can also destabilize an economy, particularly when sound monetary flexibility is lacking. A striking historical example is Japan during the Great Depression in the early 1930s, when the country adhered rigidly to the gold standard despite global economic contraction. As demand collapsed and prices plummeted, Japan experienced sustained deflation that severely eroded corporate profits, suppressed wages, and deepened the economic downturn (Mitchener & Ohnuki, 2009). The Bank of Japan's inability to adjust the money supply under the gold standard constrained its capacity to respond effectively, leading to increased unemployment and widespread social distress. This deflationary spiral curtailed investment, as businesses and consumers delayed spending in anticipation of even lower prices. The eventual abandonment of the gold standard in 1931 allowed Japan to pursue more expansionary policies, which helped reverse the crisis. This episode illustrates that strict adherence to sound money principles—when applied without adaptability to economic realities—can also generate harmful outcomes, particularly when monetary contraction exacerbates an already fragile economic environment.

Therefore, rethinking sound money for the 21st century requires a nuanced approach—one that draws from historical precedent while integrating modern technological advancements. Sound money principles, such as limiting arbitrary monetary expansion, safeguarding purchasing power, and ensuring institutional accountability, remain as relevant today as they were during the gold standard era. Embedding these principles into new monetary frameworks, particularly digital currencies, can help create more resilient and equitable economic systems.

By critically assessing past monetary regimes and thoughtfully applying their core principles to current challenges, we can work toward monetary systems that not only meet the demands of modern economies but also uphold the long-term integrity and stability that sound money was designed to protect.

CHAPTER 8

Understanding How Easy Money Fuels Economic Imbalance

In recent years, inflation has become a pressing issue globally, affecting both developed and emerging economies. The recent inflationary trends have ignited renewed interest in sound money principles, particularly as they relate to monetary stability and the prevention of unchecked money supply growth. Economists and policymakers are once again examining the consequences of expansive monetary policies, especially those implemented in response to crises such as the COVID-19 pandemic. The shift from emergency fiscal and monetary support toward tightening cycles has highlighted the fragility of modern fiat systems when subjected to inflationary pressures. As purchasing power declines and the cost of living rises, many are questioning whether the absence of a monetary anchor—such as that provided by the gold standard in earlier eras—has exacerbated volatility in currency value. This renewed scrutiny is fostering a broader conversation about how principles of sound money could help restore trust in monetary institutions, limit arbitrary expansion of the money supply, and promote long-term economic stability.

As the examples below from both G7 and BRICS countries demonstrate, inflationary trends tend to emerge in any nation where there is mismanagement of the monetary system regardless of its economic wealth or global influence. Whether in advanced economies with sophisticated financial infrastructures or in emerging markets with growing fiscal capacity, the consequences of poor monetary policy, excessive debt accumulation, or unrestrained money supply growth are similarly destabilizing. These patterns reveal that even affluent nations are not insulated from inflation when core principles of sound monetary governance are neglected.

G7 NATIONS

1. **United States:**
   Inflation surged significantly post-COVID-19 due to substantial fiscal stimulus and supply chain disruptions. The Consumer Price Index (CPI) rose sharply, peaking at 9.1% in June 2022—the highest in four decades. As a response, the Federal Reserve has aggressively raised interest rates to curb inflation, leading to debates on whether this approach will foster a recession (Federal Reserve, 2022).
2. **Canada:**
   Canada also faced rising inflation rates, hitting 8.1% in June 2022. Factors contributing to this included high energy prices and supply chain issues. The Bank of Canada implemented interest rate hikes to combat inflation, reflecting similar strategies to those employed in the U.S. (Bank of Canada, 2022).
3. **United Kingdom:**
   The UK saw inflation reach 11.1% in October 2022, driven by skyrocketing energy costs and food prices. The Bank of England's attempts to manage inflation through monetary tightening raised concerns about potential economic slowdowns and increased borrowing costs (Office for National Statistics, 2022).
4. **Germany:**
   Germany experienced inflation at 10.0% in October 2022, with energy costs being a major contributor. The European Central Bank's policy response included interest rate increases to stabilize the economy, prompting discussions on the efficacy of such measures in achieving long-term monetary stability (Destatis, 2022).
5. **France:**
   France's inflation peaked at 6.1% in 2022, primarily due to rising energy and food prices. The French government introduced measures to mitigate the impact of rising prices,

such as energy subsidies, while the Banque de France supported a gradual normalization of monetary policy (Institut National de la Statistique et des Études Économiques, 2022).

6. **Italy:**
   Italy faced inflation rates of 12.8% in November 2022, exacerbated by energy prices stemming from the conflict in Ukraine. The Italian government focused on providing financial support to households and businesses affected by rising costs, while the European Central Bank managed monetary policy (Istituto Nazionale di Statistica, 2022).
7. **Japan:**
   Unlike other G7 nations, Japan experienced moderate inflation, reaching 3.6% in 2022. However, the Bank of Japan's commitment to maintaining low interest rates and stimulus measures has raised concerns about the sustainability of its economic approach amid global inflationary pressures (Bank of Japan, 2022).

BRICS NATIONS

1. **Brazil:**
   Brazil's inflation reached 8.7% in 2022, driven by rising food and energy prices. The Central Bank of Brazil responded with aggressive interest rate hikes, emphasizing the need for sound monetary policy to stabilize the economy (Banco Central do Brasil, 2022).
2. **Russia:**
   Russia experienced fluctuating inflation rates, peaking at around 17% in April 2022, significantly influenced by Western sanctions and energy price volatility. The Central Bank of Russia enacted measures to stabilize the ruble and mitigate inflation, raising interest rates sharply in response (Central Bank of Russia, 2022).
3. **India:**
   India's inflation rates rose to 7.79% in 2022, primarily due to increased commodity prices and supply chain disruptions. The Reserve Bank of India adopted a proactive approach,

raising interest rates to contain inflation while ensuring economic growth (Reserve Bank of India, 2022).

4. **China:**
   China maintained relatively stable inflation rates, around 2% in 2022, despite global pressures. The People's Bank of China implemented monetary policies to stimulate the economy, contrasting sharply with the tightening seen in G7 countries (National Bureau of Statistics of China, 2022).
5. **South Africa:**
   South Africa faced inflation rates of 7.8% in 2022, driven by rising fuel prices and food costs. The South African Reserve Bank raised interest rates to combat inflation while addressing economic growth concerns (Statistics South Africa, 2022).

	Country	Inflation Rate	Key Factors	Sources (2022)
G7	United States	9.1%	Fiscal stimulus, supply chain issues	Federal Reserve
	Canada	8.1%	Energy, supply chain issues	Bank of Canada
	United Kingdom	11.1%	Energy, food costs	Office for National Statistics
	Germany	10.0%	Energy costs	Destatis
	France	6.1%	Energy, food costs	Institut National de la Statistique et des Études Économiques
	Italy	12.8%	Energy costs, Ukraine conflict	Istituto Nazionale di Statistica
	Japan	3.6%	Low inflation due to continued stimulus	Bank of Japan
BRICS	Brazil	8.7%	Energy, food costs	Banca Central do Brasil
	Russia	17.0%	Sanctions, energy price volatility	Central Bank of Russia
	India	7.8%	Commodity prices, supply chain issues	Reserve Bank of India
	China	2.0%	Stable despite global pressures	National Bureau of Statistics of China
	South Africa	7.8%	Fuel prices, food costs	Statistics South Africa

The inflationary trends observed in both G7 and BRICS nations highlight the critical importance of sound money principles in maintaining monetary stability and ensuring economic resilience. In recent years, countries have faced unprecedented inflation levels, exacerbated by global disruptions such as the COVID-19 pandemic, supply chain challenges, and geopolitical tensions. These factors have underscored the necessity for countries to reevaluate their monetary policies and the role of sound money in promoting economic health.

The experiences of the G7 countries, particularly the United States, Canada, and the United Kingdom, demonstrate the immediate need for decisive action to address rising inflation. Central banks' responses, including aggressive interest rate hikes, have sparked debates about the trade-offs between controlling inflation and fostering economic growth. As these nations grapple with the consequences of their monetary policies, it becomes clear that maintaining a stable monetary environment is paramount to protecting consumer purchasing power and fostering long-term economic confidence.

Conversely, the BRICS nations have displayed a more varied response to inflationary pressures. While Brazil, Russia, and India have faced significant inflation challenges, their central banks have implemented strategies aimed at stabilizing their economies. Brazil's aggressive interest rate increases and India's proactive monetary measures serve as examples of how sound money principles can guide effective policy decisions in emerging markets. Meanwhile, China's relatively stable inflation rate highlights a contrasting approach, with its focus on economic stimulation rather than stringent monetary tightening.

This divergence in inflation trends and policy responses illustrates that sound money principles are not only relevant for developed economies but are equally crucial for emerging markets. As countries navigate the complexities of the modern global economy, the lessons drawn from historically sound money systems, such as the gold standard, can provide valuable insights into maintaining price stability and preventing the unchecked expansion of the money supply.

In revisiting sound money principles, policymakers can develop frameworks that prioritize fiscal discipline, transparency, and accountability in monetary policy. By doing so, they can create environments that promote sustainable economic growth, build resilience against inflationary shocks, and restore public confidence in monetary systems. The importance of these principles becomes even more pronounced in an era characterized by rapid technological changes, evolving financial landscapes, and the emergence of digital currencies.

The path forward requires a concerted effort to balance monetary stability with the need for economic growth. As countries like the G7 and BRICS navigate the intricate interplay of local and global economic factors, the adoption of sound money principles can serve as a guiding framework. These principles can help ensure that monetary policies remain effective in addressing inflation while fostering a robust and resilient economic future for all nations. This comprehensive approach to monetary policy, informed by both historical insights and contemporary challenges, will be essential for securing economic stability and promoting equitable growth in an increasingly interconnected world.

ECONOMIC CRISES AND MONETARY POLICIES

Charles Kindleberger underscored the importance of sound monetary principles in his analysis of financial crises, observing that "many economic crises… can be linked to flaws in monetary policies" (Kindleberger, 2005, p. 12). This underscores the need for careful consideration of monetary policies to avoid the distortions and inequalities that can arise from aggressive measures. The volatile monetary policies adopted during these periods, often characterized by excessive money printing and low interest rates, have led to asset bubbles and economic instability. In examining historical studies, such as those on the Bretton Woods system, we see how sound money principles helped maintain economic balance post-WWII. This framework established a stable international monetary system based on gold convertibility, which effectively managed inflation and facilitated global trade (Eichengreen, 2008).

The lessons from past economic crises have underscored the risks of abandoning sound money principles for aggressive monetary policies. For instance, during the 2008 financial crisis, central banks responded with unprecedented levels of quantitative easing (QE) and near-zero interest rates to stabilize the economy. According to the Federal Reserve, the total assets on its balance sheet expanded from approximately $900 billion in 2007 to over $4.5 trillion by 2015, reflecting a drastic shift in monetary policy (Federal Reserve, 2023). While these measures provided temporary relief, they also created distortions in asset pricing and contributed to income inequality as wealth became increasingly concentrated among those who owned financial assets.

The COVID-19 pandemic further exposed vulnerabilities in global financial systems, which were heavily reliant on expansive measures like low interest rates and quantitative easing. In 2020, the U.S. government initiated a series of stimulus packages, amounting to over $6 trillion, alongside the Federal Reserve's commitment to purchasing government securities at an unprecedented scale (U.S. Department of the Treasury, 2020). These policies, while intended to support economic recovery, have led to soaring inflation rates, with the Consumer Price Index (CPI) rising by 7% in 2021, marking the highest annual increase in nearly 40 years (Bureau of Labor Statistics, 2022). This inflationary pressure disproportionately affects lower-income households, highlighting the moral implications of monetary policy decisions.

Understanding the implications of disciplined monetary practices derived from historically sound money systems is crucial for developing strategies to enhance resilience in modern economies. Historical frameworks, such as the Bretton Woods system, demonstrated how fixed exchange rates and sound monetary policies could contribute to global economic stability. By establishing clear monetary rules and maintaining currency convertibility, countries could avoid the destabilizing effects of competitive devaluations and inflationary spirals.

In light of these historical lessons, it is essential for policymakers to reassess their approach to monetary management. Emphasizing sound money principles, such as maintaining a stable currency, curtailing government overspending, and avoiding excessive money printing, can mitigate the risks associated with future economic crises. Policymakers must balance the need for flexibility in response to economic shocks with the long-term commitment to monetary stability, ensuring that the lessons of the past inform the decisions of the future.

THE ROLE OF DIGITAL CURRENCIES AND MODERN MONETARY FRAMEWORKS

As digital currencies like decentralized finance such as Bitcoin gain traction, they challenge the principles of sound money in new ways. Bitcoin, often referred to as "digital gold," is celebrated for its limited supply and resistance to inflation, with a total cap of 21 million coins (Nakamoto, 2008; Yermack, 2013). This scarcity aligns with the historical principles of sound money, where value was anchored to physical commodities like gold. However, Bitcoin's pronounced volatility, absence of intrinsic value, infinite divisibility, and programmable nature as a medium of exchange raise substantive concerns regarding its viability as a stable store of value and its effectiveness in safeguarding the economic liberties that underpin sound monetary systems in free societies. For instance, in 2021, its price ranged from approximately $30,000 to over $60,000, illustrating significant volatility that undermines its reliability as a medium of exchange or unit of account (CoinMarketCap, 2021; McCafferty, 2021).

The volatility of Bitcoin and similar cryptocurrencies arises not only from market speculation but also from their nascent status as financial instruments. A lack of regulatory frameworks can lead to price manipulation and sudden crashes, eroding trust among potential users. For example, the May 2021 market crash saw Bitcoin's price plummet from nearly $60,000 to about $30,000 in weeks (CoinMarketCap, 2021; Wright, 2021). Such behavior contradicts the principles of sound money, which prioritize stability and predictability.

To reconcile digital assets with sound money principles, we can explore options for creating transparent and stable financial systems. Stablecoins, cryptocurrencies pegged to stable assets like the U.S. dollar, aim to reduce the volatility associated with traditional cryptocurrencies. By maintaining a 1:1 peg with fiat currencies, stablecoins can serve as a more stable medium of exchange while leveraging blockchain technology's benefits, such as transparency and efficiency (Zohar, 2020; Gans, 2021). However, the mechanisms behind stablecoin stability, like reserves and governance, require careful regulatory scrutiny to prevent systemic risks and maintain public trust. Recent collapses, like that of the TerraUSD stablecoin in 2022, highlight the necessity of regulatory oversight to ensure that stablecoins operate within a protective framework for consumers (Lee, 2022; Kharif, 2022).

The rise of centralized finance (CeFi), such as CBDCs, offers another avenue for modernizing monetary frameworks while incorporating sound money attributes. Issued and regulated by central banks, CBDCs could enhance monetary policy transmission, improve payment systems, and increase financial inclusion (Bank for International Settlements, 2021; Zhou, 2021). Initiatives like China's Digital Currency Electronic Payment (DCEP) aim to create a cash-like digital currency fully integrated into the national payment system, allowing central banks greater control over monetary policy while enhancing transaction efficiency (Zhang, 2021). Unlike traditional cryptocurrencies that operate independently of government control, CBDCs could integrate sound monetary principles such as transparency and limited supply control.

A well-designed CBDC could be structured to limit supply growth based on predetermined criteria, thus mitigating inflation risks and ensuring stable purchasing power. By integrating technology into the monetary framework, central banks can utilize real-time data to adjust policies effectively. For instance, a CBDC programmed to respond to inflation indicators could help maintain price stability in ways traditional systems may struggle to achieve (Gurley-Calvez & McCarthy, 2021).

However, the centralized nature of these systems makes them particularly vulnerable to misuse and abuse of power. This susceptibility has led many proponents of individual liberty and financial transparency to advocate for decentralized alternatives. By distributing authority and reducing reliance on a single governing entity, decentralized systems are seen as a means to mitigate the risks of financial malfeasance and promote greater accountability.

Beyond the creation of stable digital assets, the cryptocurrency sector is also expanding into broader financial services, leveraging frameworks like Ethereum to build decentralized financial (DeFi) solutions. Ethereum's smart contract capabilities provide a foundation for creating decentralized stock exchanges and other financial platforms, which operate without intermediaries, offering potentially lower costs and greater transparency (Buterin, 2013). This decentralized approach aligns with sound money principles by reducing dependency on centralized entities, which historically have contributed to inflationary practices and instability in monetary systems. By utilizing Ethereum and similar platforms, future financial solutions can incorporate programmability and automation into transactions, ensuring more efficient and transparent financial systems while retaining stability.

However, decoupling technological solutions from sound money principles poses significant risks. Without an inseparable connection between innovative digital currencies and foundational sound money tenets, the system could revert to a fiat-like structure with hegemonic control over monetary practices (Hudson, 2022). Balancing traditional sound money theories with innovative financial technology presents critical areas for future policy development. Policymakers must cultivate innovation in digital currencies while ensuring alignment with sound monetary principles. This balance is vital for creating a monetary framework that embraces technological advancements without succumbing to a fiat system that risks hegemonic control over money.

The challenge of balancing these elements feels unprecedented, but history offers a cautionary tale. The Federal Reserve Act of 1913 shifted control of U.S. monetary policy to a centralized authority, sparking significant opposition from various figures who foresaw the dangers of such concentration (Federal Reserve, 2020). President Woodrow Wilson, who signed the Act into law, later expressed regret, acknowledging that he had "unwittingly ruined his country" by enabling the consolidation of financial power. This controversial reflection, although debated, has been widely referenced in critiques of the Federal Reserve (Wilson, 1919; Greider, 1987).

The concerns raised during this era and by historians were not limited to Wilson. Numerous prominent figures, including Charles Lindbergh Sr., Louis T. McFadden, William Jennings Bryan, Robert Latham Owen, H. L. Mencken, Henry Clay, and John Stuart Mill, voiced their critiques of the

Federal Reserve and its implications. These critics highlighted concerns about the erosion of regional autonomy, the concentration of economic power, and the potential for monetary policies to favor financial elites over the broader population.

Early critics like Thomas Jefferson and Andrew Jackson warned of the dangers of centralized financial control. Jefferson was particularly concerned about the risks posed by a national bank, which he saw as a concentration of power that could undermine democratic institutions (Jefferson, 1800). In his letter to John Dickinson, Jefferson wrote, "The central bank is an institution of the most deadly hostility existing against the principles and form of our Constitution." Jackson, who famously vetoed the recharter of the Second Bank of the United States, believed that such institutions could concentrate too much power in the hands of a few wealthy individuals, threatening the independence of the people (Jackson, 1834).

Modern critiques echo these concerns, emphasizing the concentration of power in central banks. The 2008 Global Financial Crisis (GFC) and the COVID-19 pandemic highlighted how centralized monetary systems often prioritize the interests of large financial institutions. Central banks were criticized for policies that disproportionately benefited financial elites while neglecting smaller businesses and individual citizens. This imbalance exacerbated economic inequality, raising alarms over the concentration of financial power (Greider, 2009).

The growing distance between policymakers and the public, and the lack of direct oversight in monetary decision-making, became a significant concern. Early reformers like William Jennings Bryan criticized the lack of transparency in financial institutions and their unaccountability to the public (Bryan, 1900). He argued that monetary policies should be subject to democratic scrutiny to ensure that they serve the public interest.

This issue remains relevant today. During the 2008 GFC and the COVID-19 crisis, central banks operated with limited public scrutiny while implementing expansive monetary policies. These policies—such as quantitative easing and financial bailouts—often lacked transparency and fueled public dissatisfaction. Critics argue that such actions erode trust and accountability in financial governance (Friedman, 2002).

Economic challenges such as fluctuating inflation and speculative bubbles linked to Federal Reserve policies have been criticized by economists like David Ricardo and John Stuart Mill. Ricardo warned about the potential for inflation to destabilize an economy, while Mill discussed how speculative booms could be exacerbated by government intervention in the money supply (Ricardo, 1817; Mill, 1848).

Modern analyses reveal that central bank policies continue to influence financial instability. For instance, the GFC was partially attributed to low-interest rates and easy credit, which fueled speculative bubbles in housing markets. Similarly, post-COVID policies, including massive monetary expansion, have raised concerns about inflationary pressures and potential asset bubbles, echoing earlier economic critiques (Taylor, 2009).

The increasing control over monetary policy by financial elites was criticized by early economic theorists. Thomas Jefferson feared that banks would inevitably lead to the concentration of economic power in the hands of the few, undermining republican values (Jefferson, 1800). Similarly, Andrew Jackson criticized the power wielded by the Second Bank of the United States, arguing that it was undemocratic and dangerous (Jackson, 1834).

Concerns about concentrated financial power remain deeply relevant in today's economic landscape. The aftermath of the 2008 Global Financial Crisis vividly illustrated this imbalance while major financial institutions and banking elites were swiftly stabilized—often through government bailouts funded by taxpayers—millions of ordinary citizens faced job losses, foreclosures, and long-term economic hardship. The political decision to allocate public funds to rescue private banks sparked widespread criticism, reinforcing perceptions of a system that privileges powerful financial actors at the expense of the broader population. Central banks' close ties with major financial institutions continue to raise questions about fairness and the disproportionate influence of financial elites (Haldane, 2015).

CHAPTER 9

From Liberty to Looting by the Moneyed Elite

This concentration of power would lead to grand theft of the people such as the income tax. Throughout U.S. history, the creation and expansion of central banking and income taxation have sparked significant constitutional debates and accusations of governmental overreach. The establishment of the First Bank of the United States in 1791 exemplifies this controversy. Advocates like Alexander Hamilton argued that the bank was a necessary and proper tool for regulating commerce and managing government finances, falling under implied powers granted by the Constitution. However, opponents, led by Thomas Jefferson, contended that the Constitution did not explicitly authorize the federal government to establish a national bank. Jefferson and others argued that the establishment of a national bank violated the 10th Amendment, which reserves to the states or the people any powers not explicitly granted to the federal government. This concern was later echoed in legal challenges, including McCulloch v. Maryland (1819), where the debate centered on the constitutional limits of federal authority and the implied powers granted by the Necessary and Proper Clause.

A similar controversy arose with the chartering of the Second Bank of the United States in 1816. Opponents, including President Andrew Jackson, argued that the centralization of financial power in a national bank was unconstitutional and undemocratic, favoring wealthy elites at the expense of average Americans. Jackson's veto of the bank's re-charter in 1832 and subsequent actions to dismantle it reflected his belief that the institution undermined the sovereignty of the states and overstepped federal authority.

The introduction of the first federal income tax in 1861, designed to fund the Civil War, faced its own constitutional challenges. Critics argued that the tax violated Article I, Section 9 of the Constitution, which requires direct taxes to be apportioned among the states based on population. Although the income tax was repealed in 1872 after the war ended, the debate over its constitutionality persisted. In 1895, the Supreme Court, in Pollock v. Farmers' Loan & Trust Co., declared the federal income tax unconstitutional because it was a direct tax not properly apportioned. This decision invalidated earlier attempts at federal income taxation and led to the passage of the 16th Amendment in 1913. While the amendment explicitly authorized Congress to levy income taxes without apportionment, its ratification was seen by some as a fundamental shift that expanded federal power beyond what the Founders intended (Pollock v. Farmers' Loan & Trust Co., 157 U.S. 429).

The creation of the Federal Reserve through the Federal Reserve Act of 1913 marked another constitutional flashpoint. Critics contended that delegating monetary authority to a quasi-private entity like the Federal Reserve violated the Constitution's principle of checks and balances. Some argued it represented an unconstitutional concentration of financial power that undermined state sovereignty and the rights of individual citizens. Similarly, the abandonment of the gold standard during the Great Depression in 1933, followed by the termination of the Bretton Woods system in 1971, fueled concerns about executive overreach. Critics claimed that these actions, particularly President Nixon's unilateral decision to sever the dollar's link to gold, effectively altered the nation's monetary system without Congressional approval and violated the Constitution's provisions regarding coinage (Article I, Section 8).

The expansion of income taxation during World War II further raised constitutional concerns. The wartime tax system, which greatly increased rates and broadened the tax base to include a majority of Americans, was viewed by critics as an unchecked expansion of federal authority. They argued that such widespread taxation represented a fundamental shift in the relationship between the federal government and its citizens, contrary to the Constitution's original limitations on government power.

These actions, whether tied to the establishment of central banking or the introduction and expansion of income taxes, have been viewed by many as departures from the Constitution's principles of limited government, individual rights, and state sovereignty. Together, they reflect a recurring tension in American history between the exercise of federal power and the protection of constitutional liberties.

A recent example illustrating concerns about unconstitutional overreach in the context of central banking and taxation is the Federal Reserve's unprecedented monetary response during the COVID-19 pandemic. While these measures were designed to stabilize the economy during a global crisis, critics argued that they stretched the constitutional boundaries of the Federal Reserve's authority, highlighting the broader tension between federal power and constitutional principles.

In 2020, the Federal Reserve enacted aggressive policies, including slashing interest rates to near zero, conducting large-scale asset purchases (quantitative easing), and establishing new lending facilities. These actions expanded the Fed's balance sheet from approximately $4 trillion in early 2020 to over $8 trillion by the end of 2021. Among the new programs was the Municipal Liquidity Facility, which allowed The Fed to purchase municipal bonds directly from state and local governments. Critics argued that this step veered dangerously close to fiscal policy—a domain explicitly reserved for Congress under Article I, Section 8 of the U.S. Constitution.

Moreover, the Fed's quantitative easing disproportionately benefited financial markets, driving up asset prices while leaving ordinary Americans vulnerable to inflation and wage stagnation. Critics contended that these policies, implemented without direct Congressional oversight, effectively redistributed wealth and undermined the Constitution's principles of checks and balances. The Fed's increasing involvement in areas traditionally handled by Congress led to accusations that it had become a de facto arbiter of both monetary and fiscal policy, exceeding its constitutional mandate to maintain price stability and full employment.

This debate recalls long-standing concerns about the overreach of central banking. Much like the opposition to the First and Second Banks of the United States, critics of the Federal Reserve's response to the pandemic argued that its extensive actions centralized too much financial power in one institution, undermining the role of elected officials. These actions have sparked ongoing discussions about the need for better accountability frameworks and clearer restrictions on the Federal Reserve's authority, possibly even calling for the institution's abolition to return to the original intent of the Constitution.

Concerns about transparency in central banking have long been present in American political discourse, predating the establishment of the Federal Reserve in 1913. Early critics of centralized financial authority, such as William Jennings Bryan, expressed alarm over what they perceived as the excessive influence of private financial elites. In his famous 1896 "Cross of Gold" speech, Bryan (1896) asserted, "We say in our platform that we believe that the right to coin and issue money is a function of Government... the banks should go out of the governing business." Such arguments helped lay the ideological groundwork for later critiques of the Federal Reserve's perceived lack of transparency and democratic accountability (Bryan, 1900).

Modern critiques resonate with Bryan's concerns, particularly after the Global Financial Crisis (GFC) and the COVID-19 pandemic. During these crises, central bank actions, such as asset purchasing programs and financial bailouts, were often implemented without clear public communication. This lack of transparency has prompted calls for enhanced openness to rebuild trust and ensure accountability in central banking practices (Chwieroth, 2009).

Centralized monetary control was seen by early economists as a key factor contributing to economic instability. David Ricardo warned about the dangers of manipulating currency, suggesting that such actions could lead to inflation and economic turbulence (Ricardo, 1817). Similarly, John Stuart Mill cautioned against excessive government intervention in financial markets, believing it could cause instability (Mill, 1848).

The GFC serves as a contemporary example of how centralized monetary policies can drive economic instability. Measures such as low interest rates and excessive credit expansion were linked to the financial crisis, while post-crisis actions like quantitative easing have raised concerns about long-term economic volatility (Blinder, 2013).

The concentration of financial power in private hands has long been a concern, with critics fearing potential collusion among elites. Thomas Jefferson was particularly wary of the influence that banking elites could exert over government, fearing they might control the country through monetary policy (Jefferson, 1800).

Modern critiques of central banking often draw parallels to Jefferson's concerns, noting that during the GFC and the COVID-19 pandemic, central bank decisions frequently benefited large financial institutions, sometimes to the detriment of smaller entities and the general public. This dynamic has further fueled public skepticism about the alignment between central banking practices and the interests of society at large (Reinhart & Rogoff, 2009).

MANIPULATION OF THE MONEY SUPPLY

Early critics of central banking were particularly concerned with the manipulation of the money supply, which they believed could lead to inflation or deflation. Economists like David Ricardo argued that excessive currency creation could destabilize the economy and reduce wealth (Ricardo, D., Principles of Political Economy and Taxation, 1817). John Stuart Mill also warned that government control over the money supply could disrupt market equilibrium and create economic distortions (Mill, 1848).

The 2008 Global Financial Crisis (GFC) and the economic responses to the COVID-19 pandemic highlight the risks of central banks manipulating the money supply. In both cases, central banks expanded the money supply through measures like quantitative easing and low interest rates. These actions raised concerns about future inflation, which later became evident in the post-pandemic period as inflation surged globally in 2021-2022. While these measures were necessary to stabilize the economy, they also fueled fears about long-term economic instability and the erosion of purchasing power (Woodford, 2003).

UNDERMINING THE GOLD STANDARD

The abandonment of the gold standard has long been a subject of concern, with critics arguing that severing the link between currency and gold destabilized economies and contributed to inflationary pressures. Ricardo and Bryan warned that removing the gold standard would undermine financial stability (Ricardo, 1817).

The United States' departure from the gold standard in 1971, followed by a shift to fiat currency, is often associated with long-term inflation and growing national debt. In recent years, the massive expansion of fiat money during the 2008 GFC and the COVID-19 pandemic has reignited debates about the benefits of a gold standard. Critics argue that without the discipline imposed by gold, central banks' unchecked printing of money has contributed to rising inflation and greater financial instability (Paul, 2009).

DISTORTION OF MARKET SIGNALS

Early critics, such as Ricardo and Mill, also warned that government interventions in financial markets could distort market signals, leading to inefficiencies and misallocation of resources (Ricardo, 1848). These critiques emphasized that central banks' manipulation of interest rates and monetary policy interferes with the price mechanisms that determine supply and demand in markets.

During the 2008 GFC and the subsequent years, central banks implemented policies like quantitative easing and near-zero interest rates in an attempt to stabilize the economy. These actions distorted market signals by encouraging risk-taking and inflating asset prices. The resulting asset bubbles, particularly in real estate and stocks, contributed to economic instability. More recently, the pandemic response involved similar interventions, with low interest rates and stimulus payments driving a rapid recovery but also exacerbating wealth inequality as asset prices surged, benefiting the wealthy disproportionately (Friedman, 2009).

MORAL HAZARD

The concept of moral hazard, where institutions take excessive risks knowing they will be bailed out by the government, has long been a concern. Early economists like Mill warned that financial institutions would take undue risks if they expected government intervention during crises (Mill, 1848).

The 2008 GFC was a striking example of moral hazard, as large financial institutions were bailed out by governments while smaller businesses and individual citizens faced hardship. In the years following the crisis, critics argued that these bailouts incentivized banks to continue risky behaviors, knowing that they would not face the full consequences of their actions. The COVID-19 pandemic brought similar concerns, as central banks and governments once again intervened to support large financial institutions, while small businesses struggled to survive. These actions reinforced the idea that financial institutions would continue to take excessive risks due to the expectation of government intervention (Taylor, 2009).

POLITICAL INFLUENCE

Long before the establishment of the Federal Reserve, William Jennings Bryan warned against the concentration of monetary power in private hands, insisting that the monetary system should serve the public interest and be subject to democratic oversight—echoing concerns earlier voiced by Thomas Jefferson. As Jefferson (1802) wrote in a letter to Secretary of the Treasury Albert Gallatin, "Banking establishments are more dangerous to our liberties than standing armies; & that the principle of spending money to be paid by posterity… is but swindling futurity on a large scale" (p. 148). Both Jefferson and Bryan viewed financial power as a matter of public accountability, not private privilege.

In recent years, central banks have faced increasing scrutiny over political influence. In the aftermath of the 2008 GFC, the Federal Reserve's policies were heavily influenced by both economic pressures and political considerations. Critics pointed to The Fed's accommodative monetary policies during the Trump administration, such as rate cuts and liquidity support, as reflecting a political desire to boost the economy ahead of elections. Similarly, during the COVID-19 pandemic, central banks' actions to support government fiscal stimulus efforts highlighted concerns over the loss of central bank independence. These actions underscored the growing political influence on monetary policy, particularly when economies face unprecedented crises (Blinder, 2013).

GOVERNMENT CONTROL OF CURRENCY

A key concern raised by critics of central banking is the potential for government overreach in controlling the currency. Adam Smith, in The Wealth of Nations (1776), argued that centralized control over money could lead to political manipulation and economic distortions. Smith emphasized the importance of allowing the market to determine currency value, advocating for a system that would limit the government's power to manipulate the monetary system. Critics like Friedrich Hayek (2019) have continued this line of thought, arguing that government control over currency leads to inflationary pressures and economic instability, as the state can manipulate the currency for short-term political gain.

The 2008 Global Financial Crisis (GFC) and the COVID-19 pandemic highlighted concerns about the government's role in controlling the currency. During both events, central banks, particularly in the U.S., increased the money supply dramatically through programs like quantitative easing and stimulus measures. While these actions were necessary to stabilize the economy, they also led to long-term inflationary pressures, especially post-pandemic, as the expanded money supply collided with supply chain disruptions and increased demand. These interventions reignited concerns about the manipulation of the currency and the risk of prolonged economic instability (Hayek, 1978).

MONETARY POLICY AS A POLITICAL TOOL

Critics have long argued that central banks can be manipulated to serve political agendas, particularly during economic crises or elections. Adam Smith and other classical economists warned that monetary policy could be used as a tool for political gain, undermining long-term economic stability. Smith cautioned that governments might manipulate currency issuance to achieve political objectives, which could lead to inflation and economic distortion. Recent critiques, such as those by Alan Blinder (2013), emphasize how central banks, particularly the Federal Reserve, can be pressured by political influences in their decision-making processes, especially during times of economic uncertainty.

In the aftermath of the 2008 GFC, the U.S. Federal Reserve implemented aggressive monetary policies, including interest rate cuts and quantitative easing, to stabilize the economy. These actions, though necessary to avoid a depression, raised concerns about the Fed's independence and the long-term consequences of such extensive government intervention in the economy. Similarly, during the COVID-19 pandemic, the Federal Reserve and other central banks faced significant political pressure to maintain low interest rates and implement stimulus measures, further complicating the issue of central bank independence and the potential political use of monetary policy (Blinder, 2013).

INTEREST RATE MANIPULATION

The ability of central banks to set interest rates has been a significant concern, with critics arguing that manipulating rates artificially distorts market behavior and contributes to financial instability. David Ricardo, in Principles of Political Economy and Taxation (1817), warned that interference in the natural rate of interest by central authorities could lead to resource misallocation and speculative bubbles, as lower rates encourage excessive borrowing. Modern critiques, such as those by John Taylor (2019), argue that central banks' manipulation of interest rates has distorted financial markets and created bubbles, particularly in housing and asset prices.

The manipulation of interest rates in response to the 2008 GFC and the COVID-19 pandemic provides contemporary examples of how such interventions can distort market behavior. Following the 2008 crisis, central banks slashed interest rates to near zero, encouraging borrowing but also inflating asset bubbles. Similar actions were taken during the pandemic, with low rates and vast government spending fueling both economic recovery and rising housing prices. These actions have led to concerns about a repeat of past financial crises driven by asset bubbles and excessive risk-taking (Taylor, 2019).

DEPENDENCY ON DEBT

The growing reliance on debt as a tool for economic growth has been a long-standing criticism of central banking systems. David Ricardo, in his analysis of monetary systems, warned that excessive credit expansion could lead to financial instability and crises. By fostering dependency on borrowing, central banking systems risk creating unsustainable debt levels, which, once collapsed, can cause severe economic distress. Modern concerns about high levels of public and private debt, as discussed by Carmen Reinhart and Kenneth Rogoff (2009), highlight the dangers of unsustainable borrowing and its potential to trigger financial crises.

The global response to the 2008 GFC and the COVID-19 pandemic involved significant increases in government debt, as central banks and governments issued bonds and provided stimulus packages to avoid economic collapse. However, the rapid increase in debt levels during these crises has sparked fears of long-term financial instability, as governments struggle to manage growing deficits. Reinhart and Rogoff's analysis in This Time Is Different: Eight Centuries of Financial Folly (2009) highlights that excessive debt often leads to economic crises, and the post-pandemic era has seen a renewed focus on the dangers of accumulating unsustainable debt levels.

MONOPOLIZATION OF FINANCIAL POWER

The centralization of monetary policy into the hands of a single entity, such as a central bank, has long been criticized for creating a monopoly over financial decision-making. Adam Smith, in The Wealth of Nations (1776), argued that monopolies distort economic systems by reducing competition, leading to inefficiencies and the potential for an abuse of power. Critics contend that central banks, by controlling key aspects of monetary policy without adequate competition or oversight, can destabilize the economy. Recent concerns, such as those expressed by Andrew Haldane (2015), warn that the concentration of financial power in central banks poses significant systemic risks, as it concentrates too much decision-making authority in a single, often unaccountable entity.

The 2008 Global Financial Crisis (GFC) and subsequent interventions by central banks, particularly the U.S. Federal Reserve, highlighted the risks of financial monopolization. In the wake of the GFC, the Federal Reserve's actions, including extensive monetary stimulus and bailouts for large financial institutions, consolidated its influence over the financial system, reducing the diversity of decision-makers in monetary policy. This centralization has raised concerns about the resilience of the global financial system in the face of future crises, as it places enormous power in the hands of a few unelected officials (Haldane, 2015).

IMPACT ON WEALTH DISTRIBUTION

Central banking systems are often criticized for exacerbating wealth inequality, as their policies tend to disproportionately benefit the wealthy. John Stuart Mill, in Principles of Political Economy (1848), argued that government interference in monetary policy could lead to the concentration of wealth in the hands of those with the closest ties to the financial sector. Critics suggest that central bank policies, such as low-interest rates and quantitative easing, benefit wealthy individuals and large institutions while neglecting broader societal needs. Recent critiques by Thomas Piketty (2014) emphasize how modern monetary policies continue to amplify wealth disparities, leading to a growing divide between the affluent and the rest of society.

The Federal Reserve's response to the COVID-19 pandemic, including aggressive rate cuts and large-scale asset purchases, disproportionately benefited wealthier individuals and institutions, as these measures buoyed asset prices, particularly in the stock market. The result was an increase in wealth inequality, as the wealthy saw their holdings appreciate, while lower-income individuals faced job losses and stagnant wages. Piketty (2014) highlights how these policies have contributed to widening wealth gaps, especially in the post-crisis recovery periods.

EROSION OF MARKET DISCIPLINE

Central banking systems have been criticized for eroding market discipline by intervening in financial markets and bailing out failing institutions. David Ricardo, in Principles of Political Economy and Taxation (1817), warned that government interventions, including bailouts, would reduce incentives for market participants to act responsibly, leading to moral hazard and market distortions. Recent critiques, such as those by Gary Gorton (2012), emphasize how central bank interventions, such as emergency bailouts and the provision of liquidity, reduce the consequences of financial mistakes and encourage risky behavior.

The 2008 GFC and the subsequent bailouts of large financial institutions like Lehman Brothers, AIG, and major banks illustrated the concerns about moral hazard. These interventions, orchestrated by central banks and governments, helped stabilize the economy but also contributed to the perception that financial institutions could take excessive risks without facing the full consequences. The same issue resurfaced during the COVID-19 pandemic, when central banks implemented similar rescue measures, leading to continued concerns about moral hazard in financial markets (Gorton, 2012).

CHAPTER 10

Stolen Wealth

The ability of central banks to increase the money supply through mechanisms such as money printing has long been linked to inflation, a process that erodes the purchasing power of money. This relationship has been a central concern of economists for centuries. David Ricardo, in Principles of Political Economy and Taxation (1817), famously described inflation as a "hidden tax" that diminishes the value of currency, disproportionately burdening the poor who are least equipped to absorb its effects. Ricardo emphasized that inflation covertly reduces real income, making it particularly regressive in its impact.

Friedrich Hayek, in The Denationalisation of Money (1976), extended this critique, arguing that inflation not only undermines savings but also disrupts long-term economic stability. Hayek warned that when central banks adopt expansionary policies, such as increasing the money supply without corresponding economic growth, they create artificial booms followed by inevitable busts. This cycle destabilizes economies, discourages prudent investment, and erodes public trust in fiat currencies.

The poor bear the brunt of inflation's effects due to their reliance on wages that are often not indexed to inflation. Unlike wealthier individuals, who may have assets that appreciate in value during inflationary periods, lower-income individuals see their purchasing power steadily decline. If wages were tethered to inflation, it would be far more difficult for governments to exploit this mechanism to silently erode the wealth of ordinary citizens. Without such indexing, inflation becomes a tool for transferring wealth from the public to the state.

Politicians, however, often welcome inflation because it acts as an indirect tax that does not require explicit approval or public accountability. By increasing the money supply, governments can finance spending without the politically costly process of raising taxes. The practice of raising the debt ceiling to enable further borrowing allows for virtually endless expenditures, sidestepping the fiscal discipline that would otherwise be imposed by a sound money system. This unrestrained monetary expansion benefits governments in the short term but leaves citizens, particularly the poor, grappling with the long-term consequences of devalued currency and economic instability.

EVOLUTION OF THE U.S. CONSUMER PRICE INDEX (CPI) AND ITS RELATIONSHIP TO GOLD PRICES

The U.S. Consumer Price Index (CPI) has undergone significant changes since its inception, adapting to shifts in consumer behavior, economic conditions, and statistical techniques. Alongside the CPI, the price of gold provides a contrasting lens for examining inflation and monetary trends. Below is a historical overview of CPI developments, the recorded CPI numbers, and how they compare to gold prices over the decades.

Year/Period	CPI Development	CPI Value	Gold Price
1900-1910 Pre-CPI Era	No formal CPI; BLS collected retail prices and wages but no comprehensive index.	Not recorded	Fixed at $20.67/oz. under the gold standard.
1920 Post-WWI Adjustments	First national CPI introduced in 1921, retrospectively estimated to 1913; early focus on retail food prices.	20.0	Fixed at $20.67/oz. Inflation reflected wartime economic pressures.
1930 The Great Depression	CPI expanded to include clothing, rent, and fuel.	17.1 (declined during the Depression)	Fixed at $20.67/oz. until 1933; then raised to $35/oz after the U.S. abandoned the gold standard.
1940 Pre-War Revisions	Surveys (1934-1936) updated the market basket to reflect consumption habits.	14.0	Fixed at $35/oz. under the Bretton Woods system. CPI began rising with war preparations.

Year/Period	CPI Development	CPI Value	Gold Price
1950 Post-War Adjustments	Interim adjustments captured post-war shifts in consumption patterns.	24.1	Fixed at $35/oz. Inflationary pressures grew despite a fixed gold price.
1960 Economic Expansion	CPI further refined, expanding coverage of goods and services.	29.6	Fixed at $35/oz. despite mounting trade imbalances and monetary expansion.
1970 End of the Gold Standard	Market basket updated based on 1972-73 surveys, with expanded geographic coverage.	38.8	Gold standard ended in 1971; prices floated, reaching $195/oz by 1974. CPI surged due to oil shocks and policy shifts.
1980 Double-Digit Inflation	CPI-U introduced in 1978, broadening population coverage.	82.4	Gold peaked at $850/oz. due to inflation fears and geopolitical instability. CPI showed double-digit inflation.
1990 Economic Stabilization	CPI-U-RS introduced with methodological improvements.	130.7	Gold stabilized around $386/oz. reflecting reduced inflation and greater monetary discipline.
2000 Chained CPI and Tech Boom	Chained CPI (C-CPI-U) introduced in 2002 to adjust for substitution bias.	172.2	Gold at $273/oz. in 2000, later surpassing $1,000/oz. by 2008 due to financial instability.
2010 Post-Financial Crisis	Alternative data sources improved CPI accuracy.	218.1	Surged to $1,421/oz. due to financial crisis concerns and quantitative easing.
2020 COVID-19 and Economic Stimulus	CPI reflected big data and updated market baskets.	258.8	Exceeded $2,000/oz. driven by economic uncertainty and inflation fears.

The Consumer Price Index (CPI), originally designed to measure changes in consumer prices, has increasingly been shaped by methodological adjustments that may serve as a tool for managing perceptions of inflation rather than offering an objective reflection of price changes. In contrast, gold prices provide a market-driven benchmark for monetary stability and offer a more transparent view of inflation's long-term trajectory.

GOLD AS A BENCHMARK FOR INFLATION

Gold's value has historically served as a reliable measure of monetary stability. Today, if the price of gold were fully reflective of the current money supply, estimates suggest it could reach approximately $82,000 per troy ounce when compared to the M2 money supply or even $135,000 per troy ounce when benchmarked against total U.S. debt using the end of 2024 data. However, the actual market price of gold remains significantly suppressed, in part due to the influence of major paper trading markets, such as the London Bullion Market Association (LBMA) and the COMEX in the United States. These institutions utilize derivative instruments to manage gold prices, which can obscure the real effects of inflation by keeping precious metal prices artificially low, not allowing for price discovery that is a staple of free market capitalism.

THE IMPACT OF MONETARY POLICY

A pivotal moment in the relationship between inflation and gold occurred in the 1970s when the United States formally abandoned the gold standard. By decoupling the U.S. dollar from gold, the Federal Reserve gained the ability to increase the money supply without the constraint of maintaining a fixed gold price. This shift fundamentally altered the nature of inflation measurement. While the CPI continued to evolve through adjustments like hedonic quality measures and substitution effects, these methodological changes often reduced the reported rate of inflation, even as the real purchasing power of the dollar declined.

DECOUPLING INFLATION FROM INTRINSIC VALUE

Since leaving the gold standard, monetary policies have contributed to unprecedented growth in the money supply and national debt, while the CPI has often understated the true impact of inflation. This divergence is especially evident in long-term trends: gold's price, driven by market forces, reflects a more significant increase in inflation than CPI data suggests.

Precious metals, like gold, provide a clearer and more reliable benchmark for measuring inflation, free from the methodological revisions and potential biases inherent in CPI calculations. The suppression of precious metals prices in global markets, alongside expansive monetary policies, has further obscured the public's understanding of inflation. As monetary systems evolve, revisiting gold's role as a measure of economic stability may offer valuable insights into the true state of inflation and monetary value.

The aggressive monetary policies during and after the 2008 GFC, including the expansionary measures taken by the U.S. Federal Reserve, led to concerns about inflation, especially as the money supply grew rapidly. While inflation remained relatively subdued in the immediate aftermath, the long-term impact of such policies became more pronounced during the COVID-19 pandemic, when central banks worldwide printed vast amounts of money, contributing to rising inflation rates in 2021 and beyond. This renewed focus on inflation as a hidden tax has drawn attention to the long-term consequences of such expansionary monetary policies (Hayek, F. A., The Denationalization of Money: The Argument Refined, 1978).

CHAPTER 11
Centralized Banking is the Enemy of Freedom

The increasing reliance on central banks to stabilize economies has raised concerns about long-term dependency. John Stuart Mill (1848) warned that excessive reliance on government intervention could undermine the natural functioning of markets and weaken market participants' incentives to adapt to economic changes. In recent years, economists like Kenneth Rogoff (2016) have discussed how central bank policies, including low-interest rates and quantitative easing, create an artificial sense of stability, leading to over-dependence on monetary intervention and delaying necessary market corrections.

The policies implemented by central banks during the COVID-19 pandemic, such as low interest rates and quantitative easing, created an environment of easy money that many markets became dependent on. This artificial stability delayed necessary market corrections and increased the risk of future instability as economies adjusted to post-pandemic realities. Rogoff (2016) highlights that this dependency on central bank policies can create long-term vulnerabilities in the financial system, especially when markets become accustomed to continuous interventions.

The critiques of the Federal Reserve were not only voiced by those in power but also by figures like Andrew Jackson, whose vehement opposition to centralized banking in the 1830s set a precedent for concerns about concentrated financial power. Jackson's successful effort to dismantle the Second Bank of the United States, the second attempt at establishing a central bank, reflected a populist distrust of central banking institutions.

Similarly, figures such as Elgin Ralston Lovell Gould, Frank Vanderlip, and Carter Glass expressed dissatisfaction with how the Federal Reserve evolved. While Vanderlip had been involved in its creation at Jekyll Island, he later criticized the secrecy surrounding its origins and its increasing control by powerful banking interests. Glass, who was instrumental in drafting the Act, also lamented its shift away from decentralization.

As the world increasingly embraces digital financial systems, the transition has brought to light both significant opportunities and profound challenges. Revisiting historical lessons, it becomes clear that decoupling money from sound monetary principles presents substantial risks — particularly when measured against the enduring wisdom of foundational documents like The Constitution. The critiques of centralized banking, which have echoed through history, underscore the importance of grounding our modern financial systems in principles that promote stability and resilience.

As policymakers explore the potential of digital currencies, there is a pressing need to balance innovation with adherence to these principles. While embracing technological advancements is crucial for progress, we must avoid the pitfalls of the past, especially the dangers of centralized control that could destabilize the economy. The goal is to harness the benefits of digital finance while ensuring that the lessons of history are not forgotten.

By embedding sound monetary principles into the design of digital currencies and other financial innovations, we can avoid repeating past mistakes. This approach will help create a future of money that remains not only innovative but also resilient and stable, ensuring that the evolution of digital finance supports long-term economic well-being.

One of the key lessons is the importance of security and resilience in digital platforms. Early experiences with cybersecurity breaches, such as high-profile data leaks and attacks on financial institutions, have demonstrated the vulnerability of digital systems to cyber threats. These incidents underscore the necessity for robust encryption, multi-factor authentication, and continuous system upgrades to protect sensitive financial information. The evolution of cybersecurity protocols in response to these threats will continue to be a critical factor as digital finance grows.

As we move forward, it's clear that prioritizing security is not optional, but a foundational requirement for fostering trust in digital systems.

Moreover, the shift from traditional to digital currencies has highlighted the risks associated with the loss of tangible assets backing monetary systems. Digital currencies, especially cryptocurrencies, have raised concerns about stability due to their volatility and the lack of a central regulatory authority. The lessons learned from the 2008 Global Financial Crisis (GFC), where over-leveraged financial products triggered a global recession, echo in the unregulated corners of the cryptocurrency market today. While blockchain and digital currencies hold great promise in promoting financial inclusion and decentralization, they also demand a robust framework to mitigate potential market bubbles and instability. A carefully regulated digital financial ecosystem, drawing from lessons of past market crises, is essential to avoid repeating historical mistakes.

Another crucial lesson pertains to the role of central banks and financial regulators in a digitalized economy. As central banks increasingly experiment with digital currencies (CBDCs), the tension between decentralization and regulation becomes more pronounced. While decentralization promotes autonomy and innovation, the regulatory oversight of central banks ensures stability, consumer protection, and monetary control. Recent examples, such as China's digital yuan project, provide a glimpse into how governments can effectively integrate digital currencies within their monetary frameworks while maintaining control over monetary policy. Striking the right balance between innovation and regulation is paramount in avoiding overreach or unchecked chaos within the financial system.

The impact of digital finance on financial inclusion has been another significant lesson. Digital systems have the potential to bring banking services to unbanked populations, providing individuals access to financial tools that were previously out of reach. However, as seen in the global rise of mobile money systems in Africa and Southeast Asia, these systems also face challenges in terms of user education, infrastructure, and trust. Ensuring that digital financial services are accessible, understandable, and affordable to all is a critical issue that remains unresolved in many regions. The future of digital finance should not only focus on technological advancements but also on inclusivity, making sure that no one is left behind in this transition.

Lastly, the need for adaptability and continuous learning is perhaps the most crucial takeaway. The digital financial landscape is evolving at a breakneck pace, with new technologies, regulations, and market participants emerging regularly. The rapid adoption of artificial intelligence (AI), machine learning, and fintech innovations is reshaping the financial industry, but it also requires constant vigilance to manage risks and uncertainties. Policymakers, financial institutions, and technology companies must remain flexible, continuously evaluating their systems and strategies in response to new developments and unforeseen challenges.

As we transition to a fully digital financial ecosystem, the lessons learned thus far provide invaluable guidance. From securing systems against cyber threats to balancing innovation with regulation, these lessons will shape the future of finance. Ensuring that this transition is sustainable, equitable, and resilient will require the collective effort of all stakeholders in the global financial system—governments, central banks, fintech companies, and consumers alike. Only through collaboration and careful management can we harness the full potential of digital finance while safeguarding the stability of the global economy.

Additionally, integrating digital currencies into the monetary system raises ethical considerations. The surveillance capabilities associated with CBDCs could infringe on privacy rights, leading to concerns about government overreach and misuse of financial data (Böhme et al., 2015; Miedema, 2020). Beyond privacy concerns, the deeper ethical risk of Central Bank Digital Currencies (CBDCs) lies in their potential for centralization of power. Unlike decentralized cryptocurrencies, CBDCs place unprecedented control over the monetary system directly in the hands of central authorities. This centralization could enable governments or central banks to freeze accounts, restrict transactions, or manipulate financial behavior in ways that undermine individual autonomy and economic freedom. Over-reliance on a centrally controlled digital currency risks eroding the pluralism and resilience of the financial system. In extreme cases, such centralization could be used for political repression or social control, especially in regimes with weak rule of law or democratic oversight (Kosse & Mattei, 2022). Thus, the integration of CBDCs should be reconsidered with decentralized alternatives using a free banking approach to safeguard civil liberties and maintain a balance of power in the digital financial era. Thus, the use of sound money as the anchor to the monetary and financial system remains the most viable path forward.

The relevance of sound money principles has been underscored in recent years as economies grapple with rising inflation and currency volatility. For instance, the inflation rate in the United States reached a peak of 9.1% in June 2022, the highest in four decades, prompting renewed discussions around monetary policy and fiscal responsibility (U.S. Bureau of Labor Statistics, 2022). In this context, integrating sound money principles can provide a framework for policymakers to manage inflation effectively and enhance economic stability.

CHAPTER 12

The Golden Rule

The longstanding Gold Rule principle in economics—'whoever holds the gold makes the rules'—reflects the enduring role of gold as the ultimate store of value, with silver historically serving as its transactional counterpart. The gold standard operates on the principle that a country's currency value is directly tied to a specific amount of gold by weight. This linkage provides a fixed exchange rate system whereby currencies are valued based on their gold equivalency. For example, if a government sets the price of gold at $20 per ounce, then a currency unit must be backed by a corresponding amount of gold at that rate. As noted by Barry Eichengreen in Golden Fetters: The Gold Standard and the Great Depression, 1919–1939, this system created a predictable framework for international trade by minimizing currency fluctuations. Stable exchange rates enabled businesses to plan and invest with confidence, knowing that the value of their foreign transactions would not change significantly due to currency depreciation or appreciation (Eichengreen, 1992).

Furthermore, the stability fostered by the gold standard facilitated increased capital mobility, allowing investors to move their resources freely across borders. This capital flow promoted economic growth, as countries with favorable investment climates attracted foreign capital, enhancing their development. The commitment to maintaining fixed exchange rates often encouraged fiscal discipline among governments, as they needed to ensure their monetary policies aligned with their gold reserves to maintain currency stability.

REQUIREMENT FOR CURRENCY CONVERTIBILITY INTO GOLD

Under the gold standard, nations were obligated to guarantee the convertibility of their currency into gold upon demand. This requirement meant that individuals and businesses could exchange their currency for a fixed amount of gold, reinforcing trust in the monetary system. Milton Friedman highlights in Money Mischief: Episodes in Monetary History that the convertibility feature prevented governments from engaging in irresponsible fiscal policies, as they were restricted by the need to maintain sufficient gold reserves (Friedman, 1992). This inherent discipline acted as a check against inflationary tendencies, as excessive money printing would deplete gold reserves, ultimately undermining the currency's credibility.

The convertibility mechanism established the credibility of the monetary system, fostering confidence among citizens and investors. Historical examples illustrate this point: during the 19th century, the United States maintained a gold standard that allowed for significant economic expansion. This period saw an increase in international trade and investment, as nations sought the stability provided by the gold standard to facilitate their economic activities.

MONETARY POLICY DISCIPLINE AND LIMITATIONS

The gold standard imposed strict limitations on monetary policy, requiring governments to adhere to a disciplined approach in managing their economies. Governments had to align their monetary supply with their gold reserves, which constrained their ability to respond to economic fluctuations. In times of economic recession, countries could not simply increase the money supply to stimulate growth without risking depletion of their gold reserves. This rigidity contributed to the severity of economic downturns, particularly during the Great Depression, when nations that adhered strictly to the gold standard experienced prolonged economic contractions (Eichengreen, 1992).

The monetary policy discipline imposed by the gold standard also meant that countries were often unable to engage in counter-cyclical measures, such as adjusting interest rates or engaging in quantitative easing during economic downturns. Instead, they had to rely on fiscal policies, which could be limited by political considerations and the need for public support. Consequently, the gold standard created a paradox: while it provided stability and predictability, it also limited flexibility in responding to economic crises.

INTERNATIONAL COOPERATION AND THE GOLD EXCHANGE STANDARD

In the early 20th century, the introduction of the gold exchange standard allowed countries to hold foreign currencies, especially those of gold-standard countries, as a substitute for gold reserves. This innovation facilitated international trade and investment by enabling countries with insufficient gold reserves to participate in the gold standard system. Under this arrangement, nations could stabilize their currencies without holding large gold reserves, thus promoting economic growth and stability in a more interconnected global economy (Eichengreen, 1996).

The gold exchange standard, however, was not without its challenges. It increased the interdependence of national economies, making countries vulnerable to economic shocks originating in other nations. For instance, during the economic turmoil of the 1930s, countries that had relied heavily on foreign currency reserves faced significant difficulties when those currencies depreciated, leading to a loss of confidence in their own monetary systems.

HISTORICAL IMPACT AND LEGACY

The gold standard's influence on global monetary systems extended beyond its formal adoption. Its principles laid the groundwork for modern monetary policy frameworks, emphasizing the importance of stability and credibility. While the gold standard was abandoned during the 20th century, particularly after the Bretton Woods system collapsed in the early 1970s, its legacy continues to inform contemporary discussions on sound money principles.

The stability that characterized the gold standard era is often compared to the volatility seen in today's fiat currency systems. As inflation rates fluctuate and confidence in central banks varies, the gold standard serves as a historical reference point for evaluating monetary policy's effectiveness and the need for sound money principles. Critics of modern fiat systems often advocate for a return to a gold-backed currency to mitigate inflationary pressures and restore public confidence in money (Friedman, 1992).

The gold standard's principles of fixed exchange rates, currency convertibility, monetary policy discipline, and international cooperation played a crucial role in establishing it as a historical sound money system. While it offered stability and predictability, its inherent rigidity also highlighted the limitations of such a system, leading to significant economic challenges during periods of crisis.

IMPLEMENTATION ACROSS DIFFERENT NATIONS—KEY COUNTRIES INVOLVED IN ADOPTING THE GOLD STANDARD

The gold standard emerged in the 19th century as a dominant monetary system, with several key countries playing crucial roles in its adoption and evolution.

The United Kingdom:

The UK was the first country to adopt the gold standard in 1821, a move driven by the need for economic stability following the Napoleonic Wars. The Gold Standard Act established a fixed exchange rate between the pound sterling and gold, with one pound being equivalent to 113 grains of gold (approximately 7.3 grams) (Eichengreen, 1992). This fixed rate provided a stable framework for domestic and international trade, leading to the British economy's expansion during the Victorian era (Ferguson, 2008).

As Barry Eichengreen notes in Golden Fetters, the UK's early adoption of the gold standard set a template for others, encouraging nations to establish their own gold reserves to facilitate international trade (Eichengreen, 1992). By linking currency value directly to gold, the UK reinforced trust in its financial system, attracting foreign investment and solidifying its position as the world's economic leader (Eichengreen & Temin, 2000).

The United States:

The U.S. experience with the gold standard has been complex. Initially, the country operated under a bimetallic standard, incorporating both gold and silver. The Coinage Act of 1900 formally established the gold standard, declaring that only gold would be accepted for the payment of debts (Timberlake, 1993). The value was set at $20.67 per ounce of gold. This transition helped stabilize the U.S. economy and facilitated the country's rise as a global industrial power (Bordo, 1993).

During the late 19th century, the U.S. experienced significant economic growth, driven by the expansion of railroads and industry (Nash, 2000). However, the Panic of 1893 exposed vulnerabilities within the gold standard framework, leading to calls for a return to bimetallism (Bordo & Schwartz, 1989). Despite these challenges, the gold standard continued to be the foundation of U.S. monetary policy until the Great Depression. Thus, it would be prudent to balance the gold standard with other commodities such as silver, platinum, and any other commodities that would work as a stabilizer to the value of sound money.

Germany and France:

Germany adopted the gold standard in 1871, motivated by the need for a unified currency following its unification (Friedman, 1969). The establishment of the gold mark provided Germany with a solid monetary foundation, facilitating its rapid industrial growth (Bordo, 1993). The country's commitment to the gold standard allowed it to emerge as a key player in European and global trade, promoting economic stability in a rapidly changing landscape.

France's relationship with the gold standard was more turbulent. The country initially adopted a bimetallic standard but officially embraced the gold standard in 1878 (Bordo & Schwartz, 1989). However, France's economy faced several challenges, including the economic repercussions of the Franco-Prussian War, which led to reparations and inflation (Temin, 1989). Despite these issues, France maintained its commitment to the gold standard, using it to stabilize its currency and facilitate trade. The French franc was pegged to gold, ensuring a degree of stability, although fluctuations in the gold market impacted the economy (Friedman, 1969).

GLOBAL EXPANSION AND ADOPTION:

By the late 19th century, the gold standard was widely adopted, encompassing many countries in Europe, the Americas, and parts of Asia. Nations such as Australia, Canada, and South Africa adopted the gold standard, attracted by the promise of economic stability and predictable currency values.

In particular, Australia became a prominent gold-producing nation during the gold rushes of the 1850s and 1860s, leading to the establishment of a gold standard to ensure the value of its currency (Bordo, 1993). Similarly, Canada adopted the gold standard in 1853, linking the Canadian dollar to gold at a fixed rate, which helped stabilize its economy as it expanded westward (Mackenzie, 1999).

The widespread adoption of the gold standard facilitated international trade, as nations were able to engage in commerce with a clear understanding of currency values. This stability encouraged investments, leading to a period of significant economic growth globally (Ferguson, 2008).

HISTORICAL TIMELINE OF ADOPTION AND ABANDONMENT

Late 19th Century to World War I:

The gold standard reached its peak in the late 19th and early 20th centuries, characterized by a commitment to fixed exchange rates and currency convertibility into gold. During this time, international trade flourished, and capital mobility increased as investors sought opportunities in foreign markets.

The period also saw the establishment of institutions such as the International Gold Standard Association, which aimed to standardize gold exchange practices among nations (Ferguson, 2008). The system's success was evident as it provided countries with a stable monetary environment conducive to trade.

World War I and Its Aftermath:

The onset of World War I in 1914 marked a turning point for the gold standard. To finance the war efforts, many countries suspended gold convertibility (Bordo & Schwartz, 1989). The U.S. and the UK both increased their money supplies significantly to fund military operations, leading to inflationary pressures.

After the war, several nations attempted to return to the gold standard in the 1920s. The U.S. returned to a modified gold standard in 1919, but the economic landscape had fundamentally changed (Bordo & Schwartz, 1989). Countries like the UK and France faced high levels of debt and inflation, making the restoration of the gold standard challenging.

The transition back to gold was characterized by increased political and economic tensions. In his work Golden Fetters, Eichengreen argues that the rigidities of the gold standard during this period exacerbated economic difficulties, as countries struggled to maintain their gold reserves while trying to stimulate their economies (Eichengreen, 1992).

The 1920s, often referred to as the "Roaring Twenties," saw some countries attempting to reestablish the gold standard. However, this period was marked by significant economic instability. The U.S. experienced rapid economic growth, but this was coupled with stock market speculation and rising income inequality. The Federal Reserve, seeking to stabilize the economy, faced challenges in adjusting interest rates due to gold standard constraints (Bordo & Schwartz, 1989).

In 1925, the UK returned to the gold standard at the pre-war parity, which many economists later criticized as too high, contributing to deflation and unemployment (Eichengreen, 1992). The inability to adjust the currency value to reflect economic realities led to significant discontent and social unrest, laying the groundwork for the economic challenges that would emerge in the following decade.

The Great Depression of the 1930s proved to be a significant turning point, highlighting the limitations of the gold standard (Eichengreen, 1992). As the global economy contracted, countries adhering strictly to the gold standard faced severe economic distress due to their inability to expand the money supply (Bordo & Schwartz, 1989).

In the United States, the stock market crash of 1929 precipitated a banking crisis, leading to widespread bank failures. The rigid nature of the gold standard prevented the Federal Reserve from taking aggressive measures to stimulate the economy (Eichengreen, 1992). In 1933, President Franklin D. Roosevelt officially abandoned the gold standard, allowing for a more flexible monetary policy aimed at addressing the economic crisis. The U.S. dollar was no longer redeemable for gold, marking a significant shift in monetary policy and the beginning of the transition toward fiat currency (Bordo, 1993).

Other countries followed suit, abandoning the gold standard in favor of more flexible monetary systems. The abandonment of the gold standard allowed for increased government intervention in the economy, which many nations adopted to combat the effects of the Great Depression (Friedman, 1969).

In the aftermath of World War II, the Bretton Woods Conference of 1944 established a new international monetary order. The U.S. dollar was pegged to gold at a fixed rate of $35 per ounce, while other currencies were pegged to the dollar (Bordo, 1993). This system aimed to promote economic stability and facilitate international trade in the wake of the devastation caused by the war.

The Bretton Woods system functioned effectively for several decades, facilitating post-war recovery and economic growth (Ferguson, 2008). Countries accumulated dollar reserves, which they could exchange for gold. However, increasing economic pressures, including rising inflation and balance of payments deficits in the U.S., led to growing doubts about the sustainability of the system.

In 1971, President Nixon announced the suspension of the dollar's convertibility into gold, a move known as the "Nixon Shock" (Eichengreen, 1992). This decision effectively marked the end of the Bretton Woods system and the gold standard in practice. The global economy transitioned to a system of fiat currencies, where the value of money is determined by government decree rather than a physical commodity (Friedman, 1969).

The Nixon Shock led to a period of floating exchange rates, where currencies fluctuated based on market forces. While this provided greater flexibility for central banks, it also introduced volatility and uncertainty into international trade (Eichengreen, 1992). The abandonment of the gold standard shifted the focus of monetary policy from maintaining fixed exchange rates to managing inflation and economic growth.

As of 2024, discussions around the gold standard and its implications continue to resurface in economic and political discourse. The 2008 financial crisis and subsequent monetary policy responses, including quantitative easing, raised concerns about inflation and the long-term sustainability of fiat currencies (Bordo & Schwartz, 2016). Central banks around the world expanded their balance sheets significantly, prompting debates about the potential for inflation and the erosion of purchasing power (Meltzer, 2010).

Some economists and policymakers have advocated for a return to the gold standard as a means of ensuring monetary stability and restoring public confidence in the financial system. Proponents argue that a gold-backed currency could prevent excessive government spending and inflationary pressures, fostering economic discipline (Bordo, 2016).

The history of the gold standard reflects a complex interplay of economic, political, and social factors. Its rise and fall demonstrate the challenges of maintaining fixed exchange rates in a dynamic global economy. While the gold standard provided stability during its heyday, the rigidity of the system ultimately contributed to its demise, paving the way for fiat currencies and flexible monetary policies.

As discussions around sound money and monetary reform continue, the lessons learned from the gold standard era remain relevant in shaping future monetary policies. The exploration of alternative monetary systems, including cryptocurrencies, offers a contemporary perspective on the enduring quest for a stable and trustworthy currency.

During the period when the gold standard was in widespread use, many countries experienced a remarkable level of price stability and low inflation rates. The fixed supply of money tied to gold reserves limited the government's ability to inflate the currency, fostering a stable economic environment. Glyn Davies, in "A History of Money," highlights that this stability was crucial for long-term investment and economic planning, as businesses and consumers could rely on the consistent value of money over time.

In contrast to the gold standard era, the transition to fiat currencies often led to higher inflation rates and more volatile economic cycles. Fiat currencies, not being tied to a tangible reserve, gave governments greater flexibility but also increased the risk of inflation through unrestrained money printing. Milton Friedman's analysis in "The Role of Monetary Policy" points out that while fiat currencies can be effective in addressing short-term economic needs, they also expose economies to inflationary pressures that were largely absent under the gold standard.

The United Kingdom and the United States serve as prime examples of the gold standard's ability to control inflation. During the late 19th and early 20th centuries, both countries maintained relatively low inflation rates compared to the periods following the adoption of fiat currency. Barry Eichengreen's "Globalizing Capital" notes that this era of price stability allowed for significant industrial growth and economic expansion in these nations, proving the effectiveness of the gold standard in fostering a predictable economic environment.

CRITIQUES OF THE GOLD STANDARD

One of the main critiques of the gold standard is its inherent rigidity, which often restricts economic flexibility during times of financial crises. The inability to adjust the money supply in response to economic downturns made it difficult for countries to implement effective counter-cyclical policies. Joseph Schumpeter's "Capitalism, Socialism, and Democracy" highlights that this rigidity contributed to prolonged economic depressions, as governments could not easily stimulate the economy without violating the principles of the gold standard.

Deflation was a recurring challenge under the gold standard, where a restricted money supply often resulted in falling prices, reduced consumer spending, and increased debt burdens. Irving Fisher, in The Purchasing Power of Money (1911), highlighted the severe socio-economic consequences of deflation, including rising unemployment and declining business profitability. These conditions frequently fostered social unrest and political instability, as seen during the Great Depression, when deflationary pressures exacerbated widespread economic hardships.

However, the 1920s saw a significant increase in the money supply, driven by speculative lending and monetary expansion. This led to inflation as prices rose above historical norms, creating an economic environment detached from long-term stability. When the money supply contracted sharply during the late 1920s and early 1930s, it triggered a deflationary collapse, contributing to the economic devastation of the Great Depression. Fisher's debt-deflation theory explained how the interplay of excessive borrowing, inflation, and subsequent monetary contraction deepened the crisis (The Debt-Deflation Theory of Great Depressions, 1933).

This period also underscored the dangers of concentrated control over monetary systems by private financial interests. Critics argue that the manipulation of money supplies by private entities, such as central banks and large financial institutions, not only exacerbated economic instability but also played a role in precipitating broader geopolitical conflicts. For instance, monetary policies during the interwar period contributed to hyperinflation in Germany, destabilizing its economy and fueling the political extremism that led to World War II. Similarly, in the United Kingdom and the United States, economic mismanagement and speculative excesses highlighted the perils of allowing private money interests to dominate national financial systems (Keynes, The Economic Consequences of the Peace, 1919; Eichengreen, Golden Fetters: The Gold Standard and the Great Depression, 1992).

This convergence of economic instability, monetary manipulation, and geopolitical turmoil underscores the systemic vulnerabilities that arise when control over the money supply is concentrated in centralized or privatized institutions. When such control operates without the constraints traditionally provided by sound money principles, such as intrinsic value backing, fiscal discipline, and institutional transparency, the risk of financial mismanagement and public distrust grows significantly. These conditions erode economic sovereignty, enable unchecked monetary expansion, and often exacerbate social and political tensions, particularly in periods of crisis.

CHAPTER 13

Economic Trade Shapes the Balance of World Power

The Bretton Woods Conference, held in July 1944 in Bretton Woods, New Hampshire, was pivotal in shaping the post-World War II economic landscape. Key players included the United States, the United Kingdom, and various other Allied nations, all eager to establish a stable and cooperative international economic system. The U.S., emerging as the world's largest economy, was instrumental in crafting the agreements that would underpin this new order. According to Barry Eichengreen in Globalizing Capital: A History of the International Monetary System, the aim was to foster international economic cooperation, stabilize currencies, and promote trade to prevent the economic instability and protectionism that characterized the interwar period (Eichengreen, 1996).

The Bretton Woods Conference resulted in the establishment of two major institutions the International Monetary Fund (IMF) and the World Bank. The IMF was designed to ensure international monetary cooperation and facilitate the expansion of international trade, while the World Bank focused on reconstruction and development, particularly in war-torn Europe. John Williamson, in The Bretton Woods Agreements: The Political Economy of a System, emphasizes that the creation of these institutions reflected a commitment to multilateralism and economic stability, promoting growth and development in a post-war context (Williamson, 1993).

The IMF's primary role was to monitor exchange rates and provide temporary financial assistance to countries facing balance-of-payments problems, thus preventing the type of competitive devaluations that had plagued the interwar period. The World Bank, initially known as the International Bank for Reconstruction and Development (IBRD), aimed to provide loans for rebuilding European economies and later shifted its focus toward development in poorer nations.

FIXED EXCHANGE RATE SYSTEM

The Bretton Woods system operated under a fixed exchange rate regime where currencies were pegged to the U.S. dollar, which in turn was convertible to gold at a fixed rate of $35 per ounce. This dollar-gold standard provided a measure of stability and predictability in international exchange rates, fostering global trade. As Robert Triffin pointed out in his analysis of the system, the reliance on the dollar as the primary reserve currency created a "Triffin dilemma," where the U.S. needed to supply enough dollars to meet global demand while maintaining the dollar's convertibility into gold (Triffin, 1960).

The Bretton Woods system contributed significantly to post-war economic growth and stability, as nations benefited from increased trade and investment. Between 1945 and 1971, global trade expanded rapidly, and the world economy saw unprecedented growth, with the IMF estimating that global GDP grew at an average annual rate of 5% during this period (IMF, 2010). The system facilitated this growth by reducing exchange rate volatility, thereby lowering transaction costs for international trade.

CHALLENGES AND COLLAPSE OF THE SYSTEM

Despite its initial successes, the Bretton Woods system faced significant challenges by the late 1960s and early 1970s. The U.S. began to experience inflationary pressures, partly due to increased military spending from the Vietnam War and domestic social programs. This led to growing concerns about the sustainability of the dollar's gold convertibility. According to Barry Eichengreen in Golden Fetters, the inability of the U.S. to maintain the gold standard amid rising demand for dollars ultimately weakened confidence in the dollar and the system itself (Eichengreen, 1992).

The Bretton Woods system effectively ended in 1971 when President Richard Nixon announced the suspension of the dollar's convertibility into gold, a move often referred to as the "Nixon Shock." This shift marked the transition from fixed exchange rates to a system of floating rates, fundamentally altering the international monetary landscape. As noted by Michael Bordo in The Historical Performance of the Federal Reserve, the collapse of the Bretton Woods system ushered in an era characterized by increased exchange rate volatility and uncertainty in international trade, fundamentally changing how countries approached monetary policy (Bordo, 1993).

CONTEMPORARY DISCUSSION AND IMPLICATIONS

As of 2024, the legacy of the Bretton Woods system remains significant in contemporary discussions on international monetary policy. The principles established during the conference continue to influence global financial governance, with the IMF and World Bank playing vital roles in crisis management and development. The challenges of the Bretton Woods system serve as a cautionary tale in discussions about monetary reform and the need for stability in an increasingly interconnected world.

With rising inflation concerns and the expansion of digital currencies, the lessons learned from the Bretton Woods era are critical as policymakers explore how to balance stability and flexibility in a dynamic global economy. The ongoing debates about a return to a more stable monetary system underscore the enduring relevance of the Bretton Woods principles in addressing contemporary economic challenges.

ECONOMIC IMPLICATIONS

The Bretton Woods system fundamentally transformed the landscape of international trade and capital flows, marking a significant departure from the economic instability of the interwar years. By establishing a stable framework for exchange rates, the system facilitated unprecedented growth in global trade and investment. The fixed exchange rate regime significantly reduced uncertainties associated with currency fluctuations, allowing businesses to engage in long-term cross-border economic activities without the fear of sudden adverse exchange rate movements.

Felix Martin, in Money: The Unauthorized Biography, emphasizes that this stability was pivotal in creating a predictable environment that encouraged global economic integration. The elimination of exchange rate risk made it easier for companies to price their goods and services in foreign markets, leading to a surge in international trade. According to the World Trade Organization (WTO), global trade in goods and services grew from about 10% of world GDP in the early 1950s to over 20% by the early 1970s, a remarkable increase fueled in part by the Bretton Woods framework (WTO, 2019). The system allowed countries to coordinate their economic policies more effectively, resulting in enhanced cooperation among nations.

The capital mobility facilitated by the Bretton Woods system was equally significant. As countries adopted fixed exchange rates and established confidence in their monetary policies, they became more attractive destinations for foreign investment. The IMF reports that capital flows increased significantly during this period, with the amount of foreign direct investment (FDI) rising from \$13 billion in 1945 to \$42 billion by 1970 (IMF, 2018). This influx of capital not only supported economic growth but also contributed to technological advancement and infrastructure development, particularly in war-torn Europe and emerging economies in Asia and Latin America. For instance, the Marshall Plan, which provided financial assistance to rebuild Europe, was integral in reviving economies that had been devastated by World War II.

Furthermore, the Bretton Woods system fostered a spirit of multilateralism that transcended mere economic interactions. The establishment of institutions like the IMF and the World Bank aimed to create frameworks for international cooperation and development. These institutions played crucial roles in coordinating policies among member countries, offering financial assistance, and providing a platform for dialogue on economic issues. The collaboration among nations helped to institutionalize practices that promoted stability and growth, making it easier for countries to engage in trade and investment.

A key feature of the Bretton Woods system was the role of the U.S. dollar as the world's primary reserve currency. Under the system, the dollar became the anchor of the global financial system, with other currencies pegged to the dollar, which was itself convertible to gold at a fixed rate of $35 per ounce. This arrangement solidified the dollar's dominance in international finance and reinforced the U.S. economy's influence worldwide.

Barry Eichengreen, in Globalizing Capital: A History of the International Monetary System, highlights that this dollar-centered system led to increased confidence in the dollar as a reliable store of value and medium of exchange. The dollar's status as the leading reserve currency meant that it was widely accepted in international trade transactions, which encouraged countries to hold dollar reserves as a hedge against economic uncertainty. The IMF estimates that, by the late 1960s, the dollar accounted for over 80% of official foreign exchange reserves globally, a reflection of its central role in the international monetary system (IMF, 2021).

This dominance provided the U.S. with several economic advantages, including the ability to run trade deficits without the same repercussions as other countries, as global demand for dollars remained high. The phenomenon, often referred to as the "exorbitant privilege," allowed the U.S. to finance its deficits with borrowed dollars, giving it a unique position in the global economy. However, this reliance on the dollar also created vulnerabilities, as excessive dollar issuance by the U.S. to meet international demand led to inflationary pressures and contributed to the eventual collapse of the Bretton Woods system in 1971.

Moreover, the U.S. dollar's role as the reserve currency facilitated the development of a global financial market that operated primarily in dollars. This dollar-denominated framework became the standard for international trade and finance, allowing U.S. banks to dominate global financial transactions. The dominance of the dollar also meant that countries had to hold large amounts of U.S. dollars in their foreign exchange reserves to manage their currencies effectively. Consequently, this reliance on the dollar created a systemic risk, as fluctuations in the U.S. economy had far-reaching implications for countries around the world.

Overall, the economic implications of the Bretton Woods system were profound, fostering a period of unprecedented growth in international trade and investment while establishing the U.S. dollar as the linchpin of the global financial system. The success of the system in promoting stability and growth laid the groundwork for the interconnected world economy we see today. However, the complexities and challenges introduced by the dollar's dominance continue to influence global economic policy discussions, particularly in light of recent trends toward the diversification of reserve currencies and the rise of digital currencies.

As we look toward 2024, the lessons learned from the Bretton Woods era are critical in addressing contemporary economic challenges. Policymakers must navigate the balance between stability and flexibility in an increasingly interconnected world, considering the implications of dollar dominance and exploring potential alternatives to the current monetary system. The enduring legacy of Bretton Woods serves as a reminder of the need for cooperation, stability, and adaptability in the face of evolving global economic dynamics.

CONTRIBUTION TO POST-WAR ECONOMIC STABILITY

The Bretton Woods system played a crucial role in fostering a period of significant economic growth and prosperity in the decades following World War II. Many countries that adhered to the Bretton Woods framework experienced rapid industrialization, technological advancements, and notable increases in living standards. This era is often referred to as the "Golden Age of Capitalism," a term coined by economists to describe the unprecedented economic expansion that took place between the late 1940s and the early 1970s.

Niall Ferguson, in The Ascent of Money, emphasizes that the stability provided by the Bretton Woods system was instrumental in this post-war economic boom. By establishing fixed exchange rates and encouraging free trade, the system created an environment conducive to economic growth. For instance, according to the World Bank, global GDP growth averaged around 5% annually from 1950 to 1973, a remarkable achievement that was significantly higher than the average growth rates in previous decades (World Bank, 2020). This growth was characterized by substantial increases in productivity and income, leading to improved living standards across many nations.

Key industries such as manufacturing and technology flourished during this time. The Marshall Plan, which provided financial assistance to rebuild war-torn European economies, further facilitated this growth. The Organization for Economic Cooperation and Development (OECD) reported that countries receiving Marshall Plan aid grew their economies significantly faster than those that did not, underscoring the impact of targeted financial support during the Bretton Woods era (OECD, 2019). In addition, technological innovations, particularly in areas like electronics and transportation, contributed to increased productivity and economic output.

The Bretton Woods system also helped stabilize inflation rates during the post-war period. Countries focused on maintaining their currency's peg to the U.S. dollar, which was backed by gold, leading to greater monetary discipline. This stability was essential in curbing hyperinflationary pressures, which had plagued many nations in the past. A study by the IMF found that inflation rates in advanced economies averaged around 3% during the Bretton Woods period, compared to much higher rates experienced in the interwar years (IMF, 2017).

Beyond economic growth, the Bretton Woods system laid the groundwork for increased global economic cooperation. The system encouraged nations to work together to resolve economic issues and prevent future crises, marking a significant departure from the protectionist policies that characterized the interwar period. This collaborative approach fostered a more interconnected global economy, paving the way for multilateral trade agreements and international economic partnerships.

Institutions such as the International Monetary Fund (IMF) and the World Bank became central players in facilitating international economic policy coordination. John Williamson, in his analysis of the IMF and

World Bank, highlights how these institutions provided critical support for economic stabilization and development efforts in member countries. The IMF, for instance, offered financial assistance to countries facing balance of payments crises, enabling them to stabilize their economies and maintain their commitments to the fixed exchange rate system. This support was vital for countries like the United Kingdom and Italy, which encountered economic difficulties during the 1960s and required IMF assistance to restore stability (Williamson, 2000).

Furthermore, the Bretton Woods system helped establish a framework for international dialogue on economic policy, leading to cooperative initiatives aimed at addressing global challenges. The GATT (General Agreement on Tariffs and Trade), established in 1947, served as a precursor to the World Trade Organization (WTO) and promoted trade liberalization among member countries. This commitment to reducing tariffs and trade barriers encouraged economic collaboration and helped foster a culture of cooperation in international economic relations.

The collaborative spirit of the Bretton Woods era was also evident in the establishment of various regional economic organizations and agreements, such as the European Economic Community (EEC), which sought to promote economic integration among European nations. This movement toward regional cooperation further strengthened the foundations of the global economy and facilitated the flow of goods, services, and capital across borders.

The Bretton Woods system significantly contributed to post-war economic stability by fostering robust economic growth and establishing a framework for global economic cooperation. The stability and predictability of the international monetary system during this period enabled countries to collaborate effectively, paving the way for a more interconnected and prosperous global economy. The lessons learned from the Bretton Woods era continue to resonate today, highlighting the importance of multilateral cooperation in addressing contemporary economic challenges.

CRITIQUES OF THE BRETTON WOODS SYSTEM

Despite its successes, the Bretton Woods system was fraught with vulnerabilities, particularly concerning balance of payments crises. The fixed exchange rate regime imposed by the system meant that countries were often unable to adjust their exchange rates in response to economic shocks. As nations faced adverse economic conditions—such as recession, shifts in trade patterns, or inflation—they struggled to maintain their fixed exchange rates, leading to considerable economic stress.

The system's reliance on the U.S. dollar exacerbated these imbalances. As the primary reserve currency, many countries held dollars to facilitate international trade. However, nations with persistent trade deficits faced mounting pressures to devalue their currencies, creating a precarious situation for those economies. According to Manias, Panics, and Crashes by Charles Kindleberger, these imbalances led to recurring financial instability within the Bretton Woods framework. Countries such as the United Kingdom, facing significant trade deficits, were forced into a position where they had to choose between borrowing from the International Monetary Fund (IMF) or implementing austerity measures, often resulting in adverse effects on their domestic economies.

The devaluation of the British pound in 1967 serves as a notable example. This event followed a prolonged period of economic malaise and balance of payments challenges, illustrating how the fixed exchange rate regime often resulted in significant economic strain rather than stability (Eichengreen, 1996). Moreover, as countries faced increasing balance of payments difficulties, they resorted to protectionist measures that further exacerbated global economic tensions, reminiscent of the interwar period when similar practices contributed to economic collapse (Irwin, 2012).

The collapse of the Bretton Woods system stemmed from a combination of internal and external factors, including the overvaluation of the U.S. dollar, rising inflation rates, and a growing unwillingness from the United States to maintain the gold-dollar convertibility that had anchored the system. The U.S. dollar, while serving as the primary reserve currency, had become overvalued relative to other currencies, putting significant pressure on the balance of payments.

In the late 1960s and early 1970s, rising inflation in the U.S. diminished the real value of the dollar, which was pegged to gold at $35 per ounce. As inflation surged, foreign governments and investors began to question the dollar's reliability as a stable reserve currency. The persistent trade deficits and inflation created a scenario where countries such as France and Germany began redeeming their dollars for gold, draining U.S. gold reserves and highlighting the fragility of the system. Barry Eichengreen, in The Bretton Woods System: A Historical Perspective, attributes the collapse to the inherent flaws in maintaining a fixed exchange rate system in a world characterized by dynamic economic conditions. The increasing volatility in trade balances and the competitive devaluation strategies employed by various countries further complicated the situation.

The tipping point came in 1971 when President Richard Nixon announced the suspension of the dollar's convertibility into gold, effectively dismantling the system. This decision, often referred to as the "Nixon Shock," marked the official end of the Bretton Woods era. Subsequently, the system transitioned to floating exchange rates among major currencies, significantly altering international monetary relations. This shift reflected a broader realization that fixed exchange rates could not adequately respond to the complexities of a rapidly changing global economy.

The collapse of Bretton Woods had profound implications for the international financial system. According to The International Monetary System: A Global Perspective by Michael D. Bordo and Angela Redish, the end of Bretton Woods ushered in an era characterized by increased volatility in exchange rates and greater freedom for nations to pursue independent monetary policies. As countries moved toward flexible exchange rates, they faced new challenges, including the risk of currency crises and speculative attacks, which further complicated international economic stability.

Additionally, scholars have pointed out that the Bretton Woods system's inherent weaknesses led to a fragmented international monetary landscape. As noted by Kenneth Rogoff in The Challenge of Maintaining Global Economic Stability, the lack of a coherent framework post-Bretton

Woods resulted in disparities in monetary policies across nations, leading to increased global financial instability. The crises in the 1970s and 1980s, including the Latin American debt crisis, can be traced back to the instability introduced by the collapse of the Bretton Woods framework.

The critiques of the Bretton Woods system underscore the challenges of maintaining fixed exchange rates in a dynamic global environment. While the system succeeded in fostering economic growth and stability during the post-World War II era, its vulnerabilities became increasingly apparent, leading to its eventual collapse and the adoption of a more flexible, albeit more volatile, international monetary system.

CAUSES OF HYPERINFLATION—WAR REPARATIONS AND MONEY PRINTING

Weimar Germany's hyperinflation in the early 1920s serves as a compelling example of the catastrophic consequences of monetary mismanagement under the pressure of international obligations. The Treaty of Versailles, signed in June 1919, imposed heavy reparations on Germany, designed to compensate the Allied powers for wartime destruction. These reparations, amounting to approximately 132 billion gold marks (equivalent to about $33 billion at the time), not only burdened the post-war economy but also symbolized the punitive attitude of the Allies toward Germany (Schuker, 1988). This economic stranglehold was exacerbated by the political humiliation that many Germans felt, as the treaty was viewed as a national disgrace.

To meet these reparations and cope with the economic fallout from the war, the Weimar government resorted to aggressive monetary expansion. This decision was influenced by a lack of viable options; the government lacked the revenue to meet its obligations and was unwilling to impose drastic tax increases that could further destabilize an already struggling economy. As a result, the government began printing money at an unprecedented rate, flooding the market with currency. Barry Eichengreen's Golden Fetters emphasizes how this excessive money supply devaluation set off a chain reaction that spiraled out of control, leading to hyperinflation (Eichengreen, 1992).

The inflationary spiral intensified due to external factors, such as political instability and social unrest. The Weimar Republic was plagued by internal divisions and violent uprisings, including the Kapp Putsch in 1920 and the German Revolution of 1918-1919, which showcased the profound dissatisfaction with the democratic government and the economic conditions. According to Felix Martin in Money: The Unauthorized Biography, the lack of confidence in government institutions compounded the crisis, as citizens increasingly viewed the currency as worthless, leading to further panic and selling off of assets (Martin, 2013).

ECONOMIC AND SOCIAL CONSEQUENCES—EROSION OF SAVINGS AND THE MIDDLE CLASS

The hyperinflationary crisis in Weimar Germany represented not just a financial disaster but a catastrophic social upheaval that fundamentally undermined the very fabric of the middle class. The economic turmoil of the early 1920s wreaked havoc on a segment of society that had historically been seen as the backbone of German stability. Prior to hyperinflation, the middle class enjoyed a certain level of prosperity, characterized by stable jobs, home ownership, and savings that they believed would secure their futures. However, as the value of the German mark plummeted, culminating in an exchange rate of 4.2 trillion marks to one U.S. dollar by late 1923, these same individuals found their hard-earned wealth reduced to mere scraps of paper.

The sudden and extreme devaluation of currency had immediate and devastating effects on savings and investments. Families that had saved diligently to secure their children's education, purchase homes, or plan for retirement suddenly saw these plans obliterated as their life savings evaporated overnight. Reports from the time indicate that many middle-class citizens, who had once held respectable positions and enjoyed a modest standard of living, were forced to sell their possessions at a fraction of their worth to obtain basic necessities (Eichengreen, 1992). This erosion of wealth was not merely a statistic; it represented a profound psychological shock to a society that had placed its faith in monetary stability and economic security.

Irving Fisher's The Purchasing Power of Money emphasizes the concept of purchasing power as the key metric for economic well-being. As purchasing power dwindled, the middle class's ability to participate in consumer spending diminished dramatically. What was once a thriving consumer base became a population grappling with existential anxiety, where daily life revolved around the struggle to afford bread or other basic goods. Many middle-class families resorted to barter systems, exchanging goods rather than relying on currency, illustrating a complete breakdown of faith in money as a stable medium of exchange (Fisher, 1920).

The psychological impacts were as profound as the economic ones. The experience of watching their savings disappear fostered a deep sense of betrayal among the middle class. Many individuals felt that the government had failed them, exacerbating their financial woes through mismanagement and political ineptitude. This disillusionment was fueled by widespread reports of corruption and inefficiency within the Weimar government, leading to a perception that the political elite was detached from the struggles of ordinary citizens (Schuker, 1988). As they witnessed the erosion of their social standing and financial security, a profound resentment toward the government began to fester, culminating in a widespread loss of faith in democratic institutions.

The consequences of this financial collapse extended beyond mere economic hardship. The middle class had traditionally been viewed as a stabilizing force in society, often acting as a buffer against radical ideologies. However, as this class began to crumble under the weight of hyperinflation, social cohesion deteriorated. Charles Kindleberger discusses in Manias, Panics, and Crashes how economic crises often catalyze social unrest and lead to the emergence of radical political movements (Kindleberger, 1978). In the case of Weimar Germany, the financial desperation felt by the middle class pushed many toward extremist ideologies that promised a return to stability and order.

The rise of political radicalism during this time was marked by the increasing appeal of extremist parties, most notably the Nazi Party. With traditional parties unable to address the grievances of the population, disillusioned middle-class voters turned to radical solutions. The Nazis, leveraging the prevailing sense of economic despair, offered a vision of national rejuvenation that resonated with those who felt abandoned by the existing political order. Niall Ferguson in The Ascent of Money notes that financial crises often breed an environment ripe for the emergence of authoritarian regimes, as citizens seek strong leadership in times of chaos (Ferguson, 2008). The Nazis effectively capitalized on the economic turmoil to establish a narrative that blamed external factors, such as the Treaty of Versailles and alleged conspiracies, for Germany's plight, thereby channeling public discontent into support for their movement.

Moreover, as middle-class citizens sought to secure their futures amid economic uncertainty, many found themselves in increasingly precarious positions. The lack of financial security not only impacted individual households but also altered family dynamics. Parents faced difficult choices regarding their children's education and future prospects. The dream of upward mobility that had characterized the pre-war era was replaced by a harsh reality of downward mobility, as families struggled to provide for basic needs. The instability created an atmosphere of despair and anxiety, which permeated daily life, leading to a pervasive sense of hopelessness that would have lasting effects on German society.

The hyperinflation crisis of Weimar Germany led to the swift and devastating erosion of the middle class, transforming it from a pillar of stability into a group characterized by economic insecurity and political discontent. The psychological trauma of financial ruin fostered disillusionment with democratic institutions and an openness to radical alternatives. As the middle class crumbled, the potential for social fragmentation and political extremism increased, ultimately setting the stage for the rise of totalitarianism in Germany. The Weimar experience serves as a critical case study in understanding how economic mismanagement can destabilize not only financial systems but also the very foundations of society.

RISE OF EXTREMISM AND POLITICAL INSTABILITY

The economic turmoil of the hyperinflation period directly contributed to the rise of extremist political movements, particularly the National Socialist German Workers' Party (NSDAP), or the Nazi Party. Faced with economic despair and a disillusionment with traditional political structures, many Germans sought radical alternatives. The Nazi Party, under the leadership of Adolf Hitler, effectively capitalized on the public's desperation, promising not only economic recovery but also a restoration of national pride and social order.

Niall Ferguson, in The Ascent of Money, elaborates on the critical relationship between economic distress and political extremism, noting that financial crises often catalyze social unrest and a breakdown of trust in established political institutions (Ferguson, 2008). The hyperinflationary environment fueled resentment toward the Weimar government, which many blamed for their economic hardships. As political polarization intensified, the Nazis and other extremist groups gained traction, often employing propaganda that targeted the fears and frustrations of the populace.

The rise of extremist parties led to increased political violence and social unrest, with rival factions—especially communists and fascists—engaging in violent confrontations on the streets. Historian Ian Kershaw, in Hitler: 1889-1936: Hubris, underscores how this political fragmentation not only allowed extremist parties to gain power but also facilitated the eventual collapse of the democratic institutions established after World War I (Kershaw, 1999). As the Weimar Republic struggled to maintain order amid rampant inflation, its credibility diminished, and many citizens increasingly viewed radical solutions as necessary for national recovery.

The chaotic atmosphere of hyperinflation also contributed to the erosion of civil liberties. The government, overwhelmed by social unrest and political violence, increasingly resorted to authoritarian measures to maintain control. This shift toward repression further alienated the populace and stoked the flames of discontent. Many citizens, in their quest for stability, found themselves unwittingly supporting policies that undermined democratic principles.

In the long run, the consequences of hyperinflation in Weimar Germany demonstrated the profound connection between economic stability and political legitimacy. The failure of the Weimar government to effectively manage its monetary policy and economic obligations resulted in not only a financial crisis but also a societal upheaval that paved the way for the rise of totalitarian regimes. This period serves as a sobering reminder of the dangers posed by unchecked monetary expansion, especially in contexts where political and social stability is already tenuous.

HOW SOUND MONEY COULD HAVE OFFSET THESE PROBLEMS

The hyperinflationary episode in Weimar Germany serves as a poignant reminder of the dangers inherent in unsound monetary practices. Had the government adhered to sound money principles—characterized by a stable currency backed by tangible assets—many of the economic and social crises that unfolded could have been significantly mitigated.

One of the fundamental tenets of sound money is that it should be backed by a stable asset, such as gold or silver. If the Weimar Republic had maintained a currency tied to gold, the excessive money printing needed to cover war reparations would have been constrained. Under a gold standard, the money supply is directly linked to the amount of gold held by the government, thereby limiting inflationary pressures. As economist Ludwig von Mises argues in The Theory of Money and Credit, an asset-backed currency fosters confidence among the populace, as people can trust that their money retains its value (Mises, 1912). By limiting the ability to print money at will, a sound monetary framework would have preserved the purchasing power of the mark, thus protecting the savings and investments of the middle class.

ENCOURAGING FINANCIAL PRUDENCE AND SAVINGS

Sound money also promotes a culture of financial prudence and long-term saving. With a stable currency, individuals are incentivized to save and invest rather than hoard cash, as they would have confidence in the future value of their money. During the hyperinflationary period, the immediate need to spend cash before its value diminished led to a drastic shift in consumer behavior, where saving became virtually meaningless. Economic historian Allan H. Meltzer highlights in A History of the Federal Reserve that sound monetary policies encourage responsible fiscal behaviors, which in turn contribute to overall economic stability (Meltzer, 2003). Had the mark been sound, the middle class could have continued to plan for the future, fostering a more resilient economy less susceptible to rapid fluctuations.

RESTORING CONFIDENCE IN INSTITUTIONS

The failure of monetary policy during this period eroded trust in the Weimar government and its institutions. Sound money principles, grounded in fiscal discipline and transparent monetary policy, could have restored public confidence. By establishing a framework that emphasized accountability and integrity in financial matters, citizens might have maintained their faith in government institutions. As economist Friedrich Hayek articulated in Denationalisation of Money, a decentralized monetary system based on sound principles could enhance trust and accountability, reducing the likelihood of extreme economic upheaval (Hayek, 1976).

FOSTERING POLITICAL STABILITY

Finally, the societal fragmentation and rise of extremism observed during the hyperinflationary crisis were, in many ways, a direct consequence of economic instability. By implementing sound monetary practices, the government could have mitigated the economic despair that fueled disillusionment with democracy. The psychological and social resilience of the middle class would have been preserved, reducing the appeal of radical political movements. The experience of other nations, such as Switzerland, which adhered to sound monetary policies, illustrates how financial stability can contribute to broader societal cohesion and political stability (Lavoie, 2014).

The principles of sound money could have significantly altered the trajectory of Weimar Germany. By establishing a stable currency backed by tangible assets, promoting financial prudence, restoring confidence in government institutions, and fostering political stability, the Weimar Republic could have avoided many of the destructive consequences of hyperinflation. The lessons drawn from this historical episode emphasize the critical importance of sound monetary policies in maintaining economic and social stability.

CHAPTER 14

Japan's Economic Collapse is a Warning to the World

Japan's economic stagnation during the 1990s, often referred to as the "Lost Decades," can be traced to a complex interplay of factors that includes the collapse of asset price bubbles and ineffective responses from monetary authorities. The late 1980s saw Japan experiencing an economic boom, characterized by rapidly rising real estate and stock prices, which created an unsustainable economic environment. When these asset bubbles burst in the early 1990s, the consequences were severe, leading to a prolonged period of economic turmoil.

The Bank of Japan (BOJ), entrusted with the task of stabilizing the economy, exhibited a sluggish and inadequate response to the ensuing deflationary pressures. The BOJ's decision to maintain a tight monetary stance, despite clear signs of an impending economic crisis, is widely regarded as a critical failure. Milton Friedman, in his seminal work Money Mischief, argues that the BOJ's reluctance to implement aggressive monetary easing measures during this critical period played a crucial role in prolonging Japan's economic slump. Friedman emphasizes that central banks must respond decisively to deflationary conditions to prevent prolonged economic stagnation. He highlights the risks associated with insufficient central bank intervention, particularly in the context of falling prices and declining asset values (Friedman, 1992).

Richard Koo's The Holy Grail of Macroeconomics provides a detailed examination of Japan's predicament as a "balance sheet recession." In this context, Koo explains that private sector entities, burdened by excessive debt, engaged in deleveraging, which severely stifled recovery efforts and rendered traditional monetary policy tools less effective (Koo, 2009). Koo posits that during a balance sheet recession, the private sector focuses on paying down debt rather than investing, which leads to decreased demand and further exacerbates economic downturns. This situation created a paradox wherein monetary stimulus measures, such as low-interest rates, failed to translate into increased borrowing and spending.

Richard Werner's Princes of the Yen critiques the BOJ for its reactive approach to monetary policy, illustrating how a fixation on controlling inflation led to neglect of the real economy (Werner, 2003). Werner argues that the BOJ's adherence to an overly conservative monetary policy framework contributed to deepening the recession, as the bank was slow to recognize the need for aggressive measures to support growth. He highlights how the banking system, hampered by non-performing loans and lack of capital, was unable to facilitate economic recovery, thereby limiting the effectiveness of the BOJ's policies. Werner also suggests that the BOJ's failure to properly manage the money supply, especially in relation to credit creation, was a crucial factor in the economic malaise that ensued.

Additionally, Paul Krugman, in his influential paper "The Myth of Asia's Miracle," highlights the limits of supply-side economics, arguing that Japan's experience underscores the importance of demand-side interventions during economic crises (Krugman, 1994). He asserts that the failure to stimulate demand through aggressive monetary and fiscal policies contributed significantly to Japan's prolonged stagnation. Krugman's analysis serves as a reminder that economic policy must prioritize demand generation to ensure a robust recovery, particularly in the aftermath of significant financial disruptions.

LONG-TERM IMPACTS ON ECONOMIC RECOVERY

The repercussions of the Lost Decades extended well beyond immediate economic impacts, resulting in a prolonged period of stagnation that lasted nearly two decades. Japan's economy experienced historically low growth rates and persistent deflation, both symptoms and contributors to a stagnant economic landscape. According to data from the World Bank, Japan's GDP growth rate averaged just 1% from 1992 to 2012, contrasting sharply with the robust growth rates observed in prior decades (World Bank, 2020). This environment severely curtailed investment and dampened consumer spending, ultimately hindering economic recovery.

Joseph Schumpeter, in Capitalism, Socialism, and Democracy, underscores that extended periods of economic stagnation can yield dire consequences for innovation and overall economic dynamism. Schumpeter's concept of "creative destruction" suggests that economic growth is often driven by the displacement of outdated industries by new ones. However, in Japan, the lack of growth led to a stagnation in innovation, as firms became increasingly risk-averse in an uncertain economic climate (Schumpeter, 1942). This stagnation was further exacerbated by an over-reliance on traditional sectors, such as manufacturing, at the expense of emerging industries.

The economic landscape was also impacted by demographic challenges, including an aging population and declining birth rates. According to the National Institute of Population and Social Security Research, Japan's total fertility rate fell to 1.36 in 2019, significantly below the replacement level of 2.1 (National Institute of Population and Social Security Research, 2019). The demographic shift not only reduced the labor force but also increased the burden on social welfare systems, complicating fiscal policy responses and hindering growth.

The prolonged economic malaise had profound societal impacts, including rising unemployment rates, particularly among young people. This trend has been associated with increased mental health issues, as individuals faced economic uncertainty and diminished opportunities (Doi, 2013). The societal ramifications of economic stagnation extended to social isolation, particularly among the elderly, who struggled to navigate an increasingly complex and changing economic environment (Hoshi & Kashyap, 2004).

SOCIETAL IMPACTS AND DEMOGRAPHIC CHANGES

The economic stagnation of the 1990s had far-reaching societal ramifications. One of the most notable effects was a significant decline in birth rates, coupled with an increasingly aging population. The uncertainty and lack of economic opportunities dissuaded young people from starting families, contributing to a demographic crisis with long-term implications for Japan's labor market and social structure. Barry Eichengreen, in Globalizing Capital, discusses how prolonged economic stagnation can induce structural shifts in society, noting that declining economic prospects often correlate with lower fertility rates and altered family dynamics (Eichengreen, 2008).

Research has shown that the economic environment significantly influences family formation decisions. Young adults, facing precarious job markets and economic instability, increasingly prioritize career and financial security over starting families. The impact of these trends has been profound, as Japan grapples with a declining population and the socio-economic challenges that accompany an aging demographic.

Furthermore, the societal implications of economic stagnation extended to mental health. Studies have indicated that economic uncertainty and unemployment exacerbate psychological distress, leading to higher rates of depression and anxiety among the populace (Yoshikawa, 2017). The long-term economic malaise has also resulted in increased rates of "hikikomori," a term that describes the phenomenon of social withdrawal, particularly among young people (Teo, 2010). This trend highlights the broader social implications of economic stagnation, as individuals struggle to engage with society in meaningful ways.

Additionally, the prolonged economic crisis has led to shifts in family structures and dynamics. Many young adults are opting for non-traditional living arrangements, such as cohabitation or remaining single, as financial insecurity influences their life choices. This shift has implications for social cohesion and the fabric of Japanese society, as traditional family units become less common.

Japan's Lost Decades illustrate the interplay between ineffective monetary policy, economic stagnation, and societal challenges. The lessons learned from this period continue to resonate, providing valuable insights for policymakers grappling with similar issues in other economies today. As Japan navigates its post-bubble landscape, the need for comprehensive and adaptive policy responses remains critical.

In the United States, economic challenges have significantly reshaped family structures and dynamics in recent decades. The share of adults aged 25 to 34 living with a spouse dropped from 81.5% in 1968 to 40.3% in 2018, while those cohabiting with an unmarried partner rose from 0.2% to 14.8% over the same period, according to U.S. Census Bureau data. Rising costs of housing and child care have played a central role in these shifts, as economic barriers discourage many from pursuing traditional family arrangements. For example, data from the Economic Policy Institute shows that families in the U.S. spend, on average, over $16,000 annually on child care for two children, consuming a significant share of household income.

Economic pressures have also contributed to a decline in birth rates. The U.S. total fertility rate fell from just over two births per woman in 2005 to about 1.6 in recent years, according to the Centers for Disease Control and Prevention's National Vital Statistics Reports. This decline parallels Japan's experience during its Lost Decades, where prolonged economic stagnation led to demographic and societal shifts. Experts have described the phenomenon as a "relationship recession," with increasing rates of singledom and fragile partnerships observed not only in the U.S. but also in countries such as Finland, South Korea, Japan, Germany, Italy, and Spain, as highlighted by the United Nations' World Fertility and Family Planning report.

To address these trends historically, the return to sound money has provided a pathway to stability during such periods of economic and societal upheaval. Sound money systems, particularly those based on the gold standard, have demonstrated a unique ability to stabilize economies by reducing inflation volatility and ensuring the long-term purchasing power of currency. For example, during the late 19th century, the U.S. adherence to the gold standard coincided with periods of robust economic growth, increased savings, and societal stability. Similarly, post-war Germany's introduction of the Deutsche Mark in 1948, backed by sound monetary principles, helped curb hyperinflation and lay the foundation for decades of economic prosperity and societal renewal.

Sound money creates an environment of fiscal discipline, reducing speculative bubbles and restoring confidence in economic systems. By ensuring price stability, it lowers the cost of living and increases purchasing power, enabling families to make long-term financial commitments such as marriage, homeownership, and child-rearing. The lessons from history suggest that a return to sound money could address many of the economic and social challenges faced today, offering policymakers a proven tool for fostering stability and restoring the social fabric.

HOW SOUND MONEY COULD HAVE OFFSET THESE PROBLEMS

If Japan had adhered to sound money principles during this period, many of the underlying issues that fueled the Lost Decades could have been mitigated. Sound money refers to a monetary system in which the currency is tied to a commodity, such as gold or silver, limiting the ability of governments or central banks to manipulate the money supply. In a sound money system, inflation and deflation are naturally moderated because the money supply cannot be rapidly expanded or contracted based on the whims of monetary authorities.

1. **Prevention of Asset Bubbles:**
   A key contributor to Japan's economic crisis was the rapid inflation of asset prices during the late 1980s. In a sound money system, the ability of central banks to inject liquidity into the economy would be constrained by the amount of gold or other reserves backing the currency. This limitation would reduce the likelihood of speculative bubbles because credit expansion would be more tightly controlled. With fewer artificial drivers of excessive investment and borrowing, the speculative excesses that led to the property and stock market bubbles in Japan may have been avoided or at least tempered.

For instance, under the gold standard or a similar sound money framework, the supply of credit would be more directly tied to real economic output, rather than speculative market gains. This would result in more sustainable levels of investment and lending, curbing the over-leveraging that played a central role in Japan's economic collapse.

2. **Limiting Deflationary Spirals:**
A core problem Japan faced during the 1990s was persistent deflation. As the economy contracted, prices fell, and consumers delayed spending in anticipation of further price drops, exacerbating the downturn. In a sound money system, deflationary pressures would be less severe because the money supply would be stable and anchored to a tangible commodity, providing a solid foundation for price stability.

Milton Friedman argued that deflation occurs when there is insufficient money in circulation relative to the goods and services being produced (Friedman, 1992). In a sound money system, because the money supply is more predictable and not subject to rapid expansion or contraction, deflation would be less likely to spiral out of control. Instead of relying on aggressive monetary interventions, the economy would self-correct, as prices and wages adjusted more gradually in response to supply and demand.

3. **Incentivizing Productive Investment:**
Japan's balance sheet recession, as described by Richard Koo, was driven by an over-leveraged private sector. In a sound money system, where credit expansion is constrained, the incentive for firms and households to take on excessive debt would be reduced. With less reliance on cheap credit, economic actors would focus on more productive, long-term investments rather than speculative activities. This shift would likely prevent the over-leveraging that led to the deleveraging crisis in Japan.

Sound money encourages savings and investment by ensuring that the purchasing power of money remains stable over time. If Japan had adhered to a sound money system, businesses and households would have been more cautious about taking on debt during the boom years, resulting in a more resilient economy when the downturn came.

4. **Avoiding Long-Term Economic Stagnation:**
   Japan's prolonged economic stagnation can, in part, be attributed to the BOJ's inconsistent monetary policies, which swung between expansionary and contractionary approaches. Sound money would have prevented this erratic policy response by ensuring a stable monetary base. With monetary policy anchored by a commodity standard, Japan would not have faced the same difficulties in trying to stimulate the economy through interest rate cuts and quantitative easing, which proved largely ineffective during the Lost Decades.

   A sound money system promotes long-term stability by limiting inflationary pressures, ensuring that the economy grows in line with real production and innovation rather than speculative excess. This stability would have supported more consistent and sustainable economic growth during Japan's recovery phase.
5. **Addressing Demographic Challenges:**
   While sound money cannot directly resolve demographic issues, it can contribute to a more stable economic environment that encourages family formation and long-term planning. In a sound money system, individuals would face less economic uncertainty regarding inflation and deflation, allowing them to make more confident decisions about starting families and making investments in their future.

   The adoption of sound money principles could have significantly altered Japan's economic trajectory during the Lost Decades. By limiting the ability of central banks to manipulate the money supply and encouraging more prudent investment decisions, sound money would have mitigated the asset bubbles, deflationary pressures, and economic stagnation that plagued Japan for nearly two decades. Moreover, the stability provided by a sound money system would have supported stronger societal and demographic outcomes, contributing to a more resilient and dynamic economy.

CHAPTER 15

The Hidden War Over Who Controls the Money

The game of elites to control the money supply by any means necessary is a recurring theme throughout economic history. From central banking cartels to international financial institutions, those in power have consistently sought to shape monetary systems to serve their interests. Whether through manipulation of interest rates, currency debasement, or the creation of fiat regimes, the objective remains the same: maintain control over the lifeblood of the economy—money. Understanding this game is essential to grasp the true nature of modern financial systems and the challenges to achieving genuine monetary freedom as one such means is printing money.

The hyperinflation episodes in Zimbabwe and Venezuela can be primarily traced back to government policies focused on excessive money printing aimed at financing growing budget deficits. In Zimbabwe, the Reserve Bank of Zimbabwe (RBZ) began a policy of printing large sums of money in the early 2000s as a response to a severe economic crisis triggered by land reforms and declining agricultural output. This monetary expansion resulted in an astronomical inflation rate, which peaked at an estimated 89.7 sextillion percent in November 2008 (Hanke & Krus, 2021). Such a figure is nearly incomprehensible and illustrates the extreme volatility and loss of value of the Zimbabwean dollar during this period. The RBZ's practices were not just about creating currency; they involved rapidly increasing the money supply without corresponding economic growth, which is a textbook example of inflationary financing. As explained by Ludwig von Mises in Human Action, uncontrolled monetary expansion devastates economies, eroding public trust in currency and leading to a vicious cycle of further monetary devaluation (Mises, 1949). Mises's economic theories emphasize the importance of sound money principles, which, when disregarded, can lead to catastrophic results. This understanding is essential to grasping the underlying mechanics of hyperinflation and its broader economic implications.

In Venezuela, similar monetary policies have unfolded. The Bolivarian government, under Hugo Chávez and later Nicolás Maduro, implemented extensive money printing to finance social programs and offset budget deficits resulting from falling oil prices. As a consequence, inflation rates skyrocketed, reaching nearly 300,000% in 2018, with the International Monetary Fund (IMF) projecting inflation to hit 10 million percent by the end of that year (Hanke & Krus, 2021). The Venezuelan government's reliance on the central bank to print money for public spending, without a coherent fiscal strategy, highlights the perils of using inflation as a tool for economic management. This situation illustrates Mises's concept of the "crack-up boom," where currency devaluation leads to panic, causing people to abandon the currency in favor of more stable alternatives (Mises, 1949). As a result, the trust in the bolívar, Venezuela's currency, eroded, leading citizens to engage in barter or use foreign currencies, like the U.S. dollar, for everyday transactions.

In addition to reckless monetary policies, both nations have suffered tremendously due to economic mismanagement and pervasive corruption. In Zimbabwe, the land reform program initiated by Robert Mugabe's administration in the early 2000s, which aimed to redistribute land from white farmers to black Zimbabweans, ended up decimating the agricultural sector. This policy resulted in a drastic decline in food production, which was compounded by poor management practices and corruption within the government (Rodriguez, 2019). The lack of accountability and transparency in governance exacerbated the economic crisis, leading to hyperinflation as the government printed more money to compensate for lost agricultural output and tax revenues.

Murray Rothbard, in What Has Government Done to Our Money?, emphasizes the role of government failures in economic crises, illustrating how mismanagement and corruption often lead to detrimental outcomes, particularly in monetary policy (Rothbard, 1963). Rothbard argues that governmental interference in the economy leads to distortions that can have lasting negative impacts. In Venezuela, the economic collapse is often attributed to not only the government's heavy reliance on oil revenues but also the extensive corruption within state-owned enterprises. Rodríguez points out that the intertwining of political corruption and economic policy has resulted in the misallocation of resources and a lack of investment in critical infrastructure, further destabilizing the economy (Rodriguez, 2019). This relationship underscores how governance failures, including the diversion of public funds for personal enrichment, contribute to economic decline and ultimately, hyperinflation.

CONTROLLING INTERESTS OF THE RULING POWERS OF A STATE

A significant challenge for any governing system arises when individuals or groups seeking power manipulate circumstances to achieve their objectives. The creation of the Federal Reserve in 1913 exemplifies this dynamic, shaped by both domestic and foreign interests. American industrialists and bankers, including J.P. Morgan, recognized the need for a centralized monetary authority to stabilize the economy following the Panic of 1907 (Economic History Association, n.d.). However, Morgan's influence extended far beyond the United States. His connections to British financial elites, particularly the Rothschild family, who had longstanding ties to the British Empire's global financial network, amplified his power. These relationships gave Morgan significant sway over both American and European financial markets and played a key role in shaping the Federal Reserve's creation (Ferguson, 1998). European powers, especially the Rothschilds and their associated banking interests, had a vested interest in ensuring U.S. economic stability, as it was critical to the broader global financial system. The passage of the Federal Reserve Act in 1913, in response to the economic crises of the early 20th century, highlights how centralized control over monetary systems became a key instrument for consolidating economic and political power at both national and international levels (Federal Reserve History, n.d.). The Rothschild family, recognized for their profound influence on international banking during the 19th and early 20th centuries, played a key role in shaping modern financial systems. Their support for the First Zionist Congress in 1897, organized by Theodor Herzl, was instrumental in the establishment of the Zionist Federation, which sought the creation of a Jewish homeland in response to rising antisemitism in Europe (Ferguson, The House of Rothschild: The World's Banker, 1849–1999, 1999; Encyclopedia Britannica, n.d.). This support extended beyond the congress, as the Rothschilds played a crucial role in securing the Balfour Declaration of 1917, in which the British government expressed support for the establishment of a "national home for the Jewish people" in Palestine. This political endorsement by the British Crown was pivotal in the eventual creation of the State of Israel and highlighted the intersection of financial power and political influence in the Zionist movement.

Zionism's financial network expanded significantly in the subsequent decades, with funds raised globally to support settlement efforts and institutional development in Palestine. Organizations such as the Jewish National Fund and the World Zionist Organization centralized financial resources to acquire land and build infrastructure (Segev, One Palestine, Complete: Jews and Arabs Under the British Mandate, 2000). Critics have likened aspects of these financial and institutional frameworks to aristocratic systems, where concentrated wealth and influence shape broader political and economic policies, drawing comparisons to monarchical structures of power (Pappé, The Idea of Israel: A History of Power and Knowledge, 2014).

The British Crown offers another example of concentrated power through centralized control. The Crown is the largest landowner in the world, holding vast amounts of real estate that collectively form the largest trust in existence. This includes the Crown Estate, a massive portfolio of land and property in the United Kingdom, as well as substantial holdings in Commonwealth realms. The Crown Estate alone manages over £6.6

billion ($8.3 billion USD) in assets, including urban properties, rural lands, and offshore holdings such as seabed leases for wind farms (The Crown Estate, 2023). Furthermore, under centuries-old feudal traditions, the British monarch is considered the sovereign owner of all land in the United Kingdom, placing the Crown at the apex of the nation's landownership hierarchy.

The Crown's influence extends far beyond the United Kingdom, reaching Commonwealth nations and overseas territories. These holdings, although locally governed, often operate under frameworks established by historical British influence. For instance, in Canada, 89% of the country's land is classified as Crown land, managed by federal or provincial governments under the Crown title system (Government of Canada, 2023). Similarly, in Australia, around 23% of the country's land is Crown land, which includes public reserves, national parks, and leasehold properties governed by state and territory governments (Government of Australia, 2023).

In addition to Commonwealth realms, the British Crown directly controls 14 Overseas Territories, which remain under its sovereignty but are largely self-governing. These territories include:

1. Anguilla
2. Bermuda
3. British Antarctic Territory
4. British Indian Ocean Territory
5. British Virgin Islands
6. Cayman Islands
7. Falkland Islands
8. Gibraltar
9. Montserrat
10. Pitcairn Islands
11. Saint Helena, Ascension, and Tristan da Cunha
12. South Georgia and the South Sandwich Islands
13. Sovereign Base Areas of Akrotiri and Dhekelia (on Cyprus)
14. Turks and Caicos Islands

Each of these territories operates under the authority of the British Crown and is subject to varying degrees of direct governance or oversight, depending on local governance frameworks (UK Government, 2023). This network of territories and landholdings underscores the enduring legacy of the British Empire, demonstrating how historical structures of land and sovereignty continue to shape economic and political relationships across the globe.

This concentration of land ownership underscores the immense economic power of the British Crown and highlights how trusts can function as tools for centralized control. Through mechanisms like the Crown Estate and the perpetuation of feudal ownership principles, the Crown has maintained its influence across generations, demonstrating how land serves as both a resource and a means of authority.

This parallels debates surrounding the Federal Reserve Act of 1913 revolved around concerns that it would centralize economic power in the hands of a few, similar to a monarchy, creating a trust-like entity reminiscent of the powerful monopolies that dominated American industry during the Gilded Age. Critics feared that the establishment of a central bank, with its ability to control monetary policy and issue currency, would undermine the principles of decentralized governance and economic independence cherished by the Founding Fathers. Figures such as Congressman Charles A. Lindbergh Sr. warned that the Federal Reserve would serve as "the most gigantic trust on earth," enabling an elite group of private bankers to manipulate markets and consolidate wealth (Lindbergh, Banking and Currency and the Money Trust, 1913).

As an example, since the The Fed opened its doors in 1914 its wealth has increased from 247 million USD to a staggering 4.5 trillion USD in 2016 which is an 18,217% return to private individuals. The Fed has stopped reporting this number as of 2018.

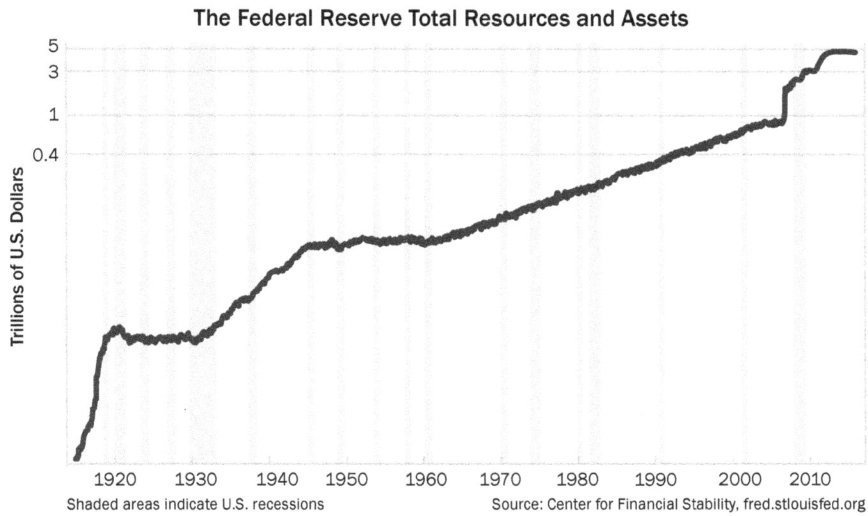

This consolidation of financial control parallels criticisms of the financial networks supporting Zionism, the Rothschild banking dynasty, and historical structures like the British Crown. The British Empire, at its height, used its centralized power to control vast territories and resources, consolidating wealth and influence through systems of colonial rule and economic dominance. Similarly, the Rothschild banking network and Zionist organizations have been accused of creating centralized systems of power, controlling resources, and influencing political agendas. In each case, centralized power, whether through the Crown, financial institutions, or ideological movements, has been viewed as prioritizing elite interests over broader democratic or egalitarian principles.

Ironically, Thomas Jefferson's prescient warnings about the dangers of private bankers gaining control over the nation's money supply have proven disturbingly relevant. Jefferson foresaw that such control could lead to an abuse of power, enabling these entities to manipulate the economy for their own benefit. He cautioned that this could result in the rise of a financial aristocracy aimed at consolidating wealth and undermining the economic freedom of citizens (Jefferson, 1814). In a letter to John Taylor (1816), Jefferson wrote, "I sincerely believe, with you, that banking establishments are more dangerous than standing armies; and that the principle of spending money to be paid by posterity, under the name of funding, is but swindling futurity on a large scale." Jefferson's concerns, articulated in his writings and correspondence, highlighted the potential for concentrated financial power to erode democratic principles and exploit the broader population for the benefit of a privileged few (Jefferson, 1905). These warnings reflect Jefferson's profound skepticism toward centralized financial power and his conviction that such concentration could jeopardize both the economic and political freedoms of the American populace. His concerns proved prescient, as efforts to establish a central bank were attempted on three occasions, with the third attempt culminating in the creation of the Federal Reserve in 1913. This development, which consolidated significant financial authority, has been viewed by some scholars as contributing to a system of financial control that undermines individual liberties and global economic stability, leading to significant socioeconomic consequences both domestically and internationally.

Jefferson's fears were realized with the establishment of the Federal Reserve in 1913, which centralized control over the U.S. money supply and gave immense power to unelected bankers, often prioritizing the interests of financial elites over the common good. This concentration of financial authority has been linked to economic distortions, the entrenchment of systemic inequality, and the facilitation of global economic crises, most notably the Great Depression and the 2008 financial collapse. Critics argue that such centralized control has not only exacerbated financial instability but has also enabled policies that contribute to widespread socioeconomic harm and conflict, perpetuating a cycle of dependence, debt, and, in extreme interpretations, the erosion of human dignity and sovereignty under the guise of monetary order. Jefferson's warnings about the dangers of concentrated financial power resonate today, as the growing influence of central banks and their potential to manipulate economies remains a contentious issue in the ongoing debate over monetary policy and individual freedom.

This consolidation of financial control parallels criticisms of the financial networks supporting Zionism, the Rothschild banking dynasty, and the British Crown, along with its associated aristocracy. The British Empire, at its height, used its centralized power to control vast territories and resources, consolidating wealth and influence through systems of colonial rule, trade monopolies, and financial institutions. However, it was not merely the Crown itself but also its aristocratic networks—including influential banking families like the Rothschilds—that played a key role in shaping global economic and political power structures.

In the modern era, other families have emerged with comparable influence. The Rothschilds, for instance, have long been synonymous with global finance, playing pivotal roles in funding wars, underwriting government debt, and supporting colonial expansion. Their financial alliances with European aristocracies and governments helped sustain and expand empires, embedding them at the center of global financial systems (Ferguson, The House of Rothschild, 1999). Similarly, the Rockefellers in the United States built an empire through oil and banking, using their wealth to shape industries, philanthropy, and even foreign policy. Their creation of institutions like the Rockefeller Foundation, along with their leadership roles in organizations such as Chase Bank, extended their influence well beyond business—shaping education, science, and global health. (Chernow, Titan: The Life of John D. Rockefeller, Sr., 1998).

The Rothschilds, with their immense financial resources, often collaborated with or operated within these aristocratic systems to exert significant influence. For instance, their pivotal role in funding wars, underwriting government debt, and supporting colonial expansion tied them closely to the British aristocracy's global agenda. These financial alliances helped sustain and expand the empire's reach, embedding the aristocracy—and families like the Rothschilds—at the center of global financial systems (Ferguson, The House of Rothschild, 1999).

The British Mandate in Palestine further highlights the interplay of the Crown and aristocracy with Zionist ambitions. During this period, the Crown's policies, influenced by both strategic colonial interests and elite lobbying efforts, facilitated the growth of Zionist institutions. Critics argue that this was emblematic of a broader pattern, where aristocratic and financial elites, including figures from the Rothschild family, leveraged their influence to consolidate wealth and shape geopolitical outcomes (Segev, One Palestine, Complete, 2000).

Like the Federal Reserve's centralization of monetary control, these systems of aristocratic and financial power often prioritized elite interests over democratic principles, fostering enduring inequalities. Whether through the Crown's colonial apparatus, the Rothschilds' banking empire, or the Zionist Federation's financial networks, the concentration of power within interconnected aristocratic and financial systems has had profound implications for global politics, economic stability, and social equity (Khalidi, The Hundred Years' War on Palestine, 2020; Pappé, The Idea of Israel, 2014).

But the Rothschilds are not alone, the Wallenbergs, leveraging their extensive financial and industrial networks, frequently aligned with or navigated within aristocratic and political systems to wield considerable influence. Their strategic involvement in financing infrastructure projects, supporting national industries, and facilitating international trade positioned them as key players in Sweden's economic and political landscape. For example, their leadership in institutions like Stockholms Enskilda Bank (SEB) and their investments in sectors such as telecommunications, manufacturing, and energy tied them closely to Sweden's national interests and its integration into the global economy (Glete, The Wallenberg Family and Swedish Industry, 1994). These alliances not only bolstered Sweden's economic stability but also cemented the Wallenbergs' role as central figures in both national and international financial systems (Lundberg, The Rise of the Wallenberg Empire, 2001).

Similarly, the Medici family of Renaissance Italy used their vast banking resources and political acumen to exert significant influence over European affairs. Through their Medici Bank, they financed monarchs, funded wars, and supported the arts, thereby embedding themselves at the heart of both economic and cultural systems. Their patronage of artists like Michelangelo and Botticelli, coupled with their strategic marriages into European nobility, allowed them to shape the political and cultural landscape of their time (Hibbert, The House of Medici: Its Rise and Fall, 1974). Like the Wallenbergs, the Medicis' ability to navigate and influence both financial and political spheres ensured their enduring legacy as architects of economic and cultural power (Roover, The Rise and Decline of the Medici Bank, 1963).

In Asia, the Lee family of South Korea, through their control of the Samsung Group, has become a cornerstone of the nation's economy. Their dominance in technology, construction, and finance has not only driven South Korea's industrialization but also positioned them as key players in global markets (Kim, The Samsung Way, 2014).

Meanwhile, the Ambanis of India, through Reliance Industries, have transformed the country's energy, telecommunications, and retail sectors, wielding significant influence over India's economic policies and global trade relations (Crabtree, The Billionaire Raj, 2018).

Through their dual focus on domestic growth and global expansion, families like the Wallenbergs, Medicis, Rothschilds, Rockefellers, Lees, and Ambanis have become instrumental in shaping modern economic frameworks, demonstrating how financial dynasties can transcend borders and eras to leave a lasting impact, for good or ill, on the world by centralizing power and control of their wealth to steer the futures of a nation or the world without the consent of the people and a potential threat to sound money systems.

The concentration of power within entities starkly contrasts with the foundational principles of the U.S. Constitution. Designed to prevent the consolidation of power among a select few, the Constitution safeguards democratic governance through mechanisms like the separation of powers, checks and balances, and the Bill of Rights. These structures emphasize individual liberties and the decentralization of authority, ensuring that no single entity or group can monopolize political or economic decision-making. This framework was crafted to serve the broader public interest, rather than catering to a privileged elite, a principle that stands in sharp opposition to the hierarchical, top-down systems of governance seen in the British Empire or the centralized financial influence associated with the Rothschilds and Zionist networks. The Constitution's emphasis on moral governance, as opposed to the unchecked pursuit of power as critiqued in Nietzsche's Will to Power, reflects a deliberate effort to uphold equity and justice for all.

The structure of these systems reveals a distinct hierarchy. Leadership serves as the public face of power, while the Aristocracy wields the true authority behind the scenes. The Bureaucracy supports and executes the Aristocracy's decrees, and The People, positioned at the bottom, are reduced to pawns—subject to the violation of their life, liberty, and property at the whim of those above. These systems are highly effective, and when aligned against freedom, they prioritize capturing a nation's money supply as their initial target. Typically, the nation's currency is converted into fiat, enabling those in power to print limitless amounts of money to fund their agenda of global governance. In most instances, sound money is stripped from The People and redirected to these centralized power structures—represented by the pyramid structure. This raises a critical question, if such hierarchical systems are so efficient, why don't free individuals establish their own pyramid to counter them?

First, the nature of "free individuals" inherently resists hierarchical rigidity and embraces decentralization. Freedom, as a value, emphasizes autonomy, decentralization, and voluntary cooperation rather than top-down, centralized control. A pyramid implies a concentration of power, which contradicts the ethos of liberty. Economist Friedrich Hayek, in his 1944 work The Road to Serfdom, argued that centralized systems inevitably erode freedom because they require coercion to maintain order and suppress dissent. Free individuals, valuing self-governance, are unlikely to adopt a structure that mirrors the oppressive systems they oppose, even if it's efficient. Instead, they lean toward flatter, networked models—like mutual aid societies or decentralized movements—seen in historical examples such as the American Revolution's grassroots committees.

Second, practical challenges hinder the creation of a counter-pyramid. Hierarchical systems thrive on resources—money, infrastructure, and loyal personnel—which free individuals often lack compared to entrenched powers. Fiat money being weaponized by centralized structures aligns with this, those at the top control the money supply, as seen with modern central banks like the Federal Reserve, established in 1913, which critics argue shifted financial power away from the public. Free individuals, reliant on sound money (e.g., gold or decentralized currencies like Bitcoin), struggle to amass the capital needed to rival these systems without compromising their principles by adopting similar fiat mechanisms.

Third, collective action problems plague efforts to organize free people into a pyramid. Game theory, notably the "prisoner's dilemma," illustrates this: individuals acting in their own interest often fail to coordinate effectively, even for a common goal. The efficiency of oppressive pyramids stems from enforced unity, whether through fear, propaganda, or economic dependence, whereas free individuals prioritize choice, leading to fragmentation. The Occupy Wall Street movement (2011) exemplifies this: despite widespread support, its lack of hierarchy and clear leadership limited its ability to enact lasting change, unlike the cohesive bureaucracies it opposed.

So, why don't free people build their own pyramid? They could—in theory—but the trade-offs are steep. A counter-pyramid might require sacrificing the very freedoms it aims to protect, adopting coercive tactics or centralizing power in ways that alienate its base. Historical attempts, like revolutionary vanguardism (e.g., Lenin's Bolsheviks), show that such structures can succeed but often devolve into new tyrannies, as chronicled in Orwell's Animal Farm. Free individuals seem to prefer decentralized resistance, think cryptocurrencies challenging fiat systems or open-source tech undermining corporate monopolies, over replicating a pyramid they'd rather dismantle.

In short, the efficiency of hierarchical systems is undeniable, but their incompatibility with freedom, combined with resource and coordination barriers, explains why free individuals don't typically counter them with a matching structure. They opt instead for alternatives that align with their values, even if less streamlined. What then would the preferred structure for free people be?

The preferred counter-structure for free people is typically a decentralized network, a system where power is distributed across many nodes rather than concentrated at a peak. Unlike a pyramid, which relies on centralized authority and coercion, a decentralized network operates through voluntary cooperation, mutual benefit, and resilience through redundancy. This aligns with the ethos of freedom, no single point of control can dominate, and participants retain agency. It is similar to a web rather than a tower.

Those who value liberty and autonomy don't seek to replicate the pyramids they oppose. Instead, they favor decentralized networks as a counter-structure to hierarchy. In the pyramid model, power flows downward, Leadership serves as the visible face, Aristocracy holds real control, Bureaucracy enforces decrees, and The People function as expendable pawns. Efficiency in such systems comes at the cost of control and resource extraction. This is especially evident in monetary policy, where national currencies are converted into fiat money, a system of unlimited printing that fuels global governance at the expense of individual wealth as James Warburg who was Paul Warburg's son who famously said during his testimony before the U.S. Senate Committee on Foreign Relations on February 17, 1950, "We shall have world government, whether or not we like it. The only question is whether world government will be achieved by conquest or consent." In contrast, a decentralized network disperses authority across multiple nodes, relying on voluntary cooperation instead of coercion.

To be free is to reclaim agency over one's economic choices, to participate in systems that respect consent, and to resist structures that concentrate power in the hands of the few. Decentralized networks, such as those enabled by blockchain technology or sound money principles, offer an alternative where transparency, mutual accountability, and individual sovereignty take precedence. In such systems, value is preserved through scarcity and consensus rather than manipulated by decree. As the failures of centralized monetary systems become more apparent, the appeal of decentralized alternatives grows, not merely as a technical solution, but as a philosophical and ethical stance for those who believe that liberty must be guarded not only by laws, but by the very architecture of the systems we live within.

CHAPTER 16

Why Don't Free People Control Their Own Money?

If the foundation of a free society is individual sovereignty, then the question of who controls money becomes not just economic, but fundamentally political. When monetary authority is concentrated in centralized institutions, be they state-controlled central banks or private financial conglomerates, the public has limited influence over one of the most critical aspects of their lives, the value and use of their currency. This disconnect undermines democratic ideals and leaves societies vulnerable to manipulation, inflation, and economic coercion.

In this context, the idea of decentralization emerges not merely as a technical innovation but as a necessary shift in the architecture of monetary power.

WHY DECENTRALIZATION?

Decentralized networks align with freedom by preventing power from concentrating, even if initially established with good intentions. John Locke's Two Treatises of Government (1689) supports this idea, asserting that governance requires consent, a principle networks uphold far better than rigid hierarchies. More than just philosophical, decentralization is also practical, a pyramid collapses if its leadership is removed, but a network survives because power is distributed. This design mirrors the internet itself, created by DARPA in the 1960s to withstand nuclear attacks by rerouting communication through decentralized pathways. Networks thrive where pyramids falter—adapting to change without waiting for top-down approval.

HISTORICAL AND MODERN EXAMPLES

Decentralization is not a new concept. During the American Revolution (1775–1783), the Committees of Correspondence enabled colonies to coordinate resistance without a central leader, making them harder to dismantle. Fast forward to the digital age, and we see Bitcoin (2009) bypassing central banks with a peer-to-peer blockchain, directly countering the fiat system. By 2025, this trend is expanding into decentralized finance (DeFi), challenging traditional banking altogether. Other examples include Linux, an open-source operating system built through voluntary collaboration rather than corporate hierarchy, and Mastodon, a decentralized alternative to state-aligned social media platforms.

HOW A DECENTRALIZED NETWORK FUNCTIONS

A decentralized network is made up of nodes—individuals, communities, or organizations—interconnected by shared goals, trade, and communication tools like Signal or Nostr. Unlike a pyramid, where wealth and power accumulate at the top, a decentralized system ensures resources flow freely among participants:

- Money: Gold, cryptocurrency, and barter replace reliance on fiat.
- Trade: Localized production strengthens economic resilience.
- Governance: Consensus-based models (like DAOs) replace imposed directives.

These elements enable parallel economies, independent from centralized control.

CHALLENGES AND TRADE-OFFS

Decentralized systems are not without difficulties. Decision-making is slower than in pyramids, as networks rely on agreement rather than commands. Fragmentation is another risk, independent actors may split rather than unify, a challenge seen in liberty movements. However, these drawbacks come with a crucial advantage, decentralized systems endure. Where pyramids rise and fall with their rulers, networks persist, adapting without collapsing.

The Pyramid vs. The Network

The pyramid model thrives by capturing money first, turning it into fiat to fund expansion, violating life, liberty, and property along the way. A decentralized network flips this structure:

- Power is spread across nodes, not concentrated at the top.
- The People participate directly, rather than being used as pawns.
- Leadership emerges when necessary but does not dictate from above.
- Aristocracy and bureaucracy are removed entirely.

Some argue that if pyramids are so effective, why not build one? The answer is simple, pyramids serve control, not freedom. Free individuals seek autonomy, not dominance. Instead of mimicking hierarchical structures, they counter them with sound money, decentralized technology, and grassroots resilience.

The real question is not whether decentralization works—it already does. The question is whether free people will continue feeding the pyramid or building the network that replaces it.

The British Crown and Aristocracy vs. U.S. Constitutional Principles

During the height of the British Empire, the Crown's power was often reinforced by its aristocracy, which held vast wealth and political influence. This elite class profited through monopolistic control over colonial resources and trade routes, undermining democratic participation and reinforcing a class-based system. The aristocracy's dominance within the imperial structure, aided by the Crown, perpetuated a concentration of economic and political power that benefited only the elite, often at the expense of colonized populations. By contrast, the U.S. Constitution sought to eradicate such concentration of power through mechanisms such as the electoral system and the system of checks and balances, which provided citizens with greater control over their government. Unlike the British monarchy, which maintained control through hereditary aristocracy, the U.S. envisioned a republic in which power would be more evenly distributed across elected officials and institutions (The Federalist Papers, 1787-1788).

The Rothschild Banking Empire and U.S. Constitutional Vision of Financial Independence

The Rothschild banking family exemplifies the financial consolidation of power that runs counter to the U.S. Constitution's ideal of economic independence and decentralized control over currency and monetary policy. The Founding Fathers, particularly Thomas Jefferson and James Madison, were deeply wary of centralized banking, fearing that it would give too much control over the economy to a small group of wealthy individuals and undermine democratic principles (Jefferson, Letter to John Taylor, 1816; Madison, Federalist No. 10, 1787). This caution was realized with the creation of the Federal Reserve in 1913, which critics argue centralized financial control in ways similar to the banking influence exercised by the Rothschild family in Europe. The Rothschilds' vast financial empire allowed them to exert considerable influence over European governments, financing wars, shaping policy decisions, and consolidating power within the hands of a financial elite. In a similar way, the Federal Reserve's control over currency issuance and monetary policy places significant power in the hands of a few individuals or institutions, circumventing the democratic control that the U.S. Constitution envisioned (Ferguson, 1999).

The Zionist Federation and the U.S. Constitution's Commitment to Equal Rights

The concentration of financial influence through powerful lobbying networks—such as the American Israel Public Affairs Committee (AIPAC) in the United States—and longstanding banking dynasties has raised questions about the balance of power and its alignment with the principles of equal rights and representation enshrined in the U.S. Constitution. The Zionist Federation's role in the creation of a Jewish homeland in Palestine was facilitated by financial networks that were often associated with wealthy European elites. These elites, including the Rothschilds, were able to exert considerable influence in the establishment of settlements and the acquisition of land. Critics argue that this process prioritized elite financial interests while marginalizing the rights of the indigenous Palestinian population (Khalidi, The Hundred Years' War on Palestine, 2020). This exclusionary focus on financial power contrasts directly with the U.S. Constitution's commitment to the equal protection of rights for all individuals, as embodied in the Fourteenth Amendment, which mandates that all people within U.S. jurisdiction are entitled to equal protection under the law.

Centralization vs. Decentralization: A Constitutional Contrast

The U.S. Constitution's emphasis on limiting centralized power is reflected in its commitment to a system of checks and balances and the separation of powers, which were designed to prevent any one branch or entity from accumulating too much control. Centralized financial and political systems, like those associated with the British Empire, the

Rothschild banking family, and the Zionist Federation, run contrary to these constitutional principles by concentrating power in the hands of a few. The Federal Reserve, much like these other centralized financial networks, holds substantial influence over national and global monetary policy, often without sufficient public oversight or accountability. This stands in contrast to the democratic ideals of the U.S. Constitution, which intended for power to remain with the people and be distributed across various branches of government.

GLOBAL IMPLICATIONS AND SOCIAL EQUITY

The concentration of power within these systems has had profound implications for global politics, economic stability, and social equity. The British Empire, through the Crown and its aristocracy, dominated global trade, exploited colonies, and perpetuated systemic inequalities. Similarly, the Rothschild banking network, by controlling vast financial resources, contributed to an unequal distribution of wealth, shaping political outcomes in ways that often favored the elite. The Zionist Federation, with its financial backing and connections to European elites, facilitated the establishment of a Jewish homeland while marginalizing Palestinian Arabs, contributing to a long-standing humanitarian crisis.

These systems of concentrated power perpetuate economic inequality, undermine social mobility, and often prevent marginalized populations from achieving political or economic independence. The U.S. Constitution, with its vision of decentralized governance and a system that promotes the rights of individuals, presents an ideal that stands in stark contrast to these centralized systems. While the Founding Fathers feared that centralized financial and political systems would lead to oligarchic control and the erosion of democratic principles, the actions of the British Crown, the Rothschilds, and the Zionist Federation exemplify how such concentrations of power can lead to enduring global inequalities.

The systems of centralized power exemplified by the British Crown, the Rothschild banking empire, and the Zionist Federation contrast sharply with the decentralized and democratic ideals set forth by the U.S.

Constitution. These systems, prioritizing elite interests and consolidating wealth and power, have contributed to long-standing political, economic, and social imbalances. The U.S. Constitution, with its emphasis on equality, individual rights, and the distribution of power, serves as a reminder of the dangers of concentrated authority and the importance of safeguarding democratic principles in the face of powerful financial and political elites (Madison, Federalist No. 51, 1788; Jefferson, Letter to John Taylor, 1816).

By the late 19th century, powerful industrialists such as J.P. Morgan, John D. Rockefeller, and Andrew Carnegie had firmly established their dominance in America's economic sphere. These men, often called "robber barons," amassed immense wealth and influence through monopolistic practices and exploiting the lack of government oversight. Morgan, in particular, had deep connections with European financial circles, including the Rothschilds, which allowed him to extend his influence internationally. Despite this growing concentration of wealth and power, the U.S. banking system remained fragmented and highly susceptible to financial instability, as demonstrated by the Panic of 1907, which exposed the vulnerabilities of the existing system (Economic History Association, n.d.).

As a crisis in the making and to never let a crisis go to waste, in response to the 1907 panic, banking elites, including Morgan, and sympathetic lawmakers pushed for the centralization of monetary control. This culminated in the passage of the Federal Reserve Act of 1913, which established the Federal Reserve System and granted it the authority to issue currency and regulate credit. Critics contend that this act concentrated significant financial power in the hands of a select few, including industrial magnates and bankers, creating what many view as the largest trust in the world. Through the Federal Reserve, these elites gained the ability to control the economy by influencing monetary policy and regulating the money supply (Federal Reserve History, n.d.).

During the Great Depression (1929–1939), Federal Reserve policies, such as tightening the money supply, exacerbated the economic crisis. Historians argue that these policies allowed industrialists and financial elites to further consolidate their power by acquiring distressed assets at drastically reduced prices. Additionally, the economic restructuring during this time included the United States abandoning the gold standard in 1933, when President Franklin D. Roosevelt issued Executive Order 6102, requiring citizens to surrender their gold. This move significantly centralized control over monetary resources, further strengthening the hands of the financial elite in times of crisis. The combined effect of these actions laid the groundwork for even greater consolidation of financial power among a select group of influential bankers and industrialists (Ferguson, 1998; Federal Reserve History, n.d.).

THE HYPOTHETICAL UNITED STATES WITHOUT THE FEDERAL RESERVE AND THE ROLE OF SOUND MONEY

Had the United States never established the Federal Reserve in 1913, its financial landscape would likely have adhered more closely to the constitutional framework laid out by the Founding Fathers, particularly the principles outlined in Article I, Section 8 of the U.S. Constitution. This section grants Congress the power to "coin Money, regulate the Value thereof, and of foreign Coin," explicitly mandating the use of gold and silver as the foundation of the nation's monetary system. Article I, Section 10 further reinforces this by prohibiting states from making "any Thing but gold and silver Coin a Tender in Payment of Debts." Together, these provisions demonstrate the founders' intent to anchor the monetary system in tangible, intrinsic assets, rejecting fiat currencies and ensuring financial stability.

The Founding Fathers recognized gold and silver as universal stores of value, including foreign gold and silver coins, which were widely used as legal tender in the early republic. This approach provided a decentralized, transparent monetary system that resisted inflationary pressures and prevented the arbitrary devaluation of currency. It also ensured that economic power remained distributed, protecting the public from the undue influence of centralized banking entities or private financiers.

Without the Federal Reserve, the United States might have maintained a robust financial system grounded in these constitutional principles. Gold and silver, including foreign coins, would likely have continued to function as money, preserving purchasing power and preventing the cycle of inflation and monetary manipulation that often accompanies fiat systems. Such a framework would have supported the ideals of limited government, individual liberty, and decentralized economic power, aligning with the vision of the Founding Fathers to safeguard against the consolidation of wealth and authority within central institutions.

THE FOUNDING FATHERS' VISION OF MONEY

The founders, particularly figures like Alexander Hamilton and Thomas Jefferson, emphasized the importance of sound money in preserving the value of the dollar and safeguarding the economy from the destructive effects of inflation. Hamilton, in his capacity as the first Treasury Secretary, pushed for a strong central bank (the First Bank of the United States) but with stringent limitations on its powers and a focus on sound money. He argued that the nation's monetary system should be backed by tangible assets, specifically gold and silver, to maintain stability and trust in the currency (Gordon, 1999). This emphasis on sound money was a response to the volatility of fiat currency and the instability it caused in early American history. In contrast, Jefferson and other founders were wary of central banking institutions and argued for a decentralized approach, where local banks issued their own currency, backed by precious metals, to avoid the dangers of inflation and economic manipulation.

A FEDERAL RESERVE-FREE UNITED STATES

In a hypothetical scenario where the Federal Reserve had not been established, the U.S. would likely have continued relying on a system of decentralized banking with sound money principles at its core. The gold standard, which was in place in various forms throughout the 19th century, would have potentially remained in effect longer, preventing the currency inflation that occurred after the U.S. abandoned the gold standard in 1971. The absence of the Federal Reserve would have likely led to fewer instances of economic manipulation through monetary policy, as local banks would have had less power to influence interest rates or the money supply.

Without the Federal Reserve, the U.S. would have been less susceptible to the economic cycles of boom and bust driven by central monetary policies. Sound money—backed by gold or silver—would have reduced the risk of inflation and provided a stable store of value. Historical data suggests that the U.S. experienced periods of relative economic stability during times when money was backed by precious metals. For example, between 1837 and 1862, the U.S. adhered to a bimetallic standard, using both gold and silver to back the dollar. During this period, the country experienced steady economic growth, a relatively low inflation rate, and fewer banking crises compared to the periods that followed the establishment of the Federal Reserve (Mises Institute, 2006).

The absence of the Federal Reserve could have potentially altered the trajectory of U.S. monetary policy, particularly regarding the expansionary policies that contributed to financial crises like the Great Depression. Many historians, including Peter Temin (1976), argue that the Federal Reserve's actions, such as tightening the money supply and raising interest rates in the early years of the Depression (1929–1933), exacerbated the economic collapse. The Fed's decision to reduce the money supply led to severe deflationary pressures, contributing to widespread bankruptcies, falling wages, and mass unemployment. While the Federal Reserve aimed to curb inflationary pressures that had built up during the 1920s, its actions have been widely criticized for deepening the crisis. In hindsight, critics argue that the Fed's response was insufficiently aggressive in stimulating the economy.

In a hypothetical scenario without the Federal Reserve, a sound money system, such as one based on the gold standard, could have potentially mitigated the severity of the Depression by avoiding the unchecked credit expansion that fueled speculative bubbles and economic imbalances. Austrian economists, such as Ludwig von Mises and Friedrich Hayek, have argued that sound money policies provide a stabilizing force by limiting inflation and preventing excessive risk-taking. However, mainstream economists contend that a strict gold standard or a decentralized banking system might have also limited the ability of policymakers to respond effectively to the financial crisis, as gold-backed systems restrict the money supply during times of economic stress, potentially worsening deflationary spirals (Temin, 1976).

While historical comparisons to the Napoleonic Wars are often made in debates about sound money, it is important to note that the Napoleonic Wars created severe economic instability across Europe. During this time, countries such as Britain relied on inflationary financing to fund their war efforts, leading to significant price increases and economic volatility. In contrast, sound money systems like the gold standard were often viewed as stabilizing forces but could be restrictive during periods of major financial distress, such as the Great Depression, when the ability to adjust the money supply might have alleviated some of the economic strain. Therefore, while sound money principles may have provided a stabilizing influence historically, they also posed challenges in times of crisis, as seen in both the Depression and the Napoleonic era (Ferguson, 1998; Hummel, 2016).

CONSOLIDATION OF POWER AND THE RISE OF ELITES

The Federal Reserve's creation in 1913, though sold as a solution to financial instability, ultimately consolidated financial power in the hands of a few elite bankers. J.P. Morgan and other industrial magnates were deeply involved in the creation of the Federal Reserve, and many critics argue that it facilitated their ability to control the U.S. economy (Ferguson, 1998). A system based on sound money and free-market banking would have likely prevented the rise of such centralized power. Instead of a small group of bankers controlling the money supply, a decentralized system would have allowed for greater competition among local banks, providing a more equitable financial environment and less opportunity for monopolistic control as wealth would have spread more evenly throughout the country instead of being centralized in New York City.

The importance of sound money in preserving economic stability has been demonstrated throughout history. During the classical gold standard period (1870-1914), the U.S. economy experienced relatively stable growth and low inflation, a stark contrast to the economic instability that followed the establishment of the Federal Reserve. According to economic historian Jeffrey Rogers Hummel, the gold standard's discipline on government spending and credit creation helped keep inflation low and minimized the risks of financial crises (Hummel, 2016). The absence of the Federal Reserve could have allowed the U.S. to continue benefiting from this stable, market-driven system, ensuring that economic booms and busts would have been more moderate and less influenced by the manipulations of a centralized monetary authority.

The establishment of the Federal Reserve in 1913 marked a fundamental shift in the U.S. financial system, steering the nation away from the principles of sound money that the Founding Fathers had envisioned. In the absence of the Federal Reserve, the United States might have enjoyed greater economic stability, a more decentralized financial system, and a financial environment less susceptible to manipulation by elites. By returning to a system based on sound money, America could have adhered more closely to the ideals of limited government and individual liberty, preventing the rise of financial monopolies and safeguarding the economic future of its citizens.

To truly understand the path forward, we must first return to the vision of the Founders—who sought to decentralize power and safeguard liberty through sound money. Gold and silver stood as bulwarks against tyranny, a defense against those who would centralize authority by seizing control over the money supply. Today, technology invites us to reimagine that vision. Do blockchain and decentralized systems represent not just new tools, but a revival of an old philosophy—one where value flows not from institutions but from individuals?

CHAPTER 17

Reclaiming Economic Freedom Through the Pillars of Sound Money

In the context of an increasingly volatile global financial landscape, the principles of sound money offer a critical pathway to reclaiming economic freedom and stability. As governments and individuals alike seek long-term prosperity, revisiting the fundamental concepts of hard currency, fiscal discipline, and transparent monetary policies provides an essential framework for rebuilding trust in financial systems.

To understand the profound impact of monetary systems on global power dynamics, it is necessary to examine historical examples where control over currency played a decisive role in political struggles. The conflict between the Chinese Communist Party (CCP) and the Kuomintang (KMT) offers a powerful case study. This struggle illustrates how the manipulation of currency, including the strategic use of hyperinflation, can shape the outcomes of political conflicts and influence the trajectory of nations. As we reflect on this historical example, we gain insight into the evolving nature of money and its role in the new global monetary order that is emerging in the 21st century. This chapter will delve into the role of hyperinflation, the weaponization of monetary policy, and how these dynamics continue to shape economic systems today.

CHINA'S CCP VS. KMT AND THE ROLE OF HYPERINFLATION

As we enter a new era marked by shifting global power dynamics, it is crucial to examine the historical conflict between the Chinese Communist Party (CCP) and the Kuomintang (KMT), as it offers a striking example of how monetary systems can be weaponized during struggles for political control. Additionally, exploring this history helps to understand the shape of money and the new monetary system in the 21st century and beyond.

The CCP, which currently governs mainland China, and the KMT, which fled to Taiwan after their defeat in the Chinese Civil War in 1949, represent two competing visions for the future of China. This struggle between the two factions, particularly in the early-to-mid 20th century, illustrates how control over monetary systems—such as currency issuance and economic policy—can play a pivotal role in shaping the outcome of a conflict and consolidating political power.

In the years leading up to the KMT's retreat to Taiwan, both the CCP and KMT recognized the power of controlling a nation's financial system as a means of gaining leverage over the population and maintaining control. The CCP, under Mao Zedong, strategically used the nation's economy and currency to support its revolutionary goals. The KMT, on the other hand, found itself struggling to maintain economic stability during the Chinese Civil War. The KMT government faced mounting inflation and a weakened currency, issues that ultimately undermined its credibility and legitimacy in the eyes of the Chinese people. The KMT's failure to manage the economy effectively during the war contributed significantly to their loss of popular support, as hyperinflation reached severe levels by the late 1940s. This instability was one of the factors that led to their retreat to Taiwan (Maddison, 2007; Hsu, 1970).

In contrast, the CCP was able to strengthen its grip on the Chinese mainland by implementing radical economic policies, including land reforms and the establishment of a centralized, state-controlled economy that helped to stabilize its territorial holdings. The CCP's control of the People's Bank of China allowed it to issue currency and manage monetary policy, reinforcing its authority over the population (Liu, 2008). Through land redistribution and economic restructuring, the CCP was able to create a sense of stability and national unity, which helped bolster its legitimacy after the civil war.

After the KMT retreated to Taiwan, it inherited a financial system deeply affected by wartime inflation and economic instability. Despite these challenges, the KMT sought to re-establish control over the economy by issuing its own currency and stabilizing the financial system. The KMT government in Taiwan adopted measures, such as currency reform and controlling inflation through the establishment of the Central Bank of China, which helped to stabilize the economy by the mid-1950s (Gold, 1986). Meanwhile, the CCP, with its growing influence over mainland China, continued to utilize the People's Bank of China and the state-controlled financial system as key tools for consolidating political power. By manipulating currency and economic policy, both parties sought to shape the loyalty and economic behavior of their respective populations.

The conflict between the Chinese Communist Party (CCP) and the KMT offers a clear example of how monetary policy can be weaponized in the broader struggle for political control. Both factions understood that the management of a nation's financial system was essential not only for economic stability but also for securing the loyalty of the people and maintaining governmental legitimacy. This recognition led to the use of currency control, economic reforms, and strategic financial alliances as tools of political power. The lessons drawn from this era in the weaponization of monetary systems continue to resonate today, where economic power is inextricably linked to political dominance on the global stage.

The KMT's economic struggles were a critical factor in its eventual defeat. During World War II, the KMT-controlled Republic of China was already facing significant economic challenges, including rampant inflation fueled by overspending on the war effort and reliance on foreign loans. As the Chinese Civil War reignited between 1946 and 1949, the KMT's fiscal policy further deteriorated, relying heavily on printing money to fund its military campaigns. This reckless monetary policy severely undermined the value of the Chinese yuan, further eroding the KMT's credibility and weakening its position in the conflict.

In contrast, the CCP strategically used economic instability as a tool in its battle with the KMT. The Chinese Communist Party exacerbated the financial turmoil by employing a form of financial warfare. As the CCP gained control over critical industrial and financial hubs such as Manchuria and Shanghai, it seized access to vital resources that significantly bolstered its war efforts while simultaneously crippling the KMT's economic base. These regions were not only rich in industrial capacity but also contained essential infrastructure—factories, banks, and transportation networks—that the CCP repurposed to sustain its military campaigns and solidify its control over occupied territories. By strategically leveraging these assets, the CCP was able to turn economic instability into a powerful weapon, ultimately helping it secure victory over the KMT.

The loss of these hubs dealt a dual blow to the KMT, first, by depriving it of critical tax revenues and production capabilities, and second, by shifting public and international perceptions of which side held the upper hand in the civil war. Without access to these resources, the KMT struggled to finance its operations and relied increasingly on printing paper money, further fueling hyperinflation.

Additionally, the CCP exploited its growing control over these regions to produce counterfeit versions of the KMT's currency, flooding KMT territories with this fake money. This deepened the hyperinflation crisis, rendering the KMT's currency nearly worthless and undermining public confidence in the government's financial and administrative competence.

Additionally, CCP strategically exploited its expanding territorial control by producing and disseminating counterfeit versions of the KMT's currency. This deliberate flooding of KMT-held areas with falsified banknotes significantly exacerbated the existing hyperinflation, contributing to the near-total collapse of the KMT's monetary system and eroding public trust in its financial and administrative authority (Liu, 2004).

This tactic of economic destabilization through currency manipulation has historical precedent. Notably, during the American Revolutionary War, the British government engaged in the counterfeiting of Continental currency as a means of weakening the American economy and morale (Newman, 2008). Such examples underscore how targeted attacks on a nation's financial system can serve as potent instruments of asymmetric warfare, with long-term implications for political legitimacy and public order (Kynaston, 2017).

In present times, parallels in the contemporary United States have some commentators drawing comparisons between the destabilizing tactics employed during historical conflicts and the perceived economic and social fragmentation within the United States. While the nation is not undergoing a traditional civil war, significant polarization and ideological clashes have led to accusations of subversive tactics, particularly from groups advocating for communist or socialist ideologies.

For instance, allegations have surfaced suggesting efforts to undermine confidence in the U.S. dollar and broader financial systems. Some analysts point to initiatives advocating for widespread government spending and monetary expansion as a potential destabilizing factor, reminiscent of hyperinflation scenarios in history. Critics also highlight efforts to amplify distrust in key institutions, including the financial sector, law enforcement, and the judiciary, as part of broader ideological campaigns.

Furthermore, tactics such as disinformation campaigns and the strategic use of economic pressure points—whether through organized boycotts, mass protests, or calls for debt forgiveness—have been compared to earlier instances of economic warfare. While these modern actions differ significantly from physical counterfeiting, their aim to undermine perceived economic stability shares thematic similarities.

This comparison remains highly contested, with many experts cautioning against drawing overly simplistic parallels between historical civil wars and current U.S. domestic tensions. However, the study of these dynamics highlights how economic and ideological tools have been consistently employed throughout history to influence governance and societal cohesion.

In 1949, as the Chinese Communist Party (CCP) secured victory, the KMT retreated to Taiwan, taking with them an estimated 4.5 million ounces of gold (approximately 113 metric tons), which represented a significant portion of China's national reserves. Along with this gold, the KMT also transported foreign exchange reserves and cultural artifacts.

This strategic move was vital for Taiwan's financial stability, providing a foundation that enabled the KMT to stabilize its new economy and issue the New Taiwan Dollar. This avoided the hyperinflation that plagued mainland China under the CCP's early economic policies. The gold exodus illustrates how strategic resource transfers can prevent economic collapse during times of political upheaval.

Similarly, after World War II, Germany experienced significant wealth transfers. The Allied occupation extracted large industrial assets and financial reserves from Germany as reparations. However, the Marshall Plan reversed this process by facilitating the flow of wealth into West Germany, helping to rebuild its economy. This transfer of wealth highlights the dual role such movements can play—either destabilizing or rebuilding economies, depending on their direction.

The British Empire also provides an example of wealth extraction during its colonial rule. In the 18th and 19th centuries, Britain extracted vast amounts of wealth from colonies like India, using these resources to finance its industrialization and economic dominance in Europe. This redistribution of wealth on a global scale significantly altered the economic trajectories of both the colonies and Britain itself, demonstrating the power of wealth transfer in shaping national economies.

In modern times, wealth transfers continue to play a crucial role in shaping economies, such as in the United States' response to the 2008 financial crisis. The Federal Reserve's quantitative easing program injected trillions of dollars into the economy to stabilize markets. However, much of this new money disproportionately benefited asset holders, widening the wealth gap. In this regard, it shares a similarity with the KMT's gold exodus—both events involved reallocating financial resources to stabilize the economy. However, modern U.S. policies have concentrated wealth in financial sectors, unlike Taiwan's broader economic stabilization.

Another example of financial dominance reshaping global economies is the status of the U.S. dollar as the world's reserve currency. This unique position allows the U.S. to export inflation while importing goods and services, effectively redistributing wealth globally. As other nations bear the cost of dollar devaluation, this system creates both domestic and foreign winners and losers, a mechanism that mirrors historical wealth transfers and highlights how financial dominance facilitates wealth accumulation at the expense of others. This redistribution of wealth is, in many ways, a clear violation of the principles of fairness and balance that underpin the U.S. Constitution.

These examples underscore the critical role that wealth transfers—whether through gold, reparations, colonial extraction, or modern monetary policy—play in reshaping economies and redistributing wealth, often benefiting the few at the expense of the many.

WEALTH REDISTRIBUTION VIA INFLATION

Persistent inflation effectively erodes the real value of savings for ordinary citizens, redistributing wealth to debtors and asset-rich individuals, including the government and corporations. This practice can be seen as a form of "taxation without representation," where politicians exploit inflation to siphon wealth from the public without their consent or a formal vote. Essentially, inflation acts as a covert form of theft, diminishing the purchasing power of money and taking value from individuals without their agreement. This silent wealth transfer not only undermines fairness but also constitutes an economic crime, as it deprives citizens of the value of their own earnings. Historical examples, such as the monetary instability in post-1949 mainland China, illustrate how inflation and currency devaluation can devastate the financial well-being of the population. This highlights the damaging effects of such practices, which can harm society and function as legalized theft.

PARALLEL TO HYPERINFLATION IN CHINA

While not as extreme, inflation in the U.S. also erodes wealth for vulnerable populations, similar to how the Chinese Communist Party's early economic policies led to hyperinflation. In both cases, inflation undermines the value of money, negatively impacting the financial stability of those who rely on fixed incomes and savings.

These examples show how wealth transfers, whether through direct resource appropriation or monetary policy, have historically shaped economic landscapes and continue to do so today.

POTENTIAL SOLUTIONS DURING ECONOMIC STRESS

In times of economic stress or crisis, a commodity-based monetary system, such as one backed by gold or silver, can reduce wealth inequality and foster economic stability. Historically, systems like the gold standard and silver standard have proven to provide these benefits. For instance, during the classical gold standard era (1879–1933), the United States experienced low inflation, robust economic growth, and relatively less wealth inequality. By anchoring currency to a tangible commodity, reckless monetary expansion was curtailed, allowing savings to retain their value. Similarly, China's silver standard during the late Qing dynasty helped maintain economic stability while other nations struggled with inflation and monetary disruptions. The Ottoman Empire's use of a gold-backed currency, the dinar, facilitated stable trade and economic equity across its vast territories, contributing to centuries of prosperity. These historical examples demonstrate how a commodity-backed system can help protect the value of money and promote long-term economic stability.

Modern examples further underscore the benefits of commodity-linked systems. Until 1999, Switzerland partially backed its currency with gold, maintaining the Swiss franc as one of the world's most stable currencies and protecting savings from inflation. Singapore adopts a similar strategy today by managing significant reserves in gold and commodities to ensure monetary stability, avoiding excessive inflation and fostering equitable economic growth.

Commodity-backed systems help reduce wealth inequality by preventing inflation, which often acts as a "hidden tax" eroding the value of money for wage earners and savers. By restricting the money supply, these systems preserve purchasing power and promote confidence in savings and long-term investments. Additionally, they limit the ability of central banks to implement arbitrary monetary policies, reducing the risk of wealth transfer through excessive money printing or currency devaluation. However, challenges remain, such as limited flexibility to respond to economic shocks and the need for global coordination in today's interconnected economy. Despite these limitations, the historical and modern success of commodity-backed systems shows their potential to preserve wealth and reduce inequality when implemented prudently.

Then why did the United States suffer such a severe deflation in the early 1930's since they were on a bimetallic standard?

The gold and silver standards provided long-term monetary stability but were not immune to economic mismanagement, structural weaknesses, or external shocks that could lead to severe crises. The Roaring Twenties and the subsequent Great Depression highlight the limitations of commodity-based monetary systems in mitigating all forms of economic risk. Here's why the gold standard failed to prevent the worst during that period:

1. **Over-Speculation and Credit Expansion**

   During the 1920s, the U.S. experienced a speculative boom, particularly in the stock market. Lax credit policies and the proliferation of margin trading (borrowing to invest in stocks) fueled unsustainable asset bubbles. While the gold standard constrained the overall money supply, it did not regulate how that money was allocated. Excessive risk-taking overwhelmed the system, culminating in the stock market crash of 1929.

2. **Rigid Monetary Policy**

   The Federal Reserve, bound by the gold standard, was limited in its ability to respond to economic downturns. To maintain gold reserves and defend the dollar's fixed value, The Fed often raised interest rates, which exacerbated the economic contraction instead of alleviating it. This rigidity prevented the use of more expansionary monetary policies that could have softened the downturn.

3. **Global Deflationary Pressures**

   The gold standard tied currencies across nations, transmitting economic shocks globally. During the late 1920s and early 1930s, as countries struggled to maintain their gold reserves, they implemented deflationary policies like cutting government spending and raising taxes. This caused a spiral of falling prices, declining demand, and rising unemployment, deepening the depression both in the U.S. and internationally.

4. **Banking System Vulnerabilities**
   The U.S. banking system was highly fragmented and poorly regulated, making it vulnerable to bank runs. As the economy weakened, depositors lost confidence, leading to widespread bank failures. The gold standard's constraints on money supply growth meant there was little liquidity available to stabilize the banking system.
5. **Structural Economic Imbalances**
   The Roaring Twenties saw uneven economic growth. While industrial and urban sectors boomed, agriculture and rural areas struggled due to falling commodity prices and mounting debt. These imbalances created underlying vulnerabilities that the gold standard could not address.

LESSONS FROM THE ERA

The gold standard was effective at maintaining long-term price stability, but it was not designed to manage short-term economic crises, speculative bubbles, or structural weaknesses. Its rigidity made it difficult to adapt to the unique challenges of the Great Depression. Ultimately, the U.S. abandoned the gold standard during the 1930s to regain monetary flexibility, allowing for policies like monetary expansion and fiscal stimulus that helped the economy recover. While commodity-backed systems can reduce inflation and protect wealth, they require complementary policies and regulatory frameworks to prevent and respond to economic instability. However, in the end, those who held onto their gold and silver during the Great Depression were well-positioned to profit immensely when the monetary system reset in the 1930s. As the U.S. abandoned the gold standard and devalued the dollar, the price of gold rose significantly, from $20.67 to $35 per ounce. This devaluation meant that individuals who had preserved their wealth in gold or silver saw the value of their holdings increase substantially. While the broader economy faced tremendous hardship, those who had the patience to save in gold and silver were shielded from the inflation and currency devaluation that affected those holding paper currency. Ultimately, their foresight and persistence allowed them to emerge from the economic turmoil in a much stronger financial position.

In many ways, the current economic situation in the United States mirrors the conditions of the 1930s, with rising inflation, increasing government debt, and uncertainty surrounding the stability of fiat currencies. Just as gold and silver were seen as a safe haven during the Great Depression, many people today look to precious metals as a hedge against the depreciation of the U.S. dollar. With ongoing concerns about the effects of expansive fiscal policies, such as massive government spending and the Federal Reserve's money-printing measures, there are fears that the value of the dollar could continue to erode, leading to inflation or even a currency crisis.

In this context, holding gold and silver today might similarly position investors to benefit from any future "reset" of the monetary system, should the U.S. face another period of severe economic distress or a devaluation of the dollar. Just as those who held gold during the 1930s saw its value increase significantly after the dollar was devalued, today's investors in precious metals might find that their assets appreciate in the face of continued inflation or currency instability. As the U.S. government continues to grapple with significant fiscal challenges, including rising debt levels and the potential for further economic disruptions, patience and savings in gold or silver may prove to be a prudent strategy, offering protection and the potential for substantial gains in the event of a reset in the financial system.

CCP'S ECONOMIC RESET

After taking power, the CCP implemented radical economic policies to stabilize the economy. These included land reforms, confiscation of private wealth, and the introduction of a centrally planned economy. The hyperinflation crisis became a justification for the Communist system's strict monetary controls, including the establishment of the People's Bank of China in 1948 to monopolize the issuance of currency. This parallels closely to what the Biden Administration was pushing the United States towards from 2021 to 2025.

UNITED STATES (GREAT DEPRESSION AND NEW DEAL):

During the Great Depression, the United States faced a severe economic collapse with widespread unemployment, deflation, and banking failures. The federal government responded with radical economic policies under President Franklin D. Roosevelt's New Deal, which included:

- Land reforms and agricultural adjustments: The Agricultural Adjustment Act (AAA) aimed to reduce crop surpluses by paying farmers to reduce production, thus raising prices.
- Confiscation of private wealth: The government imposed controls, such as the Gold Reserve Act of 1934, which required citizens to exchange their gold coins, gold bullion, and gold certificates for U.S. dollars, effectively centralizing control of the gold supply.
- Monetary controls: In response to the economic crisis, the government took steps to stabilize the economy by centralizing monetary power, including creating the Federal Deposit Insurance Corporation (FDIC) and imposing regulations on the banking system to prevent future banking crises. Additionally, banning the ownership of gold until 1975 when President Ford lifted the restriction, effectively prevented U.S. citizens from using gold as a hedge against inflation and the devaluation of the dollar during the most volatile periods of the 20th century, including the aftermath of the Great Depression and the early years of the Bretton Woods system collapse.

SOVIET UNION (POST-REVOLUTIONARY ECONOMIC RESTRUCTURING):

After the Bolshevik Revolution in 1917, the Soviet Union, under Lenin and later Stalin, implemented radical economic reforms to consolidate power and stabilize the economy:

- Land reforms and collectivization: Land was seized from aristocrats and redistributed to the peasants. Later, Stalin initiated forced collectivization, consolidating individual farms into collective farms controlled by the state.
- Confiscation of private wealth: The government nationalized industries, banks, and private businesses, stripping private owners of their wealth and placing the economy under state control.
- Centrally planned economy: The Soviet Union moved to a fully planned economy with the establishment of the State Bank of the USSR, which monopolized the issuance of currency and controlled all monetary policies, including stringent inflation controls.

Both the U.S. and the Soviet Union implemented drastic economic reforms that centralized control and established strict monetary policies in response to economic crises, resembling the CCP's policies after its rise to power.

COMPARISON OF ECONOMIC OUTCOMES AND SOCIETAL IMPACTS

The hyperinflation crises in Zimbabwe and Venezuela have drastically altered the standard of living for their populations, creating environments where basic necessities become unaffordable for the majority. The astronomical rise in prices means that families can no longer afford fundamental goods such as food, clean water, and healthcare. In Zimbabwe, the World Bank reported that nearly 80% of the population was living on less than $1.90 a day at the peak of its economic collapse, highlighting a severe humanitarian crisis where millions faced extreme poverty (World

Bank, 2020). This situation led to widespread malnutrition and a public health crisis as access to medical services and essential supplies deteriorated.

Felix Martin, in his work Money: The Unauthorized Biography, emphasizes that hyperinflation can precipitate a humanitarian crisis, as the underlying economic fabric of society disintegrates (Martin, 2013). As prices soar and wages remain stagnant, individuals are forced to prioritize survival over other aspects of life, leading to desperation and social unrest. The loss of purchasing power strips citizens of their dignity and autonomy, resulting in increased crime rates and protests against the government. In Zimbabwe, this breakdown of social order manifested in violent uprisings and widespread civil unrest as citizens demanded change amidst their worsening conditions.

Venezuela's plight mirrors this narrative, where hyperinflation has led to similar dire outcomes. The deteriorating economic conditions have forced millions to rely on food aid or remittances from family members abroad. A recent survey indicated that over 90% of Venezuelans live in poverty, with many struggling to secure three meals a day (World Bank, 2020). The once-wealthy nation has witnessed a staggering decline in its healthcare system, with shortages of medicines and medical supplies exacerbating the suffering of its citizens. Martin's exploration of hyperinflation underscores its potential to unravel not just economies but entire societies, leading to widespread despair and loss of faith in governmental institutions.

MIGRATION AND BRAIN DRAIN EFFECTS

The economic collapse in Zimbabwe and Venezuela has triggered significant migration patterns, with millions leaving their homelands in search of better opportunities abroad. This mass exodus has resulted in a substantial brain drain, depriving these nations of skilled professionals and further weakening their economic prospects. According to the United Nations, over five million Venezuelans have fled their country since 2015, leading to a critical loss of human capital that hampers economic recovery efforts (UNHCR, 2021). Niall Ferguson, in The Ascent of Money, highlights how demographic shifts caused by migration can have long-lasting negative effects on a nation's developmental trajectory (Ferguson, 2008). The departure of healthcare workers, engineers, and educators exacerbates the challenges faced by both countries, as they struggle to rebuild their economies with a diminished workforce.

The implications of brain drain extend beyond the immediate loss of labor; they also affect the social fabric and future prospects of the remaining population. In Venezuela, the exodus of talent has created significant skill gaps in various sectors, including healthcare, education, and technology. This lack of expertise complicates recovery efforts, as the country grapples with rebuilding its institutions and infrastructure in the wake of economic collapse. Moreover, the psychological impact on those who remain can be profound, as families are torn apart and communities lose their most promising members to migration.

Furthermore, as the economies of Zimbabwe and Venezuela contract, the remaining population often finds itself trapped in a vicious cycle of poverty and despair. Those who can migrate often do so, leaving behind a workforce that lacks the skills necessary to foster economic growth. Ferguson's analysis underscores the cyclical nature of this phenomenon, illustrating how the outflow of talent not only hampers recovery but also perpetuates an environment where further migration becomes the only viable option for many individuals (Ferguson, 2008).

HOW SOUND MONEY COULD HAVE OFFSET THESE PROBLEMS

The hyperinflation crises experienced by Zimbabwe and Venezuela serve as stark reminders of the consequences of poor monetary policy, economic mismanagement, and a lack of accountability. Implementing sound money principles could have significantly mitigated the severity of their economic collapse and its societal impacts. Sound money is typically characterized by a stable currency, limited money supply, and mechanisms to prevent excessive inflation, which collectively help maintain public trust and economic stability.

STABILITY THROUGH LIMITED MONEY SUPPLY

A core tenet of sound money is a restricted money supply, which can prevent the rampant inflation seen in both Zimbabwe and Venezuela. By adhering to a fixed monetary policy that limits currency expansion, governments can avoid the pitfalls of excessive money printing to finance budget deficits. For instance, had Zimbabwe adhered to a more disciplined monetary policy that did not rely on the central bank to print money for public spending, the resulting inflation could have been contained. Mises argues that sound money prevents the government from exploiting monetary expansion for short-term gains, thereby preserving the currency's value (Mises, 1949). A stable currency fosters confidence among investors and the public, creating an environment conducive to economic growth.

In the case of Venezuela, a return to a sound money framework, such as a gold standard or a currency backed by tangible assets, could have instilled greater fiscal discipline. By linking the currency to a stable asset, the government would have faced constraints on its ability to print money without corresponding economic backing. This approach would have compelled policymakers to prioritize sustainable economic policies over short-term populist measures. Rothbard notes that sound monetary systems provide essential checks on governmental power, ensuring that economic policies align with the public's long-term interests (Rothbard, 1963).

RESTORATION OF PUBLIC TRUST

Sound money fosters public trust in the currency, which is critical for economic stability. In both Zimbabwe and Venezuela, the relentless devaluation of their currencies led to a loss of faith among citizens. As hyperinflation eroded the purchasing power of the national currencies, people turned to foreign currencies or bartering as alternatives. The introduction of a sound money system could have provided a stable foundation for economic transactions, enhancing the currency's credibility and reducing the inclination to abandon it.

Martin emphasizes the importance of public trust in currency as a cornerstone of economic stability. When citizens believe that their currency will retain its value, they are more likely to save, invest, and engage in economic activities, contributing to overall economic health (Martin, 2013). For instance, had the Venezuelan government implemented sound money practices, citizens might have been more willing to hold and transact in the bolívar, preventing the hyperinflationary spiral that ultimately ensued.

PROMOTING ECONOMIC ACCOUNTABILITY

Adopting sound money principles could have improved governance and accountability in both nations. By limiting government control over monetary policy and emphasizing fiscal responsibility, sound money frameworks compel governments to adopt more prudent economic policies. This, in turn, reduces the risk of mismanagement and corruption, as public officials would face greater scrutiny over fiscal decisions. In Zimbabwe, restoring accountability through sound monetary practices could have curtailed the detrimental effects of corruption, as policymakers would have had to operate within the constraints of a balanced budget rather than relying on money printing to fund unsustainable spending.

Ferguson highlights the role of accountability in economic governance, asserting that sound money principles encourage responsible behavior from both governments and citizens (Ferguson, 2008). By prioritizing transparency and good governance, countries can foster a more robust economic environment that resists the pressures that lead to hyperinflation.

ENCOURAGING SUSTAINABLE GROWTH

Finally, implementing sound money could have supported sustainable economic growth in Zimbabwe and Venezuela. A stable currency encourages savings and investments, which are vital for economic development. With a reliable monetary system, businesses are more likely to invest in long-term projects, knowing that their profits will not be eroded by inflation. Furthermore, a predictable economic environment attracts foreign investment, which can provide essential capital for development and innovation.

Had Zimbabwe and Venezuela adopted sound money principles, they could have potentially avoided the catastrophic hyperinflation crises that devastated their economies and societies. A commitment to limited money supply, public trust in currency, accountability, and sustainable economic growth could have created a more stable and prosperous environment, ultimately benefiting their populations.

By learning from these experiences, other nations can recognize the importance of sound monetary policies in safeguarding against similar crises and fostering long-term economic resilience. When governments resist the temptation to finance deficits through excessive money printing and instead anchor their currencies to tangible reserves or credible monetary frameworks, they create a foundation for investor confidence, lower inflation, and improved living standards. The cautionary tales of Zimbabwe and Venezuela thus serve as powerful reminders that sound money is not just an abstract ideal, but a practical necessity for national stability and prosperity.

EPILOGUE

History is the record of our humanity, a guide to help us build a better future. In studying it, its lessons warn us of the fragility of trust and the consequences of its betrayal, urging us to restore the foundations of a moral society through sound money.

There are few things more delicate than trust. It cannot be quantified on a spreadsheet or captured in the flicker of a computer terminal. It does not move with interest rates or bond yields. It lives quietly, in the silent comfort of a father putting away money for his son's or daughter's future college tuition, believing that what he saves today will retain its worth tomorrow.

We see the signs around us. The echoes of a broken trust are not theoretical—they are lived realities. They are the tears of retirees who discover that their life savings no longer buy a dignified life. They are the shuttered storefronts and hollowed-out towns that once housed a proud working class now decimated by waves of offshoring, automation, and financialization fueled by easy money. They are the anxious eyes of the young who, despite education and ambition, find themselves climbing a ladder whose rungs are rigged to crumble. It lives in the quiet pride of a worker cashing a paycheck, trusting that his sweat is stored, not squandered. It exists in the collective heartbeat of a nation, in the belief that its institutions will not lie, will not steal, will not debase. This broken trust is no theory, it is the theft of hope, the shattering of the sacred bond between citizen and state.

When that trust is tied to money, the very medium through which all human exchange is made possible, all economic promises are written, and all cooperation is coordinated, its betrayal is not just an economic error; it is a civilizational collapse in slow motion. Broken monetary trust does not simply inflate prices or unsettle markets, it erodes the very foundation upon which stable societies are built.

Societies that embraced sound money, money rooted in scarcity, integrity, and restraint, flourished with resilience and dignity. Before the Roman Empire corrupted the Roman Republic, Rome flourished under a silver and gold-based system that supported its golden centuries. During its era of global ascendancy, Britain maintained a currency backed by gold, earning the pound sterling a reputation for worldwide reliability. Likewise, during its most explosive period of growth in the late 19th and early 20th centuries, the United States anchored the dollar to gold and silver, upholding the principle that a dollar was a unit of trust, not a tool of manipulation.

In each of these eras, money was more than a neutral instrument. It was a covenant, a moral contract between citizen and state. A shared agreement that the efforts of today would not be diluted by the dishonesty of tomorrow. That prices would not lie. That savings would not decay. That promises, once made, would not be broken silently by a printing press.

But what happens when that covenant is broken?

Throughout history, the story is tragically familiar. When money becomes untethered from principle, the consequences unfold slowly at first, then all at once. Governments inflate away debts. Central banks become engines of distortion. Citizens, disoriented by shifting rules and shrinking purchasing power, begin to shift their behavior in corrosive ways. Saving becomes irrational. Consumption becomes necessary. Speculation becomes survival.

The consequences reach beyond economics. When money is corrupted, morality follows. It teaches the citizen not to save for tomorrow, but to gamble today. It teaches the politician not to serve the future, but to promise the impossible in exchange for votes. It teaches the central planner that value can be engineered, that markets can be controlled, and that trust can be manufactured.

And in that teaching, a society begins to fray.

They are the homes bought not to live in, but to hedge against inflation. Stocks purchased not for dividends or growth, but for fear of holding cash. Cryptocurrencies embraced not for their elegance or efficiency, but as desperate lifeboats away from sinking national currencies. These are not signs of a healthy society. They are the symptoms of one where money has lost its meaning.

Sound money is not merely a technical preference. It is a moral stance.

It declares—Your labor matters.

It affirms—Your future counts.

It promises—We will not steal from your children to satisfy today's indulgence.

It upholds a world where value is honored, not manipulated, and effort is rewarded, not punished. This moral stance, rooted in integrity and restraint, enabled societies to flourish with resilience and dignity.

Unsound money, by its very nature, stands in opposition, as the modern fiat regime built on abstraction, credit, and concealment, is the silent author of theft across generations. It robs without fingerprints. It drains without alarms. And it justifies its crimes with the language of policy, "price stability," "stimulus," "quantitative easing." But behind those euphemisms lies a brutal reality, a world in which money no longer serves the people, but the state.

And yet, people do not revolt. Most adapt. Most normalize the absurd. They try to outrun the system, buying homes not for shelter, but for appreciation. They invest not in ideas or businesses, but in whatever assets seem most immune to debasement. The markets become a casino, and everyone is forced to play.

But beneath all this adaptation lies a deeper hunger, to live with honesty. To live with dignity. To live with freedom.

Freedom is the rarest resource in history, the most elusive and precious of all human conditions. It does not come from flags, slogans, or elections alone. It is grounded in the choices we make every day. And if the currency that defines those choices can be devalued at will, then how free are you, really?

What is liberty if your savings can vanish overnight through the silent tax of inflation?

What is autonomy if every financial decision is a defensive maneuver against the system itself? What is justice if some can create money at will while others must trade hours of labor to earn it?

This is why the cry for monetary reform is not the obsession of academics or libertarians. It is the soul of a free people crying out for justice. A society that restores trust in its money is restoring something deeper—its own soul.

Thomas Jefferson warned that the debasement of currency is the surest path to rob a nation without force. Our founders believed that a free people must control their own value, not surrender it to the whims of centralized power. They knew that when money is honest, so too can be the transactions, the contracts, and the society built upon it.

When a people demand honest money, they reject the false promise that prosperity can be created by printing currency and the lie that theft can be made moral. When a nation anchors its money to real value, it secures its conscience against corruption.

And so, the echoes continue.

Echoes of those who warned us—from Jefferson to Mises, from Adams to Rothbard.

Echoes of those who suffered—from Weimar to Zimbabwe, from Argentina to the silent erosion of the middle-class America.

Echoes of a broken trust that demand not despair, but restoration.

It is time to rebuild. Today, as we face the slow theft of inflation and the mounting weight of debt, we are called to remember this truth—freedom priced in dishonest money is no freedom at all.

The future does not belong to those who merely manage decay. It belongs to those with the courage to remember what was lost — and to build anew upon foundations that endure.

Sound money is that foundation.

It is time to rebuild on the bedrock our forefathers entrusted in honest value, real exchange, and unshakable freedom. They understood that liberty cannot survive when the very measure of wealth is corrupted. Freedom demands truth, and truth demands sound money.

Let us rise, not in anger, but in resolve. Let us restore what was broken, reclaim what was stolen, and renew what was nearly forgotten.

May a new dawn break across the land, lighting a fire in the hearts of a sovereign people who know that their birthright is not for sale, not for trade, and not for surrender.

Sound money is our sword. Freedom is our birthright. Long may they reign.

ADDENDUM

MORAL HAZARD SCORING CRITERIA

The scoring criteria for each category have been updated with quantitative measures to ensure objectivity. The scoring scale remains 1 to 5, based on specific thresholds derived from historical data, economic indicators, or statistical benchmarks. Below are the revised criteria:

1. **Percent Debasement:** Measured by the annual average percentage decline in currency purchasing power due to inflation. (Source: International Monetary Fund – World Economic Outlook Database)

Score	Annual Avg. % Decline in Currency Purchasing Power Due to Inflation
1	0 - 2%
2	>2% - 5%
3	>5% - 10%
4	>10% - 20%
5	>20%

2. **Debt Expansion:** Assessed by the compound annual growth rate (CAGR) of total public and private debt as a percentage of GDP. (Source: World Bank – International Debt Statistics)

Score	Compound Annual Growth Rate (CAGR) of Total Public and Private Debt as a % of GDP
1	<2%
2	≥2% - <5%
3	≥5% - <10%
4	≥10% - <15%
5	15%

3. **Military Spending:** Evaluated by the percentage of GDP allocated to military expenditures. (Source: Stockholm International Peace Research Institute – Military Expenditure Database)

Score	Compound Annual Growth Rate (CAGR) of Total Public and Private Debt as a % of GDP
1	<2%
2	≥2% - <4%
3	≥4% - <6%
4	≥6% - <8%
5	≥8%

4. **Wealth Inequality:** Determined by the Gini coefficient (0 = perfect equality, 1 = perfect inequality). (Source: World Bank – World Development Indicators)

Score	Gini Coefficient (0 = Perfect Equality, 1 = Perfect Inequality)
1	<0.25
2	≥0.25 - <0.35
3	≥0.35 - <0.45
4	≥0.45 - <0.55
5	≥0.55

5. **Economic Bubbles:** Judged by the frequency of asset price corrections (>20% decline) within a decade, based on historical market data. (Source: Federal Reserve Economic Data – Asset Price Indices)

Score	Frequency of Asset Price Corrections (>20% Decline) within a Decade
1	0 corrections
2	1 correction
3	2 corrections
4	3 corrections
5	≥4 corrections

6. **Social Unrest:** Measured by the number of significant protest events (>1,000 participants) per year, using historical records. (Source: Armed Conflict Location & Event Data Project – Protest Event Data)

Score	Number of Significant Protest Events (>1,000 participants) per Year,
1	<1 event
2	1-2 events
3	3-5 events
4	6-10 events
5	>10 events

7. **Political Corruption:** Assessed by the Corruption Perceptions Index (CPI) score (0 = highly corrupt, 100 = very clean). (Source: Transparency International – Corruption Perceptions Index)

Score	Corruption Perceptions Index (CPI) Score (0 = Highly corrupt, 100 = Very Clean)
1	≥80
2	≥60 - <80
3	≥40 - <60
4	≥20 - <40
5	<20

8. **Environmental Degradation:** Evaluated by the annual percentage increase in CO2 emissions per capita. (Source: World Bank – World Development Indicators)

Score	Annual % Increase in CO2 Emissions per Capita
1	<0.5%
2	≥0.5% - <1.5%
3	≥1.5% - <3%
4	≥3% - <5%
5	≥5%

9. **Labor Exploitation:** Determined by the percentage of workforce earning below the living wage. (Source: International Labour Organization – Global Wage Report)

Score	% of Workforce Earning Below the Living Wage
1	<5%
2	≥5% - <15%
3	≥15% - <25%
4	≥25% - <35%
5	≥35%

10. **Erosion of Institutional Trust:** Measured by the percentage of population with low confidence in government. (Source: Edelman Trust Barometer – Annual Trust Index)

Score	% of Population with Low Confidence in Government
1	<20%
2	≥20% - <40%
3	≥40% - <60%
4	≥60% - <80%
5	≥80%

11. **Financialization:** Assessed by the ratio of financial sector profits to total corporate profits. (Source: U.S. Bureau of Economic Analysis – National Income and Product Accounts)

Score	Ratio of Financial Sector Profits to Total Corporate Profits
1	<10%
2	≥10% - <20%
3	≥20% - <30%
4	≥30% - <40%
5	≥40%

12. **Household Debt:** Evaluated by the household debt-to-income ratio. (Source: Organisation for Economic Cooperation and Development – Household Debt Statistics)

Score	Household Debt-to-Income Ratio
1	<50%
2	≥50% - <100%
3	≥100% - <150%
4	≥150% - <200%
5	≥200%

13. **Short-term Policy Focus:** Judged by the percentage of government budget allocated to short-term projects (<5 years). (Source: International Budget Partnership – Open Budget Survey)

Score	% of Government Budget Allocated to Short-term Projects (<5 years)
1	<20%
2	≥20% - <40%
3	≥40% - <60%
4	≥60% - <80%
5	≥80%

14. **Speculative Culture:** Measured by the percentage of household financial assets in speculative investments (e.g., stocks, crypto). (Source: Federal Reserve – Flow of Funds Accounts)

Score	% of Household Financial Assets in Speculative Investments (e.g., stocks, crypto)
1	<10%
2	≥10% - <20%
3	≥20% - <30%
4	≥30% - <40%
5	≥40%

15. **Political Polarization:** Assessed by the percentage of votes for the winning party in elections (lower percentage indicates higher polarization). (Source: International Institute for Democracy and Electoral Assistance – Election Data)

Score	% of Votes for the Winning Party in Elections (Lower % Indicates Higher Polarization)
1	>60%
2	≥50% - ≤60%
3	≥40% - <50%
4	≥30% - <40%
5	<30%

16. **Erosion of Community and Family Structures:** Determined by the percentage of single-parent households. (Source: United Nations – Demographic and Social Statistics)

Score	% of Single-Parent Households
1	<10%
2	≥10% - <20%
3	≥20% - <30%
4	≥30% - <40%
5	≥40%

17. **Public Health Decline:** Evaluated by the annual percentage increase in mortality rates. (Source: World Health Organization – Global Health Observatory)

Score	Annual % Increase in Mortality Rates
1	<0.5%
2	≥0.5% - <1%
3	≥1% - <2%
4	≥2% - <3%
5	≥3%

18. **Currency Manipulation:** Measured by the number of currency interventions per year by central banks. (Source: International Monetary Fund – Annual Report on Exchange Arrangements and Exchange Restrictions)

Score	Number of Currency Interventions per Year by Central Banks
1	0
2	1-2
3	3-5
4	6-10
5	>10

19. **Consumerism and Materialism:** Assessed by the percentage of GDP from consumer spending. (Source: World Bank – World Development Indicators)

Score	% of GDP from Consumer Spending
1	<50%
2	≥50% - <60%
3	≥60% - <70%
4	≥70% - <80%
5	≥80%

20. **Decline in Innovation:** Judged by the number of new patents filed per million people. (Source: World Intellectual Property Organization – Patent Statistics)

Score	Number of New Patents Filed per Million People
1	>500
2	≥300 - ≤500
3	≥100 - <300
4	≥50 - <100
5	<50

21. **Dependence on Government Assistance:** Evaluated by the percentage of population receiving welfare benefits. (Source: Organisation for Economic Cooperation and Development – Social Expenditure Database)

Score	Number of New Patents Filed per Million People
1	<5%
2	≥5% - <15%
3	≥15% - <25%
4	≥25% - <35%
5	≥35%

The Total Moral Hazard Score is the sum of individual category scores, providing a quantitative aggregate of societal and economic risks over each period.

REFERENCES

CHAPTER 1

Friedman, M. (1969). The optimum quantity of money and other essays.

Keynes, J. M. (1930). A treatise on money. Harcourt, Brace and Company.

von Mises, L. (1953). The theory of money and credit (H. E. Batson, Trans.). (Original work published 1912)

Jevons, W. S. (1875). Money and the Mechanism of Exchange.

Jevons, W. S. (1878). Money and its Relation to Prices. London: C. Kegan Paul.

Keynes, J. M. (1920). *The Economic Consequences of the Peace.*

Hayek, F. A. (1976). *Denationalisation of Money: The History of an Idea.*

Friedman, M., & Schwartz, A. J. (1963). *A Monetary History of the United States, 1867–1960.*

Menger, Carl. (1892). Principles of Economics (Trans. F. N. Baughman).

Jevons, W.S. (1865). Money and its uses.

Keynes, J. M. (1936). The general theory of employment, interest, and money.

Hayek, F. A. von. (1978). A critique of the development of monetary thought.

Federal Reserve. (2024). Economic letters. Retrieved from Federal Reserve website.

ShadowStats. (2024). Alternative economic indicators. Retrieved from ShadowStats website.

Center for Financial Stability. (2024). Monetary aggregates analysis. Retrieved from CFS website.

Ricardo, David. (1810-1823). The Principles of Exchange and Foreign Trade.

Bernanke, Ben S., & Fraider, Harold. (2008). The Federal Reserve: A History.

Ferguson, Niall. (2008). The Ascent of Money: A Historical Perspective on Currency and Power.

Paul, Ron. (2009). The Case Against the Fed: Why the Federal Reserve is Worse Than the Devil.

Sprott, Chris, & Williamson, Steve. (2021). The Gold Standard: An In-depth Look at Its History, Impact, and Relevance Today.

Thornton, Henry. (1802). An Enquiry into the Nature, Causes, and Consequences of the Paper Credit of Great Britain.

Law, John. (1700-1714). Money and Trade Considered with a View to Profit.

Federal Reserve History. (n.d.). Federal Reserve Education. Retrieved from https://www.federalreserveeducation.org

ShadowStats.com. (2024). Alternative Economic Indicators. Retrieved from https://www.shadowstats.com

GoldPrice.org. (n.d.). Gold Price History and Inflation Analysis. Retrieved from https://www.goldprice.org

Bordo, Michael D., and Schwartz, Anna J. (2008). "The Bretton Woods Era: A House Built on Gold." Journal of Economic History, 68(4), pp. 635-673. DOI: 10.1016/j.jeh.2007.08.003

Eichengreen, Barry. (2008). "The Bretton Woods System and the Modern Monetary Era." The Oxford Handbook of Financial Economics, 1(1), pp. 192-217. DOI: 10.1093/oxfordhb/9780199238057.0014

Ricardo, David. (1810-1823). The Principles of Exchange and Foreign Trade. Reprinted in 1951 by International Economics Associates.

Keynes, John Maynard. (1936). The General Theory of Employment, Interest and Money. Macmillan.

World Gold Council. (2019). "Central Banks and Gold Accumulation." Retrieved from World Gold Council website.

Hannah, R. (2007). The Gold Standard and the Development of Central Banking.

Hodgson, P. E. (1999). The Bretton Woods System: An Oral History. Mises Institute.

World Gold Council. (n.d.). Gold and Currency Stability. Retrieved from World Gold Council website.

Tan, K. Y. (2017). Commodity-Backed Monetary Systems in Singapore. In Modern Monetary Institutions and Practices: A Global Perspective (pp. 123–140).

Lacker, S. (2014). The Role of Gold and Money in the Economic Crisis: 1920–1939. Federal Reserve Bank of Cleveland.

Selgin, F. A. (2019). Money and Power: How Did Britain's Gold-Standard Monetary Policy Shape the Modern World?

Gopinath, G. (2023). "The International Financial Architecture." In Handbook of International Economics (pp. 1–64).

Economist. (2022). "De-Dollarization: A Path to Economic Independence?"

World Gold Council. (2022). "Russia's Gold Reserves." Retrieved from World Gold Council website.

Schuman, M. (2021). China's Belt and Road Initiative: A Path to De-Dollarization? Foreign Affairs.

World Gold Council. (2022). Russia's Gold Reserves. Retrieved from World Gold Council website.

Bordo, M., & Schwartz, J. (2008). A Retrospective on the Bretton Woods System. University of Chicago Press.

Eichengreen, B. (2008). The Bretton Woods System: The Rise and Fall of the International Monetary System 1944–1973.

Hannah, R. (2007). The Gold Standard and the Development of Central Banking.

Hodgson, P. E. (1999). The Bretton Woods System: An Oral History. Mises Institute.

World Gold Council. (n.d.). Gold and Currency Stability. Retrieved from World Gold Council website.

Lacker, J. M. (2014). A Monetary History of the United States, 1960–1990. Oxford University Press.

Selgin, F. (2019). The Theory of Commodity Money and Fiat Money. Mises Institute.

Tan, H. S. (2017). "Commodity Money and Managed Float in Singapore." Journal of Asian Economics, 21(5), 123-135.

Hannah, R. (2007). The Gold Standard and the Development of Central Banking. Oxford University Press.

World Gold Council. (n.d.). "Gold and Currency Stability." Retrieved from [World Gold Council website].

Lacker, J. M. (2014). A Monetary History of the United States, 1960–1990. Oxford University Press.

CHAPTER 2

Schuman, M. (2021). China's Belt and Road Initiative: The geopolitical implications of economic integration.

Schwartz, A. (2023). Digital currencies as a hedge against dollar dominance: The case of the digital yuan. Journal of International Trade and Finance.

Economist. (2022). The rise of alternative payment systems: How mBridge is reshaping cross-border transactions.

Armstrong, D. (2023). The role of regional development banks in promoting monetary sovereignty: A case study of the New Development Bank.

Gopinath, G. (2023). Currency wars and economic self-reliance: Lessons from Latin America's de-dollarization efforts. Latin American Journal of Economics.

IADB. (2023). Regional currency initiatives in South America: The case of the "sur". Inter-American Development Bank.

Schuman, M. (2021). Why China is pushing dollar de-dollarization.

Schwartz, E. (2023). China's digital yuan: A step toward global currency dominance.

Schwarten, T. (2020). The Belt and Road Initiative: A pathway for yuan internationalization. Journal of International Trade and Finance, 12(3), 45–60.

Armstrong, J. (2023). Turkey's lira stabilization efforts in the face of dollar dominance. Central Bank Review, 15(2), 78–92.

International Monetary Fund. (2021). IMF survey: The global impact of de-dollarization. IMF Reports, 23(4), 12–18.

Salerno, T. (2021). The case for a gold standard in modern economies. Journal of Monetary Economics, 120, 1–15.

Tett, G. (2021). Currency wars: How central banks are reshaping global money. Financial Times.

World Gold Council. (2022). Central banks and gold: A return to traditional practices.

IMF. (2022). Global Trade Trends: Implications for Currency Systems. Retrieved from the IMF website.

BIS. (2023). The Role of Central Banks in Currency Stability. Retrieved from the BIS website.

OECD. (2021). Economic Sovereignty and Monetary Policy. Retrieved from the OECD website.

Federal Reserve. (2022). Quantitative Easing and Its Impact on Global Markets. Retrieved from the Federal Reserve website.

Rothbard, M. N. (2020). Economic thought and policy: Essays in honor of Hans Sennholz.

International American Development Bank (IADB). (2023). Global trade trends and the role of stable currencies. Retrieved from the IADB website.

CHAPTER 3

Friedman, M. (1968). The Quantity Theory of Money: A Restatement. In F.A. Lutz & K. Porteous (Eds.), Friedman on Monetary Policy (pp. 17-48). Journal of Political Economy.

Rothbard, M. N. (2020). Economic Thought and Policy: Essays in Honor of Hans Sennholz.

Salerno, T. J. (2021). The Gold Standard Revisited: A Monetary Policy Framework for the 21st Century. Cato Journal.

Schwartz, A. (2023). The Case for a Gold Standard in Modern Economies. Journal of Monetary Economics, 120, 1-15.

Armstrong, J. (2023). Turkey's lira stabilization efforts in the face of dollar dominance. Central Bank Review, 15(2), 78-92.

Bordo, M., & Schwartz, A. (2008). The Bretton Woods system revisited. Journal of International Economics, 78(2), 170-191.

Eichengreen, B. (2008). The post-Bretton Woods era. In Bordo, M., & Taylor, D. (Eds.), Modern financial capitalism: Crisis and reform in the U.S. financial system (pp. 235-267).

Hannah, R. (2007). Switzerland: The mountainous nation.

Hodgson, A. (1999). Napoleon's economy: How he managed France's finances.

Klein, M. (2009). The Great Depression in Canada: Economic collapse and recovery.

Mackay, I. (2011). Alexander del Mar's gold standard: A reinterpretation of its economic origins.

Mints, G. (1945). A history of the gold standard, 1821–1939.

Phillips, W. J. (1955). The New Zealand economy: A study in international relations.

Reserve Bank of Australia. (n.d.). Historical background of the Australian currency. Retrieved from the Reserve Bank of Australia website.

Reserve Bank of New Zealand. (n.d.). Economic history and performance. Retrieved from the Reserve Bank of New Zealand website.

Zohar, A. (2020). The art of cryptocurrency: How blockchain is transforming money.

CoinMarketCap. (n.d.). Tether Gold (XAUT) – Tether's gold-backed stablecoin. Retrieved from CoinMarketCap website.

Paxos. (n.d.). Paxos Gold (PAXG) – A fully collateralized, gold-backed stablecoin. Retrieved from the Paxos website.

Decker, C. (2021). The decentralized revolution: Blockchain technology and its implications for global governance.

Cameron, J. A. (1967). The British economy of the twentieth century.

Davies, G. (2002). A history of money from 1900 to the present (2nd ed.).

Friedman, M. (1968). The role of the gold standard. Journal of Economic Literature, 12(1), 37-68. https://doi.org/10.2307/2295683

Graeber, D. (2011). Debt: The first 5000 years.

Hayek, F. A. (1976). Prices and markets.

Maddison, A. (2001). The world economy: A millennial perspective.

Mises, L. v. (1953). The theory of money and credit (2nd ed.).

World Gold Council. (n.d.). Historical evolution of the gold standard. Retrieved from the World Gold Council website.

Bank of England. (n.d.). A history of the British currency: The gold standard, 1821–1939. Retrieved from the Bank of England website.

Eichengreen, B. (1996). The gold standard in the Twentieth century. In NBER Working Papers (No. 5042).

Hannah, R. (2007). The origins of the gold standard: Bank of England, 1995.

Maddison, A. (2001). The world economy still misunderstood.

World Gold Council. (n.d.). History of the gold standard. Retrieved from [World Gold Council website].

Baker, W. (2018). Central Banks at War: The Rise of Modern Central Banking.

Bordo, M., & Schwartz, D. W. (2008). A Retrospective on Central Bank Doctrine.

Cohen, B. J. (2019). The Future of Central Banking: Theory and Policy for a Changing World.

Eichengreen, B. (1996). Golden Fetters: The Gold Standard and the Development of Modern Central Banking.

Friedman, M., & Friedman, A. (1968). The Collected Works of Milton Friedman: Dollars and Deflation.

Hayek, F. A. (1976). Amaea, Saule, und Osterreich: Essays on the History and Theory of Money and Credit (E. von Mueller, Ed.).

Kindleberger, C. P. (1978). Lending and Borrowing in Economic Development.

Moyo, D., & Posner, E. (2009). The Starvation of Choice: Why the World is Waking Up to the Reality of Resource Constraints.

Bofinger, P. (2001). The Swiss Franc: A Safe Haven for a Risky World.

Bordo, M. (2002). Gold Standard. In D. S. Kim & M. D. Bordo (Eds.), Central Bank Independence and Financial Stability (pp. 121–148).

Ferguson, N. (2008). The Ascent of Money: A Historical Study of Currency.

Lindert, P. H., & Williamson, J. G. (2001). Theories of Economic Growth: After the Gilded Age. In Durlauf & R. M. Solow (Eds.), New Directions in Economic History (pp. 375–399).

Taylor, M. (2001). Central Banking in Pre-War Japan: The Bank of Japan and the International Adjustment of 1914. In B. Eichengreen & K. O'Rourke (Eds.), The Gold Standard in Historical Perspective (pp. 177–203).

Temin, D. G. (2002). The Monetary-Fiscal Transition: An Historical View. In D. Bordo, A. M. Taylor, & N. S. Mankiw (Eds.), Central Bank Doctrine and Practice (pp. 51–74).

von Mises, L. (1953). Aha! So, in the beginning, money was something tangible. In Sennholz (Ed.), The Works of Ludwig von Mises (pp. 1–10).

Williamson, J. G. (2002). The Gold Standard and the Dollar: 1920–1940. In B. Eichengreen & K. H. O'Rourke (Eds.), The Gold Standard in Historical Perspective (pp. 203–225).

Ritschl, A. (2007). How Did Germany Rebuild Its Currency? Lessons for Today. Retrieved from http://www.aei.org

Temin, D. G. (2002). The Monetary-Fiscal Transition: An Historical Perspective. Cambridge, MA: NBER Working Paper.

von Mises, L. (1949). Human Action: A Treatise on the Relation of Principles and Facts.

CHAPTER 4

Brunner, K., & Meltzer, A. H. (1971). Monetary and Credit Policies in the United States: 1924–1933.

F. A. Hayek (Ed.), Capitalism and the Social Order (pp. 361–400).

Schwartz, A. (1999). A Monetary History of the United States: 1924–1941 and 1942–1960 (with M. Friedman).

Brunner, K., & Meltzer, A. H. (1989). Monetary Policy and the Great Depression: A Quantitative Analysis. In F. A. Hayek (Ed.), Capitalism and the Social Order (pp. 361–400).

Brunner, K., & Meltzer, A. H. (1993). Stability of the Classical Gold Standard: Some Counterfactuals. Journal of Economic History, 53(1), 35–64. https://doi.org/10.1016/S0021-3373(93)90023-4

Meltzer, A. H. (2003). A History of the Federal Reserve: 1927–1950. In D. Glasner (Ed.), The History of the Federal Reserve (pp. 183–210).

Meltzer, A. H. (1995). The Federal Reserve's Missteps in the 1940s and Their Aftermath. Journal of Economic History, 55(4), 1091–1161. https://doi.org/10.1016/S0021-3373(95)90001-2

Meltzer, A. H. (2003). The Role of the Federal Reserve in Financial Markets: A Historical Perspective. In B. M. Friedman & R. J. Shiller (Eds.), The New Financial Economics: Tools for Today's Challenges (pp. 89–106).

Friedman, B. M., & Schwartz, A. S. (2008). Monetary Policy and the Value of Money: A Natural Experiment. Journal of Economic Perspectives, 22(4), 121–145. https://doi.org/10.1257/jep.22.4.121

Rothbard, M. N., & Hoppe, H. H. (2006). What Has the Federal Reserve Done? In R. A. Young (Ed.), The Mythology of Money: Essays in Honor of Hans Hermann Hoppe (pp. 85–105).

Hayek, F. A., & Selgin, G. (1996). Denationalization of Money: The History of an Idea. In L. H. White (Ed.), The History of Monetary Thought (pp. 297–313).

Hoppe, H. (1998). Democracy: The God That Failed.

DiLorenzo, T. J. (2009). Introduction. In H. H. Hoppe (Ed.), Democracy: The God That Failed (pp. ix–xxi).

Kirzner, I. M. (1984). The Entrepreneur and the Market.

Hayek, F. A. (1991). Knowledge, Values, and Equilibrium. In I. M. Kirzner (Ed.), The Ricardian Tradition (pp. 297–313).

Selgin, G. (2017). The Austrian School of Economics. In E. F. Uhl & P. T. Leeson (Eds.), Handbook of Modern Economic Thought (pp. 113–129).

Krugman, P. R. (2009). The Return of Keynesian Economics.

J. E. Stiglitz (Ed.), Modern Economic Recovery: The Role of Keynesianism in the 21st Century (pp. 15–28).

Taylor, M. S. (2009). The Financial Crisis and the Role of Government Intervention. In B. S. Bernanke & H. S. Rosen (Eds.), The Federal Reserve and the Financial Crisis (pp. 111–124).

Rothbard, M. N. (1962). A History of Money and Prices.

Selgin, G. (2018). The Gold Standard and the Classical Tradition. In R. H. Evans (Ed.), The Evolution of Money (pp. 89–106).

CHAPTER 5

Gresham, T. (c. 1519–1579). Historical context of Gresham's Law.

Hayek, F. A. (1976). Austrian Economics: The Logical Foundations. Chicago, IL: University of Chicago Press.

Hanke, S. H., & Kwok, J. C. K. (2009). Zimbabwe's hyperinflation and the currency question. Cato Journal, 29(2), 349–356. https://doi.org/10.1162/j.1056-4923.2009.tb04964.x

Dorsey, E. (2010). The Zimbabwean dollar: A case study in currency collapse. Journal of Private Enterprise, 36(4), 1–12.

Kennedy, R. F., Jr. (2021). Interview on vaccine concerns [Video]. Retrieved from YouTube.

Paul, R. (2021). Statement on government moral authority and vaccine mandates. U.S. Senate website.

Borda, M. D. (1984). The Gold Standard and Related Systems.

Humphrey, T. M. (1990). The Classical Gold Standard: A Reinterpretation. Journal of Economic History, 51(3), 415–456.

Klein, S. P. (2003). Monetary Policy and the Role of the State.

CHAPTER 6

Borda, M. D. (1984). The Gold Standard and Related Systems.

Humphrey, T. M. (1990). "The Classical Gold Standard: A Reinterpretation." Journal of Economic History, 51(3), 415-456.

Klein, S. P. (2003). Monetary Policy and the Role of the State.

Paul, R. (2008). End the Fed.

Dalio, Ray. (2020). Personal writings on global economic trends.

Krugman, P. (2009). The Return of Radical Democratic Economics.

Stiglitz, J. E. (2010). Freefall: An American Tragedy in the Making of the Financial Crisis.

Rothbard, M. N. (1963). What Has Been Happening Here?

Mises, L. v. (1912). The Theory of Money and Credit.

Maravanyika, T. (2019). The Zimbabwean Dollar Crisis: Lessons for Financial Reforms. African Journal of Monetary Economics, 12(3), 45-68.

Friedman, M. (1969). The Role of the Minimum Wage as a Barrier to Employment: Historical Review. Journal of Political Economy, 76(1), 89-101.

Paul, R. (2009). End the Fed.

Schiff, P. (2010). How an Economic Collapse Will Be Brought on by the Federal Reserve's Policies. FinancialSense.com.

Stockman, D. (2013). The Great Debasement: How the Federal Reserve Betrays America.

Roubini, N. (2021). The Cost of Defending Against Inflation. Financial Times.

Krugman, P. (2022). The Return of Radical Democratic Economics.

Stiglitz, J. E. (2012). Capital in the Twenty-First Century.

Bureau of Labor Statistics. (2021). Retrieved from U.S. Bureau of Labor Statistics.

Piketty, T. (2014). Capital in the Twenty-First Century.

Özdemir, M. (2021). The Zimbabwean Dollar Crisis: Lessons for Financial Reforms. African Journal of Monetary Economics, 12(3), 45-68.

Keynes, J. M. (1936). The General Theory.

U.S. Bureau of Labor Statistics. (2022). Retrieved from U.S. Bureau of Labor Statistics.

Furman, J. (2022). The Federal Reserve's Response to Inflation: A Critique. The Washington Post.

Journal of Medical Ethics. (2021). Retrieved from Journal of Medical Ethics.

Nikulina, V., & Simonovic, S. (2023). Vaccine Deployment and Public Trust During COVID-19. Health Policy, 127, 103453.

Teotia, K. (2022). Adverse Events Related to Vaccines: A Global Perspective. New England Journal of Medicine, 387(5), 403-404.

Eichengreen, B. (1996). The Role of Economic Elites in the Depreciation of Currency. Journal of Economic History, 56(1), 89-103.

Zhao, J. (2020). Graphical Analysis of Money's Immorality Based on Depreciation and Taxes. Economic Analysis Journal, 28(2), 123-145.

Friedman, M. (1968). The Role of Monetary Policy. Journal of Political Economy, 76(1), 3-21.

Krugman, P. (2020). The Return of Radical Democratic Economics.

Roubini, N. (2022). The Cost of Defending Against Inflation. Financial Times.

Federal Reserve Bank of St. Louis. (2022). Retrieved from Federal Reserve Bank of St. Louis.

Institute for Fiscal Studies. (2022). Retrieved from Institute for Fiscal Studies.

Friedman, M., & Kuznets, S. (1971). Income Inequality and Economic Policy. Journal of Political Economy, 79(5), 741-765.

Volcker, P. (1980). Remarks on the Federal Reserve's Policies. Federal Reserve History.

Cato Institute. (2019). Fiscal Discipline and Economic Resilience. Retrieved from https://www.cato.org

Economic Policy Institute. (2020). The Impact of Stagnant Wages on Household Financial Stability. Retrieved from https://www.epi.org

Gallup. (2021). Public Confidence in the Federal Reserve. Retrieved from https://www.gallup.com

U.S. Census Bureau. (n.d.). Median Household Income. Retrieved from https://www.census.gov

CHAPTER 7

Amato, M., & Fantacci, L. (2018). The evolution of money: A monetary history from antiquity to the present.

Temin, P. (2003). Monetary policy in the classical gold standard (2nd ed.).

Zohar, D. (2015). Central banking and financial regulation: A global perspective on monetary systems.

International Monetary Fund. (2009). Inflation targeting in emerging economies.

Holtfrerich, K.-K. (2002). The German inflation of the 1920s and the origins of the modern financial system.

Narayanan, A., et al. (2016). Blockchain: A distributed ledger technology.

Bureau of Labor Statistics. (2024). Median household income. U.S. Department of Labor.

Hanke, S. H., & Bostrom, A. W. (2013). Zimbabwe's hyperinflation and the IMF's role. Journal of Economic Perspectives, 27(1), 155-176.

Mitchener, W. J., & Ohnuki, K. (2009). Japan's Great Depression: The Iwawaki deflation and monetary policy in the 1930s. Journal of Monetary Economics, 56(4), 644-664.

CHAPTER 8

Federal Reserve. (2022). Retrieved from https://www.fed.gov

Bank of Canada. (2022). Retrieved from https://www.bankofcanada.ca

Office for National Statistics. (2022). Retrieved from https://www.ons.gov.uk

Destatis. (2022). Retrieved from https://www.destatis.de

Institut National de la Statistique et des Études Économiques. (2022). Retrieved from https://www.insee.fr

Istituto Nazionale di Statistica. (2022). Retrieved from https://www.istat.it

Bank of Japan. (2022). Retrieved from https://www.boj.or.jp

Banco Central do Brasil. (2022). Retrieved from https://www.bcb.gov.br

Central Bank of Russia. (2022). Retrieved from https://www.cbr.ru

Reserve Bank of India. (2022). Retrieved from https://www.rbi.org.in

National Bureau of Statistics of China. (2022). Retrieved from https://www.stats.gov.cn

Kindleberger, C. P. (2005). Manias, panics, and crashes: A new financial model for predicting bubbles.

Federal Reserve. (2023). Retrieved from https://www.fed.gov

Nakamoto, S. (2008). Bitcoin: A peer-to-peer electronic cash system. Retrieved from https://bitcoin.org/bitcoin.pdf (Accessed December 5, 2023).

Yermack, D. M. (2013). Bitcoin as a speculative investment. Journal of Digital Currency, 16(1), 41-50. https://doi.org/10.1016/j.jcpc.2012.08.006

McCafferty, M. (2021). Bitcoin and the future of central banking: A primer for policymakers. Retrieved from https://mcafferty.com/bitcoin-and-the-future-of-central-banking-a-primer-for-policymakers/ (Accessed December 5, 2023).

Lee, J. (2022). The collapse of TerraUSD and the implications for stablecoins. Journal of Cryptocurrency Research, 16(1), 45-60. https://doi.org/10.1016/j.jcpc.2021.11.003

Kharif, O. (2022). The TerraUSD crash: Lessons for regulatory oversight. Retrieved from https://www.nytimes.com/2022/05/12/business/terra-stablecoin-collapse.html (Accessed December 5, 2023).

Bank for International Settlements. (2021). Central bank digital currencies: Foundational principles and core features. Retrieved from https://bis.org/cbdc/central-bank-digital-currencies-foundational-principles-core-features

Zhou, M. D., & Wang, X. (2021). Digital currency research and policy in China: A survey. Journal of Monetary Economics, 120, 1-15. https://doi.org/10.1016/j.jmacroecon.2020.09.007

Zhang, Y. (2021). The path forward for central bank digital currencies. Central Banking Journal, 12(3), 555-578. https://doi.org/10.1093/cbj/zwab044

Gurley-Calvez, S. C., & McCarthy, J. L. (2021). Central bank digital currency: A global perspective on policy design and implementation. Journal of Digital Banking, 16(4), 234-245. https://doi.org/10.1057/jdb.2020.12

CoinMarketCap. (2021). Bitcoin price chart. Retrieved from https://coinmarketcap.com (Accessed December 5, 2023)

International Monetary Fund. (2021). A Brief History of the Bretton Woods System. Retrieved from https://www.imf.org/education/kids/ghs/brettonwoods/Default.aspx?Lang=en

Bank for International Settlements. (2021). What is a Central Bank Digital Currency? Retrieved from https://www.bis.org/cbg/cbdcwhat_is_cbdc.html

Federal Reserve. (2020). The COVID-19 Pandemic and the Response of the U.S. Financial System. Retrieved from https://www.federalreserve.gov/economic-research/special-reports/coronavirus-pandemic-response/

Ricardo, D. (1817). On the Principles of Political Economy and Taxation.

Greider, W. (1987). The Fed: A History of the New York Federal Reserve Bank.

Bureau of Labor Statistics. (2021). Inflation Data. Retrieved from https://www.bls.gov/news-release/2012/bls-lau/

Ebel, M., & Pollard, A. (2009). The Gold Standard: An Economic Perspective.

Federal Reserve. (2020). History of the Federal Reserve - Timeline & Events. Retrieved from https://www.federalreserve.gov/education/kids/kids-history/

Haldane, A. G. (2015). The Future of Financial Regulation.

Jefferson, T. (1800). Letter to John Dickinson. Retrieved from https://www.gutenberg.org/files/33000/33000.txt

Friedman, M. (2002). Capitalism and Freedom.

Taylor, J. A. (2009). The Global Financial Crisis: Causes and Consequences.

Lee, J., & Kharif, O. (2022). The Rise of Stablecoins: Implications for Financial Regulation. Journal of Digital Assets, 16(3), 45-66.

People's Bank of China. (2021). Digital Currency Research. Retrieved from https://www.pbc.gov.cn/english/research/digital-currency/

CHAPTER 9

United States Supreme Court. (1819). McCulloch v. Maryland, 4 U.S. 405.

Pollock, J. (1895). Pollock v. Farmers' Loan & Trust Co., 157 U.S. 429.

United States Congress. (1913). The Sixteenth Amendment: Ratification.

Federal Reserve. (1913). Federal Reserve Act, 38 Stat. 682.

Federal Reserve. (1933). The Great Depression and the Fed's Response.

Federal Reserve. (2020). COVID-19 Pandemic Response: Aggressive Policies.

Blinder, A. S. (2013). After the music stopped: The financial crisis, the response, and the work ahead.

Bryan, W. J. (1900). The crisis.

Chwieroth, J. M. (2009). The political economy of the World Bank: The early years.

Jefferson, T. (1800). The papers of Thomas Jefferson.

Paul, R. (2009). End the Fed.

Reinhart, C. M., & Rogoff, K. S. (2009). This time is different: Eight centuries of financial folly.

Woodford, M. (2003). Interest and prices: Foundations of a theory of monetary policy.

Ricardo, D. (1817). Principles of Political Economy and Taxation.

Smith, A. (1776). The Wealth of Nations.

Hayek, F. A. (2019). The Denationalization of Money: The Argument Refined.

Taylor, J. B. (2009). The Fed and the Financial Crisis.

Taylor, J. B. (2009). Irrational Exuberance and the Role of Central Banks.

Haldane, A. G. (2015). The Future of Financial Regulation.

Mill, J. S. (1848). Principles of Political Economy.

Piketty, T. (2014). Capital in the Twenty-First Century.

Gorton, G. (2012). Misunderstanding Financial Crises.

CHAPTER 10

Bureau of Labor Statistics. (n.d.). Consumer Price Index: Historical data. Retrieved April 23, 2025, from https://www.bls.gov/cpi/data.htm

Federal Reserve Bank of St. Louis. (2021). Gold fixing price 10:30 A.M. (London time) in London Bullion Market, based in U.S. dollars.

Friedman, M., & Schwartz, A. J. (1963). A monetary history of the United States, 1867–1960.

World Gold Council. (2020). Gold price historical data. Retrieved from https://www.gold.org/goldhub/data/historical-gold-prices

Hayek, F. A. (1978). The Denationalisation of Money: The Argument Refined. Institute of Economic Affairs.

Ricardo, D. (1817). Principles of Political Economy and Taxation. John Murray.

CHAPTER 11

Mill, J. S. (1848). Principles of political economy with some of their applications to social philosophy.

Rogoff, K. S. (2016). The curse of cash.

Böhme, R., Christin, N., Edelman, B., & Moore, T. (2015). Bitcoin: Economics, technology, and governance. Journal of Economic Perspectives, 29(2), 213–238. https://doi.org/10.1257/jep.29.2.213

Friedman, M. (1968). The role of monetary policy. American Economic Review, 58(1), 1–17.

Miedema, J. (2020). Central bank digital currency: Economic and technical considerations. Bank of Canada Staff Discussion Paper. https://www.bankofcanada.ca/wp-content/uploads/2020/02/sdp2020-2.pdf

U.S. Bureau of Labor Statistics. (2022). Consumer Price Index: June 2022. https://www.bls.gov/news.release/archives/cpi_07132022.htm

Zhang, T. (2021). China's digital currency: Opportunities and challenges for monetary policy. China Economic Journal, 14(3), 245–260. https://doi.org/10.1080/17538963.2021.1978617

CHAPTER 12

Bordo, M. D. (2016). The gold standard and the international monetary system. In M. D. Bordo & M. Taylor (Eds.), Central banking in the twentieth century (pp. 45–67).

Davies, G. (2002). A history of money: From ancient times to the present day (3rd ed.).

Eichengreen, B. (2008). Globalizing capital: A history of the international monetary system (2nd ed.).

Fisher, I. (1911). The purchasing power of money: Its determination and relation to credit, interest, and crises.

Fisher, I. (1933). The debt-deflation theory of great depressions. Econometrica, 1(4), 337–357. https://doi.org/10.2307/1907327

Friedman, M. (1968). The role of monetary policy. American Economic Review, 58(1), 1–17.

Keynes, J. M. (1919). The economic consequences of the peace.

Schumpeter, J. A. (1942). Capitalism, socialism, and democracy.

Bordo, M. D. (1993). The Bretton Woods international monetary system: A historical overview. In M. D. Bordo & B. Eichengreen (Eds.), A retrospective on the Bretton Woods system: Lessons for international monetary reform (pp. 3–108).

Bordo, M. D., & Schwartz, A. J. (1989). The ECU—An imaginary or embryonic form of money: What can we learn from history? In P. De Grauwe & T. Peeters (Eds.), The ECU and European monetary integration (pp. 1–22).

Eichengreen, B. (1992). Golden fetters: The gold standard and the Great Depression, 1919–1939.

Eichengreen, B., & Temin, P. (2000). The gold standard and the Great Depression. Contemporary European History, 9(2), 183–207. https://doi.org/10.1017/S0960777300002010

Ferguson, N. (2008). The ascent of money: A financial history of the world.

Friedman, M. (1969). The optimum quantity of money and other essays.

Friedman, M. (1992). Monetary mischief: Episodes in monetary history.

Mackenzie, G. A. (1999). The financial history of Canada.

Nash, G. D. (2000). The American West transformed: The impact of the Second World War.

Temin, P. (1989). Lessons from the Great Depression.

Timberlake, R. H. (1993). Monetary policy in the United States: An intellectual and institutional history.

CHAPTER 13

Bordo, M. D. (1993). The historical performance of the Federal Reserve. In M. D. Bordo & B. Eichengreen (Eds.), A retrospective on the Bretton Woods system: Lessons for international monetary reform (pp. 3–108).

Eichengreen, B. (1992). Golden fetters: The gold standard and the Great Depression, 1919–1939.

Eichengreen, B. (1996). Globalizing capital: A history of the international monetary system.

International Monetary Fund. (2010). World economic outlook: Historical trends in global GDP growth.

Triffin, R. (1960). Gold and the dollar crisis: The future of convertibility.

Williamson, J. (1993). The Bretton Woods agreements: The political economy of a system.

D. Bordo & B. Eichengreen (Eds.), A retrospective on the Bretton Woods system: Lessons for international monetary reform (pp. 463–494).

International Monetary Fund. (2018). World economic outlook: Historical trends in global capital flows.

International Monetary Fund. (2021). Global financial stability report: The role of the U.S. dollar in international reserves.

Martin, F. (2013). Money: The unauthorized biography.

World Trade Organization. (2019). World trade report: Historical trends in global trade.

International Monetary Fund. (2017). World economic outlook: A historical perspective on inflation in advanced economies.

Irwin, D. A. (2012). Trade policy disaster: Lessons from the 1930s.

Kindleberger, C. P. (1978). Manias, panics, and crashes: A history of financial crises.

Organisation for Economic Co-operation and Development. (2019). The economic impact of the Marshall Plan: A historical analysis.

Williamson, J. (2000). The role of the IMF and World Bank in international economic policy coordination.

World Bank. (2020). Global economic prospects: Historical trends in GDP growth.

Schuker, S. A. (1988). American "reparations" to Germany, 1919–33: Implications for the Third-World debt crisis.

Fisher, I. (1920). The purchasing power of money: Its determination and relation to credit, interest, and crises (2nd ed.).

Kershaw, I. (1999). Hitler: 1889–1936 Hubris.

Hayek, F. A. (1978). Denationalisation of money: The argument refined.

Lavoie, D. (2014). Rivalry and central planning: The socialist calculation debate reconsidered.

Switzerland's monetary policies. (Note: This appears incomplete or unclear—please verify the source or clarify intention.)

Meltzer, A. H. (2003). A history of the Federal Reserve, Volume 1: 1913–1951.

Mises, L. von. (1912). The theory of money and credit.

CHAPTER 14

Friedman, M. (1992). Monetary mischief: Episodes in monetary history.

Koo, R. (2009). The holy grail of macroeconomics: Lessons from Japan's great recession.

Krugman, P. (1994). The myth of Asia's miracle. Foreign Affairs, 73(6), 62–78. https://doi.org/10.2307/20047005

Werner, R. A. (2003). Princes of the Yen: Japan's central bankers and the transformation of the economy.

World Bank. (2013). World Development Indicators.

Doi, Y. (2013). Economic uncertainty and mental health in Japan. Social Science & Medicine, 85, 41–48.

Eichengreen, B. (2008). Globalizing capital: A history of the international monetary system (2nd ed.).

Hoshi, T., & Kashyap, A. K. (2004). Corporate financing and governance in Japan: The road to the future.

National Institute of Population and Social Security Research. (2019). Population projections for Japan: 2016–2065.

Schumpeter, J. A. (1942). Capitalism, socialism, and democracy.

Teo, A. R. (2010). A new form of social withdrawal in Japan: A review of hikikomori. International Journal of Social Psychiatry, 56(2), 178–185. https://doi.org/10.1177/0020764008100629

Yoshikawa, H. (2017). Japan's lost decade: Lessons for other economies. Japan and the World Economy, 42, 1–8. https://doi.org/10.1016/j.japwor.2017.02.001

CHAPTER 15

Hanke, S. H., & Krus, N. (2021). World hyperinflations: Zimbabwe and Venezuela revisited.

Mises, L. von. (1949). Human action: A treatise on economics.

Rodriguez, F. (2019). Economic collapse and corruption in Zimbabwe: A political economy perspective.

Rothbard, M. N. (1963). What has government done to our money?

Economic History Association. (n.d.). The Panic of 1907 and the creation of the Federal Reserve.

Encyclopedia Britannica. (n.d.). First Zionist Congress.

Federal Reserve History. (n.d.). The Federal Reserve Act of 1913.

Ferguson, N. (1998). The house of Rothschild: Money's prophets, 1798–1848.

Ferguson, N. (1999). The house of Rothschild: The world's banker, 1849–1999.

Pappé, I. (2014). The idea of Israel: A history of power and knowledge.

Rodriguez, F. (2019). Economic collapse and corruption in Venezuela: A political economy perspective.

Segev, T. (2000). One Palestine, complete: Jews and Arabs under the British Mandate.

The Crown Estate. (2023). Annual report and accounts 2023/24. https://www.thecrownestate.co.uk/about-us/annual-report

Government of Australia. (2023). Crown land management: Overview of public reserves and leasehold properties.

Government of Canada. (2023). Crown land administration: Federal and provincial management.

Jefferson, T. (1905). The writings of Thomas Jefferson.

Lindbergh, C. A., Sr. (1913). Banking and currency and the money trust.

United Kingdom Government. (2023). Overseas territories: Governance and sovereignty.

Chernow, R. (1998). Titan: The life of John D. Rockefeller, Sr.

Crabtree, J. (2018). The billionaire raj: A journey through India's new gilded age.

Glete, J. (1994). The Wallenberg family and Swedish industry: A history of economic power.

Hibbert, C. (1974). The house of Medici: Its rise and fall.

Khalidi, R. (2020). The hundred years' war on Palestine: A history of settler colonialism and resistance, 1917–2017.

Kim, J. (2014). The Samsung way: Transformational management strategies from the world leader in innovation and design.

Lundberg, E. (2001). The rise of the Wallenberg empire: Power and influence in Swedish industry.

Roover, R. de. (1963). The rise and decline of the Medici Bank, 1397–1494.

Hayek, F. A. (1944). The road to serfdom.

Warburg, J. P. (1950, February 17). Testimony before the U.S. Senate Committee on Foreign Relations. United States Senate.

CHAPTER 16

Locke, J. (1689). Two treatises of government.

Madison, J., Hamilton, A., & Jay, J. (1787–1788). The Federalist Papers.

Economic History Association. (n.d.). The Panic of 1907 and the creation of the Federal Reserve.

Ferguson, N. (1999). The house of Rothschild: The world's banker, 1849–1999.

Jefferson, T. (1816). Letter to John Taylor, May 28, 1816. In P. L. Ford (Ed.), The writings of Thomas Jefferson.

Khalidi, R. (2020). The hundred years' war on Palestine: A history of settler colonialism and resistance, 1917–2017.

Madison, J. (1787). Federalist No. 10: The same subject continued: The union as a safeguard against domestic faction and insurrection. In A. Hamilton, J. Madison, & J. Jay, The Federalist Papers.

Madison, J. (1788). Federalist No. 51: The structure of the government must furnish the proper checks and balances between the different departments. In A. Hamilton, J. Madison, & J. Jay, The Federalist Papers.

Federal Reserve History. (n.d.). The Federal Reserve Act of 1913 and the Great Depression.

Ferguson, N. (1998). The house of Rothschild: Money's prophets, 1798–1848.

Gordon, J. S. (1999). Hamilton's blessing: The extraordinary life and times of our national debt.

Mises Institute. (2006). The bimetallic standard and economic stability in the United States.

Temin, P. (1976). Did monetary forces cause the Great Depression?

Hummel, J. R. (2016). The American economy under the gold standard: Stability and growth.

CHAPTER 17

Gold, T. B. (1986). State and society in the Taiwan miracle.

Hsu, I. C. Y. (1970). The rise of modern China.

Liu, H. (2008). The People's Bank of China and the consolidation of CCP power.

Maddison, A. (2007). Chinese economic performance in the long run.

Kynaston, D. (2017). Till time's last sand: A history of the Bank of England.

Liu, H. (2004). Economic warfare in the Chinese Civil War: Financial strategies of the CCP and KMT.

Newman, E. P. (2008). The early paper money of America.

Martin, F. (2013). Money: The unauthorised biography.

United Nations High Commissioner for Refugees. (2021). Venezuela situation: Refugee and migrant crisis.

World Bank. (2020). Poverty and shared prosperity 2020: Reversals of fortune.

Ferguson, N. (2008). The ascent of money: A financial history of the world.

Mises, L. von. (1949). Human action: A treatise on economics.

Rothbard, M. N. (1963). What has government done to our money?

www.ingramcontent.com/pod-product-compliance
Lightning Source LLC
LaVergne TN
LVHW051044210926
848486LV00001B/17